PAL
3.22

D1553740

DISCARDED

Dr. Johnson and the English Law

Dr. Johnson
and the
English Law

E. L. McAdam Jr.
New York University

Syracuse University Press

To My FATHER and MOTHER

Preface

This book is an attempt to draw a complete picture, long
overdue, of Dr. Johnson's relations with lawyers, his conversations about the law, and his references to it in his
writings. All readers of Boswell are aware of Johnson's interest in the subject, though some may have skipped the
legal briefs which Johnson dictated to his biographer. But
Boswell passes over with the merest reference the fact that
Johnson twice during his life seriously considered studying
the law and practicing it. And although Johnson's writings
are larded with a thousand references to legal topics, no
thorough investigation of the subject has ever been made.
Except for a short paper read before the Johnson Club over
thirty years ago, no one had written upon the matter until I
discovered that Johnson had actually collaborated with
Robert Chambers in composing the Vinerian Lectures on the
English Law delivered at Oxford between 1767-1774. After
the appearance of my two articles on the subject, Sir Arnold
McNair published his *Dr. Johnson and the Law*, which is a
good introduction, but which neglects the Vinerian manuscripts of Chambers, Johnson's *Dictionary*, and many other
sources of information. The desirability of a complete study
seemed to me to predicate the quotation of all important
passages from existing materials, since these are scattered
over more than fifty volumes, of which eighteen are still in
manuscript in the British Museum. I have provided these with
links of comment, and have tried to trace Johnson's legal
interests in this was throughout his career. The reader will
find that the middle section of the book is more Johnson's
than mine: for this, Johnsonians will require no apology.

Acknowledgements

My thanks are warmly offered to the John Simon Guggenheim Foundation for a fellowship on which I was able to write this book; to the Trustees of the British Museum for the use of the Chambers manuscripts; to the Libraries of New York University, and especially to Mr. William A. Finn; to the Library of the New York Bar Association; to Dr. Helen McMaster; and most of all to Mr. George Milne, whose encouragement and advice have aided me at every stage of the work.

List of Short Titles

Letters: The Letters of Samuel Johnson, ed. G.B. Hill, 2 v., 1892; referred to by serial number.

Life: James Boswell, *The Life of Samuel Johnson*, ed. G.B. Hill and L.F. Powell, 6 v., 1934-1950.

Misc.: Johnsonian Miscellanies, ed. G.B. Hill, 2 v., 1897.

Works: The Works of Samuel Johnson, 13 v., 1787.

Works, 1825: *The Works of Samuel Johnson*, 11 v., 1825, for works not included in the first edition.

Johnson's *Dictionary* and his edition of Shakespeare are quoted from the first editions; Blackstone's *Commentaries* from the seventh ed., 1775.

Contents

Dr. Johnson and the English Law

"Never think it clever to call physic a mean study, or law a dry one."[1] When Johnson made this remark at Mrs. Thrale's house, at the height of his fame, it was a serious expression of his life-long respect for the legal profession, based not only on his wide and intimate acquaintance with lawyers, but also on his own study of the law. Poverty had prevented his finishing at the university, and had thereby prevented his becoming a lawyer, but his interest in legal matters only increased with the years.

Before entering on an examination of Johnson's writings, with the eventual aim of estimating the importance of the law in Johnson's thinking, we may survey briefly the state of legal education in the eighteenth century, both to show what obstacles lay in the way of Johnson's study of the law and to prepare for his contribution to legal education in his collaboration in the Vinerian Lectures.

The student who wished to qualify himself as a lawyer in the eighteenth century was confronted at the outset with a choice between Roman, or as it was usually termed civil, law and English law, frequently called common or municipal law. The division had existed since the twelfth century, when the study of Roman law was introduced at Oxford and made the basis for the ecclesiastical courts. The state, however, had resisted its introduction into secular courts, and since the Reformation both the civil law and the ecclesiastical courts had existed under the control and by permission of the secular constitution. A student, then, enrolled at either

1. *Misc.*, 1. 314. I have normalized spelling and punctuation throughout.

1

of the universities, proceeded to a degree in the civil law, attended the courts at Doctors' Commons at Westminster for a year in order to familiarize himself with procedure, and was admitted advocate by license of the archbishop. Before the Reformation, the slight regard in which English law was held by the Church had prevented its introduction into the universities, and by the end of the fifteenth century a rival system of legal studies was in full sway, the Inns of Court and Chancery, associations of barristers and sergeants, with their students of English law.

The eighteenth century student might still enroll in one of the Inns of Court, though they had sadly degenerated from their zenith in the days of the last three Henries, when, as "juridical universities" under royal protection and enjoying a monopoly of teaching the common law, they had supervised the performance of exercises and the reading of lectures, and had conferred degrees. As Blackstone says, "the degrees were those of barristers (first styled apprentices from *apprendre*, to learn) who answered to our bachelors: as the state and degree of a sergeant *servientis ad legem*, did to that of doctor."[2] At that time the Inns of Chancery were preparatory schools for the Inns of Court, and the students in both were sons of noblemen or gentlemen, who, for the most part, did not attend the universities. But by the middle of the eighteenth century, it was fashionable to spend four years at a university, with the result that attendance at the inns had fallen to perhaps a quarter of the two thousand students said to be enrolled in an earlier century. Blackstone comments, "the Inns of Chancery, being now almost totally filled by the inferior branch of the profession, are neither commodious nor proper for the resort of gentlemen of any rank or figure; so that there are very rarely any young students entered at the Inns of Chancery; . . . in the Inns of Court all sorts of regimen and academical superintendence, either with regard to morals or studies, are found impracticable and therefore entirely neglected: . . . persons of birth and fortune, after having finished their usual courses at the universities, have seldom

2. *Commentaries*, 1.23-24

eisure or resolution sufficient to enter upon a new scheme
of study at a new place of instruction." (pp. 25-26.)

Yet it was still possible to enter the law by this route,
which consisted largely of making commonplace books and
voluminous extracts out of the old authorities. Blackstone
gives a picture of a student under this system, which is confirmed several times by Johnson's sketches of young lawyers
in the *Rambler:*

> A raw and unexperienced youth, in the most dangerous
> season of life, is transplanted on a sudden into the midst
> of allurements to pleasure, without any restraint or check
> but what his own prudence can suggest; with no public di-
> rection in what course to pursue his enquiries; no private
> assistance to remove the distresses and difficulties which
> will always embarrass a beginner. In this situation he is ex-
> pected to sequester himself from the world, and by a tedious
> lonely process to extract the theory of law from a mass of
> undigested learning; or else by an assiduous attendance
> on the courts to pick up theory and practice together, suf-
> ficient to qualify him for the ordinary run of business. (p.31.)

Blackstone himself had combined an Oxford and a Middle
Temple education, and had learned enough in a total of six
years to qualify himself in both civil and English law. It may
be added parenthetically that barristers and sergeants (who
were barristers of sixteen years' standing) were collectively
called counsel at this time, and sometimes advocates, at
which point it became necessary to distinguish the civilians
by calling them advocates of the civil law.

The second method of entering the practice of the common
law was by means of a clerkship to an attorney (who in chancery was known as a solicitor). Blackstone, who spoke above
of the attorneys as "the inferior branch of the profession,"
refers to this method as merely learning the mechanical forms
of the law without any study of its principles. But it had become common by the second quarter of the century, when
Ephraim Chambers wrote in his *Cyclopaedia* that no attorneys
"are admitted to act without having served a clerkship for
five years, taking the proper oath, being enrolled, and examined by the judges." Part of Blackstone's (and Pope's and
Johnson's) contempt for attorneys may be accounted for by
he presumed lack of learning in that branch of the profession,

and part, perhaps, by the fact that attorneys and solicitors worked for hire. Counsel received gratuities only, and were therefore treated as legal officers of much higher standing. Attorneys were also allied to scriveners, with whom they shared the business of conveyancing.

It may be assumed, I believe, that in this period the course of study was not particularly rigorous in either the universities, the Inns of Court, or the attorneys' offices. The examination before the judges was certainly oral, probably brief, and perhaps perfunctory. The civilian had, of course, the great Roman and later continental authorities to study, but the low state of the English universities in this century will suggest how casual this study might have been. It will be remembered that Gray, who was Regius Professor of Modern History at Cambridge, never delivered a lecture during his incumbency of several years.

It was in such an atmosphere that Blackstone, in 1753, decided to give some lectures on the common law at Oxford. He says that he was "induced" to give them, but one may be permitted to suspect that this young man of thirty was more influenced by his failure in the practice of law than by the supposititious urging of his colleagues. As he stated in his *Analysis of the Laws of England*, which appeared three years later, his lectures were intended "not only to the use of such students, as were more immediately designed for the profession of the common law; but also of such other gentlemen, as were desirous of some general acquaintance with the constitution and legal polity of their native country [p. iv]." In the year this was published an eccentric old lawyer, Charles Viner, died and left the unsold sets of his enormous *Abridgment of Law and Equity* to Oxford to found a professorship of the common law "that young gentlemen who shall be students there and shall intend to apply themselves to the study of the common laws of England, may be instructed and enabled to pursue their studies to their best advantage afterwards when they shall attend the courts at Westminster, and not to trifle away their time there in hearing what they understand nothing of, and thereupon perhaps divert their thoughts from the law to their pleasures . . . ."[3] The university acted promptly, perhaps at Blackstone's insistence; statutes were drawn up, and in 1758 Blackstone, as the first Vinerian Professor, began the series of lectures which were later expanded and published as his *Commentaries on the Laws of England.* In the introductory lecture, from which I have already quoted, Blackstone portrayed the current state of legal education and showed also why he planned his lectures for a wider audience than that originally contemplated by Viner. Landed gentlemen, he says, should have some knowledge of estates and conveyancing to form "some check and guard upon a gentleman's inferior agents, and preserve him at least from very gross and notorious imposition [1.7]." Everyone, moreover, should have some knowledge of the wording and attestation of wills. Furthermore, "some legal skill" is requisite for jurors. (Some of his colleagues might have denied the desirability of this.) All members of Parliament should know something of law, and all justices of the peace, although a legal training had not been mandatory for either office (pp. 8-11). How scandalous was the ignorance of many of the magistrates, Blackstone did not point out, but Fielding, who was himself a lawyer and a magistrate, had seriously suggested a few years earlier that magistrates who were not lawyers should employ clerks who knew something of the law, in order to avoid the most egregious blunders.[4] The peerage should know the law, continues Blackstone, because the House of Lords is the final court of appeal. The clergy and the practitioners of civil law should know the English law as well, since it limits and controls the operation of the other (pp. 11-14).

Though Blackstone's introduction of English law into the university curriculum was to have a permanent effect on legal education, it was too late to affect Johnson's career, except indirectly. For Chambers, Blackstone's successor, was to apply for Johnson's help in writing the next series of Vinerian lectures, which Johnson, though his training was desultory, was qualified to give. How he qualified himself, the next chapter will partly explain.

3. Viner's will, Bodl. Gough 96 (14)
4. *Tom Jones,* Bk. 6, Ch. 9.

Johnson's Early Interest in the Law

No evidence exists to show that Johnson's interest in the law was precocious. No childhood bon mots have been recorded, though they might have been invented had his Lichfield friends later realized how extensive was his connection with legal matters. But one may suggest that some incitements to interest were at hand during his young manhood, without insisting too greatly on them.

His father's bookstore undoubtedly contained a few law books, either as part of its regular stock or as occasionally ordered from London through the store. One example may be cited: in 1727, when Johnson was seventeen, and still in Lichfield, Gilbert Walmsley bought "Aliffs Canon and Civill Law" at the shop, as a receipted bill shows.[1] Surely Johnson must at least have turned the pages of such books, and it is significant that he owned Ayliffe's *Parergon juris canonici Anglicani* in later life. We know that his habits of omnivorous reading were early acquired. Furthermore, since we do not know when he first began to read such authors as Pufendorf, Burlamaqui, Hale, and Selden, it is at least possible that he acquired some familiarity with them early in life.

Besides the bookstore, Lichfield had other more definite attractions to stimulate an interest in law. In 1779 Johnson wrote that he had visited the leet court at Lichfield for the first time in fifty years (Letter 616). This court, a survival of feudalism, was held out of doors on Whitmonday. It existed largely as a merely formal part of the Whitsun celebration, followed by morris dancing, and had little remaining

1. *Letters*, 127 n.

6

legal significance except as an occasion to "sight" the
eligible voters of the town. Nevertheless, it was a famous
local event, and I cannot doubt that Johnson had enquired as
to its origin when he first visited it, not later, as his letter
shows, than his twentieth birthday.

More important was Johnson's acquaintance with Walmsley,
then Register of the Ecclesiastical Court of Lichfield. In a
small cathedral town, the importance of the ecclesiastical
court would be much more obvious to the casual citizen than
would be true in London, and Walmsley, one of the prominent
figures of the town, took a strong interest in Johnson—entertained him at his house, advised him in his early career, and
wrote a letter of recommendation for him when he went to
London with Garrick to make his fortune. How extensive was
Walmsley's learning in canon and civil law I do not know,
other than what would have been the minimum for his holding
such a position. Johnson does not comment on the matter.
Nevertheless I believe it safe to assume that Walmsley discussed civilian problems in Johnson's hearing, perhaps the
very book which he had purchased from Johnson's father.

Another friend nearer Johnson's age was Charles Howard,
a proctor in the Ecclesiastical Court of Lichfield, in whose
mother's house Johnson was made welcome. It is impossible
to believe that Howard did not take Johnson to visit the Court
in session, and they must have talked about it more than
once. Johnson had a high opinion of Howard's ability, since
some thirty years later he recommended that Taylor consult
him about his marital difficulties.

At this same early period Johnson also knew the Rev.
Samuel Carte, Surrogate of the Chancellor and Prebend of
Lichfield, who may also have discussed ecclesiastical law
with him.

While Johnson was still in secondary school he became
friendly with John Taylor, whose father was a lawyer and
who was himself destined for the law. Johnson cherished his
friendship for the rest of his life, and though Taylor seems
to have been rather uncongenial, it is impossible to believe
that the two young men did not frequently discuss Taylor's

chosen profession. After leaving Oxford, Taylor practiced as an attorney for a while, but soon took holy orders and settled down to a long career in the church. He later consulted Johnson on several legal questions, though he, rather than Johnson, was the man with the formal legal training and even experience. Another college friend of Johnson's, perhaps better known than Taylor, was Oliver Edwards, who became a London solicitor. He is the earnest man who tried to be a philosopher, but found that cheerfulness was always breaking in. He, like Taylor, may have talked over his future profession with Johnson.

What books on the law Johnson may have read in the thirteen months which made up the whole of his college education, it is impossible to say. But that the study of law was at least in his mind at this time is strongly suggested by a conversation reported in Boswell's *Hebrides:* Talking of the transferability of talents from one occupation to another, Johnson said, "I could as easily apply to law as to tragic poetry." Boswell: "Yet, sir, you did apply to tragic poetry, not to law." Johnson: "Because, sir, I had not money to study law."[2] Which was the reason why he left college.

After his marriage and the failure of his venture into teaching, Johnson went to London and within about two years (1737-1739) published his poem *London,* failed to get his tragedy *Irene* performed, found a precarious and meager occupation as a hackwriter on the *Gentleman's Magazine,* and applied for a schoolmastership. But an M.A. degree was a requisite, and neither Oxford nor Dublin saw fit to grant it to him at this time. In this rather desperate searching for a livelihood, Johnson did not neglect the law:

About this time [says Boswell] he made one other attempt to emancipate himself from the drudgery of authorship. He applied to Dr. Adams, to consult Dr. Smalbroke of the Commons, whether a person might be permitted to practice as an advocate there, without a doctor's degree in Civil Law. "I am (said he) a total stranger to these studies; but whatever is a profession, and maintains numbers, must be within the reach of common abilities, and some degree of industry." Dr. Adams was much pleased with Johnson's design to

2. *Life,* 5.35

employ his talents in that manner, being confident he would
have attained to great eminence. And, indeed, I cannot conceive a man better qualified to make a distinguished figure
as a lawyer; for, he would have brought to his profession a
rich store of various knowledge, an uncommon acuteness,
and a command of language, in which few could have
equalled, and none have surpassed him. He who could display eloquence and wit in defence of the decision of the
House of Commons upon Mr. Wilkes's election for Middlesex, and of the unconstitutional taxation of our fellow-
subjects in America, must have been a powerful advocate
in any cause. But here, also, the want of a degree was an
insuperable bar. *(Life*, 1.134.)

At this time Johnson seems not to have known Smalbroke
or perhaps anyone practicing in Doctors' Commons, and his
friend Adams at Oxford, where civil law was taught, was a
natural person to supply such information. Many years later,
Johnson referred his friend Taylor to Smalbroke as a proper
counsel in case Taylor's wife sued for separate maintenance.[3]
It is to be noted in Boswell's account that Johnson mentions
practicing civil not common law, to which the lack of a degree was not a bar, if he knew that fact. Lichfield and Oxford had exercised their influence, and that of London had
hardly begun. Moreover, Johnson may have been mildly pre-
judiced at this time against attorneys—Taylor was one and
Johnson had slight regard for Taylor's intelligence. Pope had
called them "vile attorneys, now an useless race," and
Johnson remembered the remark a few years later and quoted
it in the *Dictionary*. And to article himself at the age of thirty
to some attorney in London with the distant hope of a future
practice of the English law—with a wife to support—must
have seemed like embracing starvation. The alternative of
enrolling as a student for several years in one of the Inns of
Court must have seemed equally bleak, though it might have
been thought possible, if Johnson had investigated, to carry
on his hackwork and study at the same time. He could not
know that Fielding, who was two years older than he and also
had a family to support, would be called to the bar in 1740,
only two and a half years after entering the Middle Temple,
during which time he seems to have carried on his literary
work without serious interruption. The study must have been

3. *Letters*, No. 159

rather perfunctory. But under the circumstances, and perhaps knowing little about the Inns of Court and their students at this date, it is no wonder that Johnson chose to work for Cave on the *Gentleman's Magazine* rather than begin life again as a law student.

Even on the magazine Johnson was not for long at a great distance from the law. In the June 1739 issue Cave had published the first installment of an abridgment of Joseph Trapp's sermons "on the nature, folly, sin, and danger of being righteous overmuch," a work of much public interest from its bearing on the Methodists. Apparently a threat of prosecution resulted, and Cave asked Johnson's advice. Johnson thereupon drew up a list of "Considerations" for the guidance of Cave or his lawyer. These are of great interest, for they are not only Johnson's first writings on the law, but the question of abridgments was not covered by any existing law, nor had it been raised in the courts. It is also worthy of note that these were written within about a year of Johnson's application to Adams discussed above. Further, since the date of that application is not known, it is at least possible that it was subsequent to these "Considerations." One may well imagine Cave, after reading them, asking his friend, "Why not pursue the law as a profession?" The points made by Johnson are:

1. That the copy of a book is the property of the author, and that he may, by sale, or otherwise, transfer that property to another, who has a right to be protected in the possession of that property, so transferred, is not to be denied.

2. That the complainants may be lawfully invested with the property of this copy, is likewise granted.

3. But the complainants have mistaken the nature of this property; and, in consequence of their mistake, have supposed it to be invaded by an act, in itself legal, and justifiable by an uninterrupted series of precedents, from the first establishment of printing among us, down to the present time.

4. He that purchases the copy of a book, purchases the sole right of printing it, and of vending the books printed according to it; but has no right to add to it, or take from it, without the author's consent, who still preserves such a right in it, as follows from the right every man has to preserve his own reputation.

5. Every single book, so sold by the proprietor, becomes the property of the buyer, who purchases, with the book, the right of making such use of it as he shall think most convenient, either for his own improvement or amusement, or the benefit or entertainment of mankind.

6. This right the reader of a book may use, many ways, to the disadvantage both of the author and the proprietor, which yet they have not any right to complain of, because the author when he wrote, and the proprietor when he purchased the copy, knew, or ought to have known, that the the one wrote, and the other purchased, under the hazard of such treatment from the buyer and reader, and without any security from the bad consequences of that treatment, except the excellence of the book.

7. Reputation and property are of different kinds; one kind of each is more necessary to be secured by the law than another, and the law has provided more effectually for its defence. My character as a man, a subject, or a trader, is under the protection of the law; but my reputation, as an author, is at the mercy of the reader, who lies under no other obligations to do me justice than those of religion and morality. If a man calls me rebel or bankrupt, I may prosecute and punish him; but, if a man calls me idiot or plagiary, I have no remedy; since, by selling him the book, I admit his privilege of judging, and declaring his judgment, and can appeal only to other readers, if I think myself injured.

8. In different characters we are more or less protected; to hiss a pleader at the bar would, perhaps, be deemed illegal and punishable, but to hiss a dramatic writer is justifiable by custom.

9. What is here said of the writer extends itself naturally to the purchaser of a copy, since the one seldom suffers without the other.

10. By these liberties it is obvious that authors and proprietors may often suffer, and sometimes unjustly: but as these liberties are encouraged and allowed for the same reason with writing itself, for the discovery and propagation of truth, though, like other human goods, they have their alloys and ill consequences; yet, as their advantages abundantly preponderate, they have never yet been abolished or restrained.

11. Thus every book, when it falls into the hands of the reader, is liable to be examined, confuted, censured, translated, and abridged; any of which may destroy the credit of the author, or hinder the sale of the book.

12. That all these liberties are allowed, and cannot be prohibited without manifest disadvantage to the public, may be easily proved; but we shall confine ourselves to the liberty of making epitomes, which gives occasion to our present inquiry.

13. That an uninterrupted prescription confers a right will be easily granted, especially if it appears that the pre-

scription, pleaded in defence of that right, might at any time have been interrupted, had it not been always thought agreeable to reason and to justice.

14. The numberless abridgments that are to be found of all kinds of writings afford sufficie | evidence that they were always thought legal, for they are printed with the names of the abbreviators and publishers, and without the least appearance of a clandestine transaction. Many of the books, so abridged, were the properties of men who wanted neither wealth, nor interest, nor spirit, to sue for justice, if they had thought themselves injured. Many of these abridgments must have been made by men whom we can least suspect of illegal practices, for there are few books of late that are not abridged.

15. When Bishop Burnet heard that his History of the Reformation was about to be abridged, he did not think of appealing to the court of chancery; but, to avoid any misrepresentation of his history, epitomised it himself, as he tells us in his preface.

16. But, lest it should be imagined that an author might do this rather by choice than necessity, we shall produce two more instances of the like practice, where it would certainly not have been borne, if it had been suspected of illegality. The one, in Clarendon's History, which was abridged, in 2 vols. 8 vo.; and the other in Bishop Burnet's History of his Own Time, abridged in the same manner. The first of these books was the property of the University of Oxford, a body tenacious enough of their rights; the other, of Bishop Burnet's heirs, whose circumstances were such as made them very sensible of any diminution of their inheritance.

17. It is observable, that both these abridgments last mentioned, with many others that might be produced, were made when the act of Parliament for securing the property of copies was in force, and which, if that property was injured, afforded an easy redress: what then can be inferred from the silence and forbearance of the proprietors, but that they thought an epitome of a book no violation of the right of the proprietor?

18. That their opinion, so contrary to their own interest, was founded in reason, will appear from the nature and end of an abridgment.

19. The design of an abridgment is, to benefit mankind by facilitating the attainment of knowledge; and by contracting arguments, relations, or descriptions, into a narrow compass, to convey instruction in the easiest method, without fatiguing the attention, burdening the memory, or impairing the health of the student.

20. By this method the original author becomes, perhaps, of less value, and the proprietor's profits are diminished; but these inconveniencies give way to the advantage received by mankind, from the easier propagation of knowledge; for as an incorrect book is lawfully criticised, and

false assertions justly confuted, because it is more the interest of mankind that error should be detected, and truth discovered, than that the proprietors of a particular book should enjoy their profits undiminished; so a tedious volume may, no less lawfully, be abridged, because it is better that the proprietor should suffer some damage, than that the acquisition of knowledge should be obstructed with unnecessary difficulties, and the valuable hours of thousands thrown away.

21. Therefore, as he that buys the copy of a book, buys it under this condition, that it is liable to be confuted, if it is false, however his property may be affected by such a confutation; so he buys it, likewise, liable to be abridged, if it be tedious, however his property may suffer by the abridgment.

22. To abridge a book, therefore, is no violation of the right of the proprietor, because to be subject to the hazard of an abridgment was an original condition of the property.

23. Thus we see the right of abridging authors established both by reason and the customs of trade. But, perhaps, the necessity of this practice may appear more evident, from a consideration of the consequences that must probably follow from the prohibition of it.

24. If abridgments be condemned, as injurious to the proprietor of the copy, where will this argument end? Must not confutations be, likewise, prohibited for the same reason? Or, in writings of entertainment, will not criticisms, at least, be entirely suppressed, as equally hurtful to the proprietor, and certainly not more necessary to the public?

25. Will not authors, who write for pay, and who are rewarded, commonly, according to the bulk of their work, be tempted to fill their works with superfluities and digressions, when the dread of an abridgment is taken away, as doubtless more negligences would be committed, and more falsehoods published, if men were not restrained by the fear of censure and confutation?

26. How many useful works will the busy, the indolent, and the less wealthy part of mankind be deprived of! How few will read or purchase forty-four large volumes of the transactions of the Royal Society, which, in abridgment, are generally read, to the great improvement of philosophy!

27. How must general systems of sciences be written, which are nothing more than epitomes of those authors who have written on particular branches, and whose works are made less necessary by such collections! Can he that destroys the profit of many copies be less criminal than he that lessens the sale of one?

28. Even to confute an erroneous book will become more difficult, since it has always been a custom to abridge the author whose assertions are examined, and, sometimes, to transcribe all the essential parts of his book. Must an inquirer after truth be debarred from the benefit of such con-

futations, unless he purchases the book, however useless, that gave occasion to the answer?

29. Having thus endeavored to prove the legality of abridgments from custom, and the necessity of continuing that custom from reason, it remains only that we show, that we have not printed the complainant's copy, but abridged it.

30. This will need no proof, since it will appear, upon comparing the two books, that we have reduced thirty-seven pages to thirteen of the same print.

31. Our design is, to give our readers a short view of the present controversy; and we require, that one of these two positions be proved, either that we have no right to exhibit such a view, or that we can exhibit it, without epitomising the writers of each party. 4.

These were posthumously published in the *Gentleman's Magazine* in 1787, and the manuscript still exists. The position taken by Johnson was upheld by 1 Bro. 451, 2 Atk. 141, and Christian in his note on Blackstone's *Commentaries*, 2. 407. Cave did not continue his abridgment, perhaps thinking the matter not worth controversy.

Shortly afterwards Cave furnished Johnson with another task with considerable bearing on the law. Cave had been employing a hack named Guthrie to report the debates in Parliament, and in 1741 Johnson took over this task. The publication of what the members considered the discussions of a private club was a dangerous and indeed at that time an illegal matter; Cave had hit upon the title *Debates in Lilliput,* using some names from Swift's novel, and disguising others by means of anagrams, to which the reader was furnished a key at the end of the year. Johnson himself did not attend the sessions of Parliament more than once to obtain notes, but used the services of a messenger, who supplied him with materials. From these meager sources—not stenographic reports—Johnson wrote some of the most brilliant speeches of the day, which were posthumously reprinted as two volumes of his collected works. He cannot, I think, be held responsible for any particular argument used in a given speech; neither, in many cases, can it be proved that he did not supply some of the arguments. The phraseology is wholly his own. The principal importance of the matter, it seems to me, is that Johnson

4. 1825. 5. 462-7

was obliged, for a period of three years, to consider legal and political questions with some care, and to write on them extensively, whether from his own point of view or not. Later, indeed, he said jocularly that he did not let the Whig dogs get the best of it. It was, at any rate, good training in the ability to see both sides of a question, and to argue on either side—an ability important for a lawyer or a judge, and one in which Johnson later demonstrated his proficiency.

The titles of the debates are sometimes not at all indicative of their contents: For example, that on the Bill for the Punishment of Mutiny and Desertion has nothing to do with that subject. It concerns an amendment to the act of that title, and deals only with the payment to innkeepers for quartering soldiers. Hence, one cannot guess without reading the debates what legal questions they may concern. Many, of course, deal with personalities and with political matters not strictly legal, though it is not easy to draw a firm line between laws and politics when dealing with the legislature and the court of last appeal. It will be remembered that the years covered by the debates saw the war with Spain in progress, the downfall of Walpole, and the fear of war with France over the Pragmatic Sanction. The titles of the debates are as follows:

On the Bill for prohibiting the Exportation of Corn.
On a seditious Paper.
On incorporating the new-raised Men into the standing Regiments.
On taking the State of the Army into Consideration.
Respecting Officers on Half-pay.
On an Address for Papers relating to Admiral Haddock.
Regarding the Departure of the French and Spanish Squadrons.
On addressing his Majesty for the Removal of Sir R. Walpole.
On cleansing the City of Westminster.
On the Bill to prevent Inconveniences arising from the Insurance of Ships.
On the Bill for the Encouragement and Increase of Seamen.
On the Bill for the Punishment of Mutiny and Desertion.
On addressing the King.
On supporting the Queen of Hungary.
On the Choice of a Speaker.
On an Address to the King.
On a Motion for enquiring into the Conduct of public Affairs.
On a Motion for indemnifying Evidence relating to the Conduct of the Earl of Orford.

On the Security and Protection of Trade and Navigation.
On an Address to the King.
On granting Pay for 16,000 Hanoverian Troops.
On the Army.
On the King's Conduct.
On Spirituous Liquors.

For the purposes of this study, neither a chronological arrangement nor one according to speakers seems profitable. I have accordingly extracted the points which seem to bear most directly upon the law, and arranged them under four heads: 1. Law in general; 2. international, foreign, military, and maritime law; 3. the King and Parliament; 4. rights and duties of the subject.

1.

"The end of law is the redress of wrong, the protection of right, and the preservation of happiness."[5] Thus the Duke of Argyle in the debate on indemnifying evidence. From this splendid generalization, it is a long step to a statement attributed to Lord Hervey, "To promote trust ... is the apparent tendency of all laws, [13.395]" but the second is particularly interesting to a commercial nation, and not less interesting as a foreshadowing of Johnson's own attitude toward trade and law. A rough definition of common law was contributed by Walpole: "The whole common law of this nation is nothing more than custom, of which the beginning cannot be traced [12.318]." The question of mutability of law was admitted by both sides in one debate, but the issue joined on the matter of reconciling the need for stability with the requirements of new situations. (We would now call such an issue conservatism vs. progress, but the eighteenth century was not sure that change and progress were identical.) For the conservatives:

The claims of the public are founded, first, upon right, which is invariable; and next, upon the law, which though mutable in its own nature is, however, to be so far fixed as that every man may know his own condition, his own property, and his own privileges, or it ceases to be law, it ceases

5. *Works*, 13. 143

to be the rule of government, or the measure of conduct. (13.161)

And for the opposition:

> Laws may, by those who have made the study and explana-
> tion of them the employment of their lives, be esteemed as
> the great standard of right; they may be habitually rever-
> enced, and considered as sacred in their own nature, with-
> out regard to the end which they are designed to produce.

> But others, my Lords, whose minds operate without any im-
> pediment from education, will easily discover that laws are
> to be regarded only for their use; that the power which made
> them only for the public advantage ought to alter or annul
> them, when they are no longer serviceable, or when they
> obstruct those effects which they were intended to pro-
> mote.[6]

The purpose of the legal profession was rather narrowly
limited in a speech given to Walpole. Lawyers exist, he says,
"to understand the laws that have been already made, and to
support the practices which they find established [12.319]."
There is no hint that jurists modify law through interpretation,
or that better laws might be made by lawyers than by laymen.
Another speaker is willing to concede that precedents may be
lacking:

> Though our constitution is in the highest degree excellent,
> I never yet heard that it was perfect, and whatever is not
> perfect may be improved. Our laws, however wise, are yet
> the contrivances of human policy; and why should we de-
> spair of adding somewhat to that which we inherit from our
> ancestors? Why should we imagine that they anticipated
> every contingency, and left nothing for succeeding ages?
> (13.170.)

One bill was attacked in the House of Lords—perhaps it
was not drawn up by a lawyer—because it lacked "one of
the most essential properties of a law, perspicuity and de-
terminate meaning [13.129]." The Corn Bill was attacked as
ex post facto legislation:

> That where there is no law there is no transgression, is a
> maxim not only established by universal consent but in it-
> self evident and undeniable; and it is, Sir, surely no less
> certain that where there is no transgression there can be
> no punishment. (12.22.)

6. *Ib.*, 13. 164; in the text, the first sentence erroneously has
"with which."

And in another debate the same question arose: ``How can any man defend his conduct, if having acted under one law, he is to be tried by another?'' (13.124.)

The general question of imprisonment for debt was to agitate the century increasingly, though not to the point of reaching a satisfactory solution of the problem. Johnson himself was able to speak from experience, and later wrote two essays on the subject. We may suppose, then, that he wrote with unusual feeling, when he put these words into the mouth of Gage:

> Sir, it is well known that by the laws of this nation poverty is in some degree considered as a crime, and that the debtor has only this advantage over the felon, that he cannot be pursued into his dwelling, nor be forced from the shelter of his own house. (12.285.)

Ignorance of the law is no defense, but how can the nation inform itself if a law passed today is made effective tomorrow? So argued Walpole in opposition to the proposal that maximum wages for merchant seamen be fixed on the very next day (12.290). The question is a practical one, of some nicety, and not quite as simple as it appears, although Fox tried to resolve it by making a distinction between restraints and punishments.

An instance where restraint might have been possible, though punishment had proved not to be, was the Gin Act. Prohibition was labeled an experiment even then, and the government was experiencing great difficulty with its sumptuary legislation. Hervey attacked the government's new tax bill, which in effect repealed the Gin Act, stating that the magistrates had ``quickly experienced . . . the folly of those laws which punish crimes instead of preventing them [13.392].''

2.

References in the debates to international, foreign, military, and maritime law are infrequent, and may be noticed briefly. In discussing the Spanish army, hemmed in between neutral states and the sea, it was pointed out that ``the law of nations bars their entrance'' to the neutral states (13.221). Later Pufendorf, who had written on the law of nations, and

with whose works Johnson later showed familiarity, was referred to as "the best writer on the German constitution,"
and one of his remarks on the empire paraphrased (13.318).
In one of several heated debates on the question of a standing army, Viner, who was in the process of publishing his
monumental *Abridgment*, and who founded the Vinerian Professorship of Law at Oxford in the next decade, stated that
the British soldiers "are deprived of the benefits of the constitution, and subjected to rigorous laws, from which every
other individual is exempt." He added that "The principal of
these laws, which all the rest are intended to enforce, required from every soldier an unlimited and absolute obedience
to the commands of his officers . . . ." This position was
very properly rebutted by quoting from the law to the effect
that soldiers shall "obey all the LAWFUL orders of their
commanders [12.95]."

Two points of maritime law developed incidentally in the
debate on a bill to prohibit insuring enemy merchant vessels.
The subject opened the question of frauds in marine insurance, particularly the practice of insuring "interest or no interest," "when an imaginary value is put upon the ship or
cargo, often much above its real worth [12.212-213]," a de-
vice necessitated by the fact that cargoes were often impossible to estimate in advance, when they were picked up piece-
meal in many ports, and subject to variation in amount. Walpole asserted that this was mere gambling, and as such should
be prohibited [12.222]. Barnard, representing the merchants
of the City, insisted that "there will always be circumstances
in which there can be no security against frauds, but common
faith [12.213]." The practice of bottomry was also attacked,
not because it is essentially fraudulent to hypothecate a ship
but because the ship sometimes was insured above its real
value, and the captain might therefore "gain by neglecting
the care of his vessel [12.218]." Barnard's comment on the
previous matter is equally applicable to this.

3.

The royal prerogative and the increase of ministerial power were hotly debated, though with less openness than Junius and Wilkes did some thirty years later. Pulteney opened his speech on the Corn Bill by stating that it had always been "the great business of this house to watch against the encroachments of the prerogative, and to prevent an increase of the power of the minister," yet he opposed the bill on the ground that the king already had power to impose an embargo in emergencies (12.2-6). He seems to have been more willing to trust the king with vaguely defined powers than to put definite authority into the hands of Walpole. He was echoed by the advocate Campbell:

> The chief use of the prerogative is to supply the defects of the laws, in cases which do not admit of long consultations, which do not allow time to convoke senates, or enquire into the sentiments of the people. (12.17.)

Barnard brought out the important difference between a proclamation and a penal law:

> By a proclamation His Majesty may prevent in some cases what he cannot punish; he may hinder the exportation of our corn by ordering ships to be stationed at the entrance of our harbors; but if any should escape with prohibited cargoes, he can inflict no penalties upon them at their return. (12.22.)

The King's relationship with his Electorate of Hanover brought up some vexing constitutional questions. Though the original Act of Settlement had prohibited the King from visiting Hanover, that clause had been repealed, and the annual royal visits to that place caused much discontent (13.67). The Act nevertheless still forbade England to interfere in behalf of Hanover in the continental quarrels, and the aid to the Queen of Hungary in her attempt to gain the Austrian throne was interpreted by the opposition as contrary to the Act. Shippen, indeed, declared in the Commons (12.380) that if the promise to defend Hanover had been foreseen at the time of the Act it "would perhaps have for ever precluded from the succession that illustrious family to which we owe

such numberless blessings, such continued felicity."—A fine
example of the threat as compliment or irony, perhaps to be
attributed to that staunch Tory, Johnson.

The next year it was discovered that the government had
hired 16,000 Hanoverian troops, who were stationed on the
continent in readiness to maintain the Hungarian cause. It
was openly charged that the purpose of the deal was merely
to fill the Hanoverian treasury, and the constitutional question was raised whether the ministry had a right to enter into
such a contract without the previous consent of Parliament.
The government insisted that it was a matter of royal prerogative:

> To make treaties, as to make war, is the acknowledged and
> established prerogative of the crown. When war is declared,
> the Senate is indeed to consider whether it ought to be
> carried on at the expense of the nation; and if treaties re-
> quire any supplies to put them in execution, they likewise
> fall properly at that time under senatorial cognizance: but
> to require that treaties shall not be transacted without our
> previous concurrence is almost to annihilate the power of
> the crown . . . . (13.370.)

The ministerial proposal to increase the size of the army
brought forth the usual fears that the troops would be employed to suppress popular liberty, and the government
shrewdly countered with the fact that the king was commander-
in-chief, and was therefore being attacked. Argyle defended
himself from the accusation by the following neat summary of
the doctrine that the king can do no wrong:

> My Lords, it is necessary to clear myself from misrepre-
> sentations... by reminding the noble lord, that His Majesty
> is never to be introduced into our debates, because he is
> never to be charged with wrong, and by declaring to your
> lordships, that I impute no part of the errors committed in
> the regulation of the army to His Majesty, but to those min-
> isters whose duty it is to advise him, and whom the law
> condemns to answer for the consequences of their coun-
> sels. (12.108.)

After the King had regretfully removed Walpole from the
government, an attempt was made to shield him from investigation by the Commons by declaring that any inquiry into the
expenditures from the civil list would be an infringement of
the prerogative: if such an investigation took place, "His

Majesty must be reduced to a state below that of the meanest
of his subjects; he can enjoy neither freedom nor property,
and must be debarred forever from those blessings which he
is incessantly laboring to secure to others [13.140]." This
emotional appeal was ably rebutted by Chesterfield (erroneously said to be Carteret in the collected editions):

It is indeed expressed in the act, that the grants of the
Civil List are without account, by which I have hitherto
understood only that the total is exempt from account; not
that the ministers have a right to employ the Civil List to
such purposes as they shall think most conducive to their
private views. For if it should be granted, not only that the
nation has no right to know how the *whole* is expended,
which is the utmost that can be allowed, or to direct the
application of any part of it, which is very disputable, yet
it certainly has a claim to direct in what manner it shall
not be applied, and to provide that boroughs are not cor-
rupted under pretence of promoting the dignity of the
Crown. (13.155.)

It is not a far cry from this speech to Johnson's attack on
pensions in the *Dictionary* a few years later.

Of the prerogatives of Parliament not in conflict with those
of the king, less was said. When it was proposed that the
author of a seditious paper distributed to the members of the
House of Commons be turned over to the courts for trial,
Howe objected that "we, and we only, are the judges of our
own rights, and we only, therefore, can assign the proper
punishment when they shall be presumptuously invaded," and
further that cognizance of the crime was placed in the Commons by "perpetual prescription and the nature of our constitution [12.31-32]." The house agreed.

The method by which the Commons proposed to investi-
gate the conduct of Walpole brought sharp dispute in the
Lords. Since it was found that witnesses would not testify
before the investigating committee unless indemnified, the
question arose whether the lower house was erecting itself
into a court of judicature, and thus infringing on the Lords.
It was affirmed that the Commons could not administer an
oath, and that therefore no committee of that house could.
Carteret, representing the majority of the Lords, said:

That they cannot, my Lords, in their own right administer

an oath, they apparently confess by the practice of calling in on that occasion a justice of the peace, who, as soon
as he has performed his office, is expected to retire. This,
my Lords, is an evident elusion, for it is always intended
that he who gives an oath, gives it in consequence of his
right to take the examination; but in this case the witness
takes an oath, *coram non judice*, before a magistrate that
has no power to interrogate him, and is interrogated by
those who have no right to require his oath. (13.127.)

As a corollary to this argument, it was pointed out that no
one could be protected from false accusation in such a committee, "for there is no provision made by the laws for the
punishment of a man who shall give false evidence before a
committee of the House of Commons [13.129]."

The well-established right of the Commons to initiate
money bills was used by the ministry on a later occasion to
force through the Lords the bill for reducing the licence fees
for retailing spirituous liquors. Lonsdale objected that the
house was not obliged to comply with all proposals sent up
by the Commons for raising money, "however destructive to
the public, or however contrary to the dictates of our conscience, or conviction of our reason," and added that to do
so would be "to vote ourselves useless, . . . destroy the constitution of the government, and give up that liberty which our
ancestors established [13.270]." He was strongly seconded
by Chesterfield:

It is not only the right, but the duty of either house, to deliberate without regard to the determinations of the other;
for how would the nation receive any benefit from the two
distinct powers that compose the legislature, unless their
determinations are without influence upon each other? If
either the example or authority of the Commons can divert
us from following our own convictions, we are no longer
part of the legislature; we have given up our honors and
our privileges, and what then is our concurrence but slavery,
or our suffrage but an echo? (13.491.)

4.

The rights and duties of the subject were treated principally in the debates on impressing seamen and indemnifying
evidence. It will be convenient first to discuss some general
rights, and then search, arrest, trial and punishment.

In the debate on a seditious paper, the Attorney General

stated that "it is indeed the incontestable right of every Briton to offer his petition at the bar of the house, and to deliver the reasons upon which it is founded. This is a privilege of an unalienable kind, and which is never to be infringed or denied." (12.36.) In the debate on impressment, Barnard declared that the proposed law was unconstitutional because impressment was tantamount to slavery (12.239). Walpole admitted the unusual nature of the law, but, by implication, denied its unconstitutionality:

> This power, in its present state, must be allowed to have no foundation in any law, and by consequence to be unlimited, arbitrary, and easily abused, and upon the whole, to be justifiable only by necessity: but that necessity is so frequent that it is often exercised, and therefore ought to be regulated by the legislature; and by making such regulations, we may rather be said to remove than introduce a grievance. (12.252.)

Pulteney replied that the law would hinder many persons from voting, and was therefore unconstitutional (12.260). He was confuted by the Attorney General:

> Sir, the practice of impressing . . . is not only founded on immemorial custom, which makes it part of the common law, but is likewise established by our statutes; for I remember to have found it in the statutes of Queen Mary . . . . (12.263.)

The "immemorial custom," he went on to say, was that of requiring every man to repair to the royal standard in emergencies. Viner tried to refute him by claiming that *prêt*, if it did occur in some old statute, meant *ready*, and had nothing to do with the more recent practice of impressment. In this he was mistaken.

The most controversial clauses of the bill for impressment empowered justices of the peace "to issue warrants to the constables, &c. to make general privy searches, by day or night, for finding out and securing such seamen and seafaring men as lie hid or conceal themselves; . . . to force open the doors of any house, where they shall *suspect* such seamen to be concealed, if entrance be not readily admitted . . . [12.245]." Barnard declared this wide power of search "oppressive and unconstitutional [12.250]," apparently because it singled out a particular class of men as its object, and because no appeal was allowed from the magistrate's decision. Walpole pointed out that the power of search was already in the hands of the magistrates for the relatively trifling purpose of preserving game, and that the exigencies of war made the new bill necessary (12.277).

In the debate on indemnifying evidence, Carteret discussed the three essentials "which the wisdom of our ancestors has made indispensably previous to the arrest of the meanest Briton": "that there is a crime committed, that the person to be seized is suspected of having committed it, and that the suspicion is founded upon probability." The first and third he expanded:

> First, that there is a *corpus delicti*, a crime really and visibly committed; thus before a process can be issued out for inquiring after a murderer, it must be apparent that a murder has been perpetrated, the dead body must be exposed to a jury, and it must appear to them that he died by violence. It is not sufficient that a man is lost, and that it is probable that he is murdered because no other reason of his absence can be assigned; he must be found with the marks of force upon him, or some circumstances that may make it credible that he did not perish by accident, or his own hand. (13.122.)

To the third point he added that "whoever apprehends or molests another on suspicion of a crime, shall be able to give the reasons of his suspicion and to prove them by competent evidence."

Chesterfield (erroneously Carteret in collected editions) replied that though a *corpus delicti* might not appear, yet the existence of a *corpus suspicionis* justified an inquiry. Hardwicke retorted that he had never heard the term and did not know what it meant, that it appeared to signify the *body of a shadow*, ''the substance of something which is in itself nothing [13.158-159].''

The qualifications of witnesses were canvassed in the same debate. It was stated that to be credible, a witness must be disinterested, "that his own cause be not involved in that of the person who stands at the bar, that he has no prospect of advancing his fortune, clearing his reputation, or securing his life [13.123].'' Bathurst elaborated somewhat upon this:

Every court, my Lords, examines the credibility of a witness; and the known corruption of these men may be properly pleaded at the trial, where your Lordships will balance
every circumstance with your known impartiality, and examine how far every assertion is invalidated by the character of the witness, and how far it is confirmed by a cor-
roboratory concurrence of known events, or supported by
other testimonies not liable to the same exception. (13.173.)

Argyle urged indemnifying witnesses as the only solution of
the dilemma "that the public has a claim to every man's evidence," and yet that "no man is obliged to accuse himself [13.142]." The use of secondary witnesses, testifying to
their belief in a fact, was stated to be legally limited to the
identification of the handwriting of a dead person (13.128).

As to the defence, first, "no man's oath will be admitted in
his own cause, though offered at the hazard of the punishment
inflicted upon perjury [13.125]." Next, self-incrimination was
frequently opposed: "Every Briton is exempted from the necessity of accusing himself, and . . . is entitled to refuse an
answer to any question which may be asked with a view to
draw from him a confession of an offence which cannot be
proved [12.25]." In the bill for impressing seamen, a clause
empowered magistrates to examine constables under oath and
punish them for "any neglect, offence, or connivance [12.264]."
Barnard denounced this as obliging a man to make oath against
himself. Winnington admitted that the clause was unconstitutional, and proposed an amendment to obviate the fault (12.268).
In the preliminary investigation of Walpole's regime, Paxton,
who was suspected of being the agent used in the purchase
of boroughs, had stood upon his rights, and refused to answer
questions of the committee "because the answer might tend to
accuse himself [13.120]." His action was defended by Carteret: "It is an established maxim that no man can be obliged
to accuse himself, or to answer any questions which may have
any tendency to discover what the nature of his defence requires to be concealed [13.123]." And Argyle stated later
that "the constitution of Britain allows no man's evidence
to be extorted from him to his own destruction [13.142]."

Whether common fame might be allowed in evidence against
a man, was hotly argued. Abingdon: "Common fame, my Lords,

is admitted in courts of law as a kind of auxiliary or supple-
mental evidence, and is allowed to corroborate the cause
which it appears to favor [12.157]." Newcastle: "If the
sudden blasts of fame may be esteemed equivalent to attested
accusations, what degree of virtue can confer security
[12.159]?" Finally Marlborough moved:

> That any attempt to inflict any kind of punishment on any
> person without allowing him an opportunity to make his de-
> fence, or without any proof of any crime or misdemeanor
> committed by him, is contrary to natural justice, the fund-
> amental laws of this realm, and the ancient established
> usage . . . . (12.201.)

The bill for indemnifying evidence, though strongly opposed, was reasonably supported by two similar precedents,
"the daily practice of promising pardon to thieves, on condition that they will make discoveries by which their confeder-
ates may be brought to justice [13.133]," and previous bills
of indemnity "to those by whom any discoveries should be
made" of frauds committed by the agents of trading companies (13.143).

The necessity for exact definition of a crime was happily
brought out in the debate on the Hanoverian troops. Horace
Walpole had carelessly spoken of "treason, or sentiments
very nearly bordering upon treason [13.260]," and was thus
demolished by Nugent:

> Treason is happily defined by our laws, and therefore every
> man may know when he is about to commit it, and avoid the
> danger of punishment by avoiding the act which will expose
> him to it; but with regard to the *borders* of treason, I be-
> lieve no man will yet pretend to say how far they extend,
> or how soon, or with how little intention he may tread upon
> them. Unhappy would be the man who should be punished
> for *bordering* upon guilt, of which those fatal *borders* are
> to be dilated at pleasure by his judges. The law has hither-
> to supposed every man who is not *guilty*, to be *innocent;*
> but now we find that there is a kind of medium in which a
> man may be in danger without guilt, and that in order to se-
> curity [!], a new degree of caution is become necessary;
> for not only crimes, but the borders of crimes are to be
> avoided. (13.262.)

An interesting point in trial procedure was raised in the
debate on a seditious libel. Yonge had urged that the printer
as well as the author of a libel should be punished, espec-

ially as this particular printer, though often offending, had long gone unpunished. Barnard objected to the comment, and Winnington insisted that "the chief question at a trial [is] the past conduct of the person at the bar [12.34]." Whether this was meant as a hit at the conduct of the courts, is not wholly clear; at any rate, Barnard responded with this fine statement:

> The character of the prisoner is never examined, except when it is pleaded by himself, and witnesses are produced to offer testimony in his favor; that plea, like all others, is then to be examined, and is sometimes confuted by contrary evidence. But the character of a criminal, though it may be urged by himself as proof of his innocence, is never to be mentioned by his prosecutor as an aggravation or proof of his guilt. It is not required by the law that the general character of a criminal, but that the particular evidence of the crime with which he stands charged, should be examined; nor is his character ever mentioned but by his own choice.

A suggestion that drunkenness might be used as a defence is implicit in Hervey's remarks in the debate on spirituous liquors:

> Those that propose the promotion of public happiness . . . ought to take care that the laws may be known, for how else can they be observed? And how can they be known, or, at least, how can they be remembered in the heats of drunkenness? (13.393.)

"No punishment is heavier than infamy." With these words, Hervey pointed out (12.200) that, in asking the King to remove Walpole as minister, the man was actually being punished without being accused of a crime. Another sort of punishment was thought too severe, when the bill to limit the maximum pay of merchant seamen was amended so that the seaman would not suffer equally with the merchant who had hired him above the legal rate. It had been suggested that the courts would grant the seaman such of his pay as he was adjudged to deserve, a *quantum meruit*, but it was noted that this was not likely to happen in cases of fraudulent contract, and the statute of usury was instanced: "He that stipulates for higher interest than is allowed, is not able to recover his legal demand, but irrecoverably forfeits the whole [12.304]." In a later debate appears a general statement on contracts which might have been relevant to this question: "All contracts,. . . whether between states or private persons, are to be understood according to the known intention of the two parties." (13.240.)

In general, the debates do not refer to many previous acts by title, except briefly. Thus the Act for preventing Bribery and the Act of Settlement are mentioned,[7] and 9 Geo. II (no cap.) on spirituous liquors and 6 Anne (no cap.) on navigation are referred to (13.386,216). This may reflect the actual debates, but if Johnson had given the full titles or references, the result would have been mere annoyance for the readers of the magazine, which, it must be remembered, was of general, not legal, character. The same comment applies to the relative scarcity of specialized legal terms, a fair sample of which appear above.

The debates, then, represent Johnson's apprenticeship in the law. It was not a systematic training, but it at least may be said to have accustomed Johnson to the use of some legal terms, and the handling, if in more or less popular style, of many legal questions. And if any stimulus was needed for Johnson's ability and willingness to argue on either side of an issue, here was stimulus enough.

In the fifteen years following Johnson's work on the *Gentleman's Magazine* he became acquainted with several lawyers, some of whom were intimate friends. Since this is a period of which little is known of Johnson's life — he was not to meet his great biographer till later — it is not easy to estimate the degree of influence which these men may have exercised upon him. We lack the conversations so illuminatingly presented after 1763. But even so, the list of names itself is suggestive.

In 1749 Johnson founded the Ivy Lane Club, the first of his clubs, and John Hawkins was a member. They may have known each other earlier, but Hawkins, who wrote an official biography of Johnson, is weak on dates, and is silent on this point. Hawkins was an attorney, later drew up Johnson's will, and was one of the executors. He was also responsible in

7. *Ib.*, 13. 146, 149; 12. 380, 13. 67

some measure for the booksellers' edition of Johnson's works.
The two men appear not to have been intimate, if one may
judge by the fact that Hawkins never met Johnson's wife, who
died in 1752. But the friendship was lasting, and Hawkins became a member of The Club, the second, though he later with-
drew. He seems to have been rather more interested in his
History of Music than in the law, perhaps because of lack of
success in his profession.

At about the same time Johnson knew Joseph Simpson,
whom Boswell mistakenly describes as his schoolfellow.
Simpson was a Lichfield man, about twelve years Johnson's
junior, and a barrister of Lincoln's Inn, to whom Johnson referred some business at Lichfield in 1752. He was a man of
good parts, says Boswell, but "fell into a dissipated course
of life, incompatible with that success in his profession
which he once had." [8] Later befriended by Johnson and Garrick, Simpson is principally remembered for the fact that his
tragedy *The Patriot* was published as Johnson's by an un-
scrupulous bookseller after Johnson's death.

Arthur Murphy, Irish actor, dramatist, and wit, met Johnson
in 1754 and was a valued friend for thirty years. Murphy had
been refused at the Middle Temple in 1757 because of his
connection with the stage, but was admitted to Lincoln's Inn
by the influence of Henry Fox, and became a barrister. For
some years his practice was rather small, but in 1774 he drew
up the appellants' case in the question of perpetual copyright
before the Lords, a case in which Johnson was deeply interested. He is, of course, the author of *An Essay on the Life
and Genius of Samuel Johnson*, 1792.

A most important piece of information about another lawyer
friend comes from Boswell:

On my expressing my wonder at his discovering so much of
the knowledge peculiar to different professions, he told me,
"I learnt what I know of law, chiefly from Mr. Ballow, a
very able man. I learnt some too from Chambers; but was
not so teachable then. One is not willing to be taught by a
young man." When I expressed a wish to know more about
Mr. Ballow, Johnson said, "Sir, I have seen him but once
these twenty years. The tide of life has driven us different
ways." (*Life*, 3.22.)

8. *Life*, 3.28

Boswell places this conversation in 1776, which would put
the acquaintance in the early 'fifties. Henry Ballow, two
years Johnson's senior, had been called to the bar in 1728,
had published his *Treatise of Equity* anonymously in 1737,
and had perhaps at some time presented Johnson with a copy,
since it is listed in his library. Hawkins describes Ballow,
whom he apparently knew, as frequenting Tom's Coffee House
in Devereux Court—

> a lawyer by profession, but of no practice; he having, by
> the interest of some of the Townshends to whom he had
> been a kind of law tutor, obtained a place in the Exchequer,
> which yielded him a handsome income and exempted him
> from the necessity of attending Westminster Hall. (*Works*,
> 1.244-245.)

He was a man of "deep and extensive learning, but of vulgar
manners" and splenetic temper—"a little deformed man,
well known as a saunterer in the park, about Westminster,
and in the streets between Charing Cross and the Houses of
Parliament." It is possible that Hawkins introduced him to
Johnson; at any rate Ballow somehow stimulated Johnson in
this dark decade to a new interest in the law. One may imagine how the study proceeded: the men walked in the park
discussing legal questions which had arisen in connection
with the day's news, and Ballow recommended books for
Johnson's study. Many of their talks must have turned on the
question of the place of equity in English law, and it is not
surprising to find Johnson dictating to Chambers on that subject a few years later.[9] Ballow was the recognized authority
on equity of the period, and they could not have avoided his
specialty.

Robert Chambers, mentioned above by Johnson as a man
from whom he also learned some law, is fully dealt with in
the fourth chapter. Johnson knew him from 1754 onwards, but
they did not delve into the law together till twelve years
later. Nevertheless, the fact that the young Chambers was
studying law at Oxford may have increased Johnson's interest
in the subject at this time.

9. V. Ch. IV

It was probably at this period that Johnson met Saunders Welch, High Constable of Holborn during the magistracy of Henry Fielding, and Fielding's chief assistant, who was appointed to the Commission at Westminster in 1775. Fielding called him "one of the best officers who was ever concerned in the execution of justice,"[1] and Boswell says that his friendship with Johnson was long and intimate. Since Johnson referred to him on one occasion as the justice "who was once High Constable of Holborn [Life, 3.401]," I think it possible that he had known him from that time, that is, before 1755. Boswell also states that Johnson "attended Mr. Welch in his office for a whole winter, to hear the examination of the culprits [3.216]," but what winter we are not told. One incident of this attendance was related to Boswell by Reynolds, who accompanied Johnson on one visit during the examination of "a little blackguard boy":

> Welch, who imagined that he was exalting himself in Dr. Johnson's eyes by using big words, spoke in a manner that was utterly unintelligible to the boy; Dr. Johnson, perceiving it, addressed himself to the boy, and changed the pompous phraseology into colloquial language. Sir Joshua Reynolds, who was much amused by this procedure, which seemed a kind of reversing of what might have been expected from the two men, took notice of it to Dr. Johnson as they walked away by themselves. Johnson said, that it was continually the case; and that he was always obliged to *translate* the Justice's swelling diction, (smiling,) so as that his meaning might be understood by the vulgar from whom information was to be obtained. (*Life*, 4.184.)

Whatever Johnson learned from Welch about the law in a magistrate's court he amply repaid in 1776 when, through his friendship with Chamier, Under Secretary of State, he procured a leave of absence for Welch to go abroad for his health.

One very great friend of Johnson's may be mentioned in this period, though we do not know just when they became acquainted. Edmund Burke, whose father was an attorney, had come to London in 1750 to keep terms at the Middle Temple. Though he soon abandoned the study of law, he had mastered enough to play his part in the constitutional struggles which followed. Johnson's friend Murphy reviewed Burke's *Inquiry*

1. *Life*, 3.514

into the Origin of our Ideas on the Sublime and Beautiful for
The Literary Magazine in 1756 when Johnson was editing that
journal, and it is conceivable that Johnson met Burke either
through Murphy or through Dodsley, who was Burke's publisher as well as Johnson's. Burke was one of the original
members of The Club (1764), an honor not lightly granted.
Johnson saw the magnitude of Burke's genius early, and when
someone expressed surprise on Burke's election to Parliament,
Johnson said, "Now we who know Burke, know, that he will
be one of the first men in this country [*Life*, 2.450]." Burke's
opinion of Johnson was equally high, and one must believe
that they taught each other a good deal, notwithstanding the
diversity of their political views. It is interesting to note
that when Burke tired of his six apprentice years as a sort of
secretary to Hamilton, Johnson followed him in a somewhat
similar position.[2]

During the years under consideration, Johnson's writings
contain many references to the law. The first, in his violent
anti-Hanoverian satire, *Marmor Norfolciense* (1739), is a
blast at the profession, quite unlike Johnson's later respect
for it:

> It is well known to be the constant study of the lawyers
> to discover, in acts of parliament, meanings which es-
> caped the committees that drew them up, and the senates
> that passed them into laws, and to explain wills into a
> sense wholly contrary to the intention of the testator . . . .
> A man accustomed to satisfy himself with the obvious
> and natural meaning of a sentence does not easily shake
> off his habit; but a true-bred lawyer never contents him-
> self with one sense, when there is another to be found.[3]

In the *Life of Blake* in the next year, there is a single
reference to the law of nations: the Dutch, instead of admit-
ting Blake to treat, "fired upon him from their whole fleet,
without any regard to the customs of war, or the law of nations."[4] In the *Life of Drake* which follows, Johnson makes
a similar point: Hawkins was attacked by the Spaniards "with-

2. V. Ch. III
3. 1825. 6. 109
4. *Works*, 4.364

out any declaration of hostilities," and in violation of the peace between Spain and England (4.381). But Drake was more civilized: "He was a rigid observer of the laws of war, and never permitted his arrows to be poisoned [4.388]." The Moors were less well bred: during some peaceful trading they seized one of Drake's men, and he was naturally "disgusted at this breach of the laws of commerce (4.417)." In this same book Johnson refers in passing to the Six Articles Act (1539), without comment (4.379).

In the *Account of the Harleian Library* (1742) Johnson gives a brief summary of the legal books in the collection:

> The laws of different countries, as they are in themselves equally worthy of curiosity with their history, have, in this collection, been justly regarded; and the rules by which the various communities of the world are governed, may be here examined and compared. Here are the ancient editions of the papal decretals, and the commentators on the civil law, the edicts of Spain, and the statutes of Venice.

> But with particular industry have the various writers on the laws of our own country been collected, from the most ancient to the present time, from the bodies of the statutes to the minutest treatise; not only the reports, precedents, and readings of our own courts, but even the laws of our West-Indian colonies, will be exhibited in our catalogue. (9.345-346.)

Since Johnson is said by Boswell to have supplied the Latin accounts of books in the catalogue which followed, it seems likely that he acquired some familiarity with these works from handling and glancing into them.

In a review of Du Halde's *China* written for the *Gentleman's Magazine* in 1742, Johnson comments with approval on the fact that the emperors of China did not consider themselves above the law, but submitted to the reproof of their ministers when they had deviated from the law (1825.6.2).

The *Life of Savage* (1744) is unique in Johnson's career, since its subject was able to impose himself on Johnson as the son of the Countess of Macclesfield, a claim now almost universally considered fraudulent. Johnson's sympathy for the apparently unfortunate, and his friendship with Savage, in this one instance disabled his skepticism. Lady Macclesfield, in order to gain her freedom from her husband, alleged that the father of the child she was carrying was Earl Rivers. Her husband applied to Parliament for an act dissolving the marriage and illegitimating his wife's children. This he obtained, though, says Johnson, "without the approbation of some, who considered marriage as an affair only cognizable by ecclesiastical judges," and he quotes the dissent of Halifax and Rochester.[5] This occurred two months after the birth of her son, who, later, Savage claimed to be. (The actual son is believed to have died in childhood.) The subsequent behavior of Savage's supposed mother Johnson adjudges worse than infanticide, the punishment for which, he says, is well known, "nor has its justice ever been contested[3.259]." (It is perhaps well for the lady that Johnson was not a prosecuting attorney.)

The trial of Savage for murder during a tavern brawl is reported by Johnson rather dispassionately. His analysis of the testimony of the witnesses is typical.

> There was some difference in their depositions; one did not see Savage give the wound, another saw it given when Sinclair held his point towards the ground; and the woman of the town asserted that she did not see Sinclair's sword at all: this difference, however, was very far from amounting to inconsistency; but it was sufficient to show that the hurry of the dispute was such that it was not easy to discover the truth with relation to particular circumstances, and that therefore some deductions were to be made from the credibility of the testimonies. (3.267.)

Johnson's final comment on the trial, which ended in a conviction, after a prejudicial charge by the notorious Page, is: "Thus had Savage perished by the evidence of a bawd, a strumpet, and his mother, had not justice and compassion procured him an advocate of rank too great to be rejected unheard, and of virtue too eminent to be heard without being believed [3.272-273]." The Countess of Hertford appealed to the Queen, he was admitted to bail, and soon pardoned.

In discussing one of Savage's poems, Johnson says that "the poet is employed in a more pleasing undertaking than that of proposing laws which, however just or expedient, will never be made, or endeavoring to reduce to rational schemes of government societies which were formed by chance, and are conducted by the private passions of those who preside

5. *Works*, 3.246

in them." One of Johnson's characteristic attitudes toward colonization appears when he notes that Savage exposes "the enormous wickedness of making war upon barbarous nations because they cannot resist [3.320-321]." Finally Johnson records one of the curious aspects of the debtors' law, on the occasion when Savage was confined late in life: "He took care to enter his name according to the forms of the court, that the creditor might be obliged to make him some allowance, if he was continued a prisoner." (3.362-363.)

In *The Plan of an English Dictionary*, 1747, Johnson explains that the dictionary will contain some alien words because the purchasers will expect to find them, such as, in the common law, capias, habeas corpus, praemunire, nisi prius (9.170). In the latter part of the essay Johnson amusingly compares the rules of language to those of common law: "I shall therefore, since the rules of style, like those of law, arise from precedents often repeated, collect the testimonies on both sides, and endeavor to discover and promulgate the decrees of custom, who has so long possessed, whether by right or by usurpation, the sovereignty of words." (9.185.)

The *Preface to the Preceptor* (1748) gave Johnson an opportunity to recommend some law books to the young student:

The principles of laws and government come next to be considered; by which men are taught to whom obedience is due, for what it is paid, and in what degree it may be justly required. This knowledge, by peculiar necessity, constitutes a part of the education of an Englishman, who professes to obey his prince according to the law, and who is himself a secondary legislator, as he gives his consent, by his representative, to all the laws by which he is bound, and has a right to petition the great council of the nation, whenever he thinks they are deliberating upon an act detrimental to the interest of the community. This is therefore a subject to which the thoughts of a young man ought to be directed; and that he may obtain such knowledge as may qualify him to act and judge as one of a free people, let him be directed to add to this introduction Fortescue's *Treatises*, N. Bacon's *Historical Discourse on the Laws and Government of England*, Temple's *Introduction*, Locke on *Government*, Zouch's *Elementa Juris Civilis*, *Plato Redivivus*, Gurdon's *History of Parliaments*, and Hooker's *Ecclesiastical Polity*. (9.419.)

A rather formidable list for the beginning student, but
Johnson was no friend to coddling. In the *Rambler*, however,
we find him handling the law with more lightness. In No. 8,
for instance, apropos of the snares of the imagination: "To
pick and cull among possible advantages is, as the civil law
terms it, *in vacuum venire*, to take what belongs to nobody;
but it has this hazard in it, that we shall be unwilling to quit
what we have seized, though an owner should be found."
In No. 9, talking of the partiality of each man for his own
profession, he attacks the superficial contempt for religion
characteristic of some lawyers:

> The truth is, very few of them have thought about religion;
> but they have all seen a parson; seen him in a habit dif-
> ferent from their own, and therefore declared war against
> him. A young student from the Inns of Court, who has often
> attacked the curate of his father's parish with such argu-
> ments as his acquaintances could furnish, and returned
> to town without success, is now gone down with a resolu-
> tion to destroy him; for he has learned at last how to man-
> age a prig, and if he pretends to hold him again to syllogism,
> he has a catch in reserve, which neither logic nor meta-
> physics can resist.

In No. 13, Johnson, in accord with his feeling that attorneys represented the lowest species of lawyer, brackets them
with office clerks, ladies of the bed-chamber, chamber-maids,
and footmen. In No. 18, a satirical portrait of Polyphilus, who
flitted from one profession to another, lawyers are treated
with more understanding. Polyphilus, going on impulse into
Westminster Hall where a case was being tried,

> found himself able to produce so many arguments, which
> the lawyers had omitted on both sides, that he determined
> to quit physic for a profession in which he found it would
> be so easy to excel, and which promised higher honors,
> and larger profits, without melancholy attendance upon
> misery, mean submission to peevishness, and continual
> interruption of rest and pleasure.

> He immediately took chambers in the Temple, bought a
> commonplace book, and confined himself for some months
> to the perusal of the statutes, year-books, pleadings, and
> reports; he was a constant hearer of the courts, and began
> to put cases with reasonable accuracy. But he soon dis-
> covered, by considering the fortune of lawyers, that prefer-
> ment was not to be got by acuteness, learning, and elo-
> quence. He was perplexed by the absurdities of attorneys,
> and misrepresentations made by his clients of their own

causes, by the useless anxiety of one, and the incessant importunity of another; he began to repent of having devoted himself to a study which was so narrow in its comprehension that it could never carry his name to any other country, and thought it unworthy of a man of parts to sell his life only for money.

We later find this same young man, unable to find any profession without faults, "collecting a vocabulary of the obsolete terms of the English law," which may be an amused reference to Johnson's current occupation with his dictionary. In No. 20, an essay on affectation, Johnson remarks that a correspondent using the name Chloris reveals his true profession and sex by allusions to Bracton and Plowden. (Plowden was one of the law books in Johnson's library, and he may be assumed to have had a nodding acquaintance with Bracton.) In No. 23, we find an interesting proof that Johnson had considered some of a lawyer's problems in addressing the court:

> It is observed by the younger Pliny that an orator ought not so much to select the strongest arguments which his cause admits as to employ all which his imagination can afford; for, in pleading, those reasons are of most value, which will most affect the judges; and the judges, says he, will always be most touched with that which they had before conceived.

In No. 26, speaking with disapprobation of the young man who was easily convinced that he could not "submit to the drudgery of the law," Johnson shows that he knows how necessary such drudgery is. In No. 57, speaking of frugality, Johnson remarks that "the civil law ranks the prodigal with the madman, and debars them equally from the conduct of their own affairs." Suspirius, the screech-owl who tries to destroy the peace of mind of all his acquaintance, tells the lawyer "of many men of great parts and deep study, who have never had an opportunity to speak in the courts" (No. 59). One might paraphrase Johnson's attitude by saying that no profession is without its difficulties, but that no difficulties are so insuperable that work, brains, and a little luck cannot overcome them. The notion is anticipatory of his advice to Boswell when that young man was filled with difficulties about entering the law.

Johnson's familiarity with the writings of Sir Matthew Hale is suggested by the presence of at least one of Hale's books in his library, and is strengthened by reference to Hale's religious practices in No. 14. In No. 60 Johnson quotes him: "'Let me remember,' says Hale, 'when I find' myself inclined to pity a criminal, that there is likewise a pity due to the country.'" This, says Johnson, is analagous to the duty a biographer owes "to knowledge, to virtue, and to truth."

Legal maxims are not uncommon in the *Rambler*. In No. 77, "To believe no man in his own cause, is the standing and perpetual rule of distributive justice." And in No. 79: "a Greek writer of sentences has laid down as a standing maxim, that *he who believes not another on his oath, knows himself to be perjured.*" Toward the end of the same essay, Johnson applies this idea of the importance of mutual trust to warfare:

> But surely war has its laws, and ought to be conducted with some regard to the universal interest of man. Those may justly be pursued as enemies to the community of nature, who suffer hostility to vacate the unalterable laws of right . . . .

In discussing the apparently contradictory claims of benevolence and justice (No. 81), Johnson insists on the importance of public safety:

> The magistrate, therefore, in pardoning a man unworthy of pardon, betrays the trust with which he is invested, gives away what is not his own, and, apparently, does to others what he would not that others should do to him. Even the community, whose right is still greater to arbitrary grants of mercy, is bound by those laws which regard the great republic of mankind, and cannot justify such forbearance as may promote wickedness, and lessen the general confidence and security in which all have an equal interest, and which all are therefore bound to maintain. For this reason the state has not a right to erect a general sanctuary for fugitives, or give protection to such as have forfeited their lives by crimes against the laws of common morality equally acknowledged by all nations, because no people can, without infraction of the universal league of social beings, incite, by prospects of impunity and safety, those practices in another dominion, which they would themselves punish in their own . . . . Justice is indispensably and universally necessary, and what is necessary must always be limited, uniform, and distinct.

In Nos. 61 and 95 we find satirical portraits of frivolous
law students in London, Mr. Frolick and Pertinax. In neither
instance is there much comment on the law; they are just
young men released from the discipline of the home or the
university who are able to divert themselves in the city without hindrance from the law societies. In No. 113, attorneys
are again the object of implied criticism, when Hymenaeus
feels himself justified in breaking with his fiancee "because
she gave my attorney a bribe to favor her in the bargain" on
the settlements.

The next *Rambler* consists of a vigorous argument against
vindictive laws, and especially against capital punishment
for theft, which may surprise some persons who have not read
the essay recently, and are accustomed to think of Johnson
as a rigid defender of the rights of property. He begins by a
shrewd suggestion that mere arrogance, rather than the requirements of the state, is sometimes behind "the desire of
investing lawful authority with terror," and continues:

> A slight perusal of the laws by which the measures of vin-
> dictive and coercive justice are established, will discover
> so many disproportions between crimes and punishments,
> such capricious distinctions of guilt, and such confusion of
> remissness and severity, as can scarcely be believed to
> have been produced by public wisdom, sincerely and calmly
> studious of public happiness . . . .

> It has always been the practice, when any particular species
> of robbery becomes prevalent and common, to endeavor its
> suppression by capital denunciations. Thus, one generation
> of malefactors is commonly cut off, and their successors
> are frighted into new expedients; the art of thievery is aug-
> mented with greater variety of fraud, and subtilized to high-
> er degrees of dexterity, and more occult methods of con-
> veyance. The law then renews the pursuit in the heat of
> anger, and overtakes the offender again with death. By this
> practice, capital inflictions are multiplied, and crimes very
> different in their degrees of enormity are equally subjected
> to the severest punishment that man has the power of exer-
> cising upon man.

> The lawgiver is undoubtedly allowed to estimate the mal-
> ignity of an offence, not merely by the loss or pain which
> single acts may produce, but by the general alarm and
> anxiety arising from the fear of mischief and insecurity of
> possession: he therefore exercises the right which so-
> cieties are supposed to have over the lives of those that
> compose them, not simply to punish a transgression but

to maintain order and preserve quiet; he enforces those
laws with severity that are most in danger of violation,
as the commander of a garrison doubles the guard on that
side which is threatened by the enemy.

This method has been long tried, but tried with so little
success that rapine and violence are hourly increasing:
yet few seem willing to despair of its efficacy, and of
those who employ their speculations upon the present corruption of the people, some propose the introduction of more
horrid, lingering, and terrific punishments; some are inclined to accelerate the executions; some, to discourage
pardons; and all seem to think that lenity has given confidence to wickedness and that we can only be rescued from
the talons of robbery by inflexible rigor and sanguinary
justice.

Yet since the right of setting an uncertain and arbitrary
value upon life has been disputed, and since experience
of past times gives us little reason to hope that any reformation will be effected by a periodical havoc of our fellow-
beings, perhaps it will not be useless to consider what
consequences might arise from relaxations of the law, and
a more rational and equitable adaptation of penalties to
offences.

. . . . To equal robbery with murder is to reduce murder
to robbery, to confound in common minds the gradations
of iniquity, and incite the commission of a greater crime
to prevent the detection of a less. If only murder were
punished with death, very few robbers would stain their
hands in blood; but when, by the last act of cruelty no
new danger is incurred, and greater security may be obtained, upon what principle shall we bid them forbear?

It may be urged, that the sentence is often mitigated to
simple robbery; but surely this is to confess that our laws
are unreasonable in our own opinion; and, indeed, it may be
observed that all but murderers have, at their last hour, the
common sensations of mankind pleading in their favor . . . .

The gibbet, indeed, certainly disables those who die upon
it from infesting the community; but their death seems not
to contribute more to the reformation of their associates
than any other method of separation. A thief seldom passes
much of his time in recollection or anticipation, but from
robbery hastens to riot, and from riot to robbery; nor, when
the grave closes upon his companion, has any other care
than to find another.

The frequency of capital punishments, therefore, rarely
hinders the commission of a crime, but naturally and commonly prevents its detection, and is, if we proceed only
upon prudential principles, chiefly for that reason to be
avoided. Whatever may be urged by casuists or politicians,
the greater part of mankind, as they can never think that to

pick the pocket and to pierce the heart is equally criminal, will scarcely believe that two malefactors so different in guilt can be justly doomed to the same punishment: nor is the necessity of submitting the conscience to human laws so plainly evinced, so clearly stated, or so generally allowed, but that the pious, the tender, and the just, will always scruple to concur with the community in an act which their private judgment cannot approve.

He who knows not how often rigorous laws produce total impunity, and how many crimes are concealed and forgotten for fear of hurrying the offender to that state in which there is no repentance, has conversed very little with mankind. And whatever epithets of reproach or contempt this compassion may incur from those who confound cruelty with firmness, I know not whether any wise man would wish it less powerful, or less extensive.

If those whom the wisdom of our laws has condemned to die, had been detected in their rudiments of robbery, they might, by proper discipline and useful labor, have been disentangled from their habits, they might have escaped all the temptations to subsequent crimes, and passed their days in reparation and penitence; and detected they might all have been, had the prosecutors been certain that their lives would have been spared. I believe every thief will confess that he has been more than once seized and dismissed; and that he has sometimes ventured upon capital crimes because he knew that those whom he injured would rather connive at his escape than cloud their minds with the horrors of his death.

All laws against wickedness are ineffectual, unless some will inform, and some will prosecute; but till we mitigate the penalties for mere violations of property, information will always be hated, and prosecution dreaded. The heart of a good man cannot but recoil at the thought of punishing a slight injury with death; especially when he remembers that the thief might have procured safety by another crime, from which he was restrained only by his remaining virtue.

The obligations to assist the exercise of public justice are indeed strong; but they will certainly be overpowered by tenderness for life. What is punished with severity contrary to our ideas of adequate retribution, will be seldom discovered; and multitudes will be suffered to advance from crime to crime, till they deserve death, because, if they had been sooner prosecuted, they would have suffered death before they deserved it.

In No. 125 Johnson quotes in passing "one of the maxims of the civil law, that *definitions are hazardous.*" In a rather infrequent mood of pessimism as to the state of contemporary society, he regrets the necessity of protecting contracts from fraud (No. 131):

If we consider the present state of the world, it will be found that all confidence is lost among mankind, that no man ventures to act, where money can be endangered upon the faith of another. It is impossible to see the long scrolls in which every contract is included, with all their append-ages of seals and attestation, without wondering at the depravity of those beings who must be restrained from violation of promise by such formal and public evidences, and precluded from equivocation and subterfuge by such punctilious minuteness. Among all the satires to which folly and wickedness have given occasion, none is equally severe with a bond or a settlement.

The tribulations of the poor were of constant concern to Johnson. In *Rambler* 142, depicting the life of a brutal country squire, he shows how unequal were the poor before the law:

His next acts of offence were committed in a contentious and spiteful vindication of the privileges of his manors, and a rigorous and relentless prosecution of every man that presumed to violate his game. As he happens to have no estate adjoining equal to his own, his oppressions are often borne without resistance, for fear of a long suit, of which he delights to count the expenses without the least solicitude about the event; for he knows that where noth-ing but an honorary right is contested, the poorer antag-onist must always suffer, whatever shall be the last de-cision of the law . . . . It is his common practice to pro-cure his hedges to be broken in the night, and then to demand satisfaction for damages which his grounds have suffered from his neighbor's cattle. An old widow was yesterday soliciting Eugenio to enable her to replevin her only cow then in the pound by squire Bluster's order, who had sent one of his agents to take advantage of her calamity, and persuade her to sell the cow at an under rate.

In No. 148 Johnson describes the same sort of injustice on a larger scale:

Politicians remark that no oppression is so heavy or last-ing as that which is inflicted by the perversion and ex-orbitance of legal authority. The robber may be seized, and the invader repelled, whenever they are found; they who pretend no right but that of force, may by force be punished or suppressed. But when plunder bears the name of impost, and murder is perpetrated by a judicial sentence, fortitude is intimidated, and wisdom confounded; resistance shrinks from an alliance with rebellion, and the villain remains secure in the robes of a magistrate.

He proceeds to compare such tyranny with the behavior of some parents, noting that in early Rome there was no punish-ment set for parricide, since the Romans could not conceive of such wickedness; conversely, that punishment of children was left in the hands of their fathers. But with a growing experience in human depravity, the Romans were obliged "to deter the parricide by a new law, and to transfer capital punishments from the parent to the magistrate."

In the next essay, Johnson gives a good example of the judicial quality of his mind: "There is always danger lest the honest abhorrence of a crime should raise the passions with too much violence against the man to whom it is imputed. In proportion as guilt is more enormous, it ought to be ascertained by stronger evidence." In No. 156 Johnson makes a remark which indicates his political principles, and also shows where those principles met Burke's: "Every government, say the politicians, is perpetually degenerating towards corruption, from which it must be rescued at certain periods by the resuscitation of its first principles, and the re-establishment of its original constitution."

In No. 197 Johnson gives an uncomplimentary portrait of an attorney, a sharper who made himself necessary to three rich relatives, and had endeared himself to one of them "who once rashly lent an hundred pounds without consulting him, by informing her that her debtor was on the point of bankruptcy, and posting so expeditiously with an execution, that all the other creditors were defrauded." He was also a kind of steward to the squire, and "had distinguished himself in his office by his address in raising the rents, his inflexibility in distressing the tardy tenants, and his acuteness in setting the parish free from burdensome inhabitants, by shifting them off to some other settlement." This picture is in accord with Johnson's other comments on attorneys, and may contain the internal evidence why he did not class them with the respectable and honorable members of the profession. In the office of rent collectors, especially, I suspect, in country districts, they must have been conspicuously unpopular.

Except for one quotation from Cujacius, the French civilian, which is not relevant to the law, but suggests that Johnson had read him, this ends my gleaning in the *Rambler*. The *Adventurer*, which came soon afterward, contains in No. 50

an interesting paragraph by Johnson:

> There is, I think, an ancient law of Scotland, by which
> leasing-making was capitally punished. I am, indeed, far
> from desiring to increase in this kingdom the number of ex-
> ecutions; yet I cannot but think that they who destroy the
> confidence of society, weaken the credit of intelligence
> and interrupt the security of life, harass the delicate with
> shame and perplex the timorous with alarms, might very
> properly be awakened to a sense of their crimes by denun-
> ciations of a whipping-post or pillory: since many are so
> insensible of right and wrong that they have no standard
> of action but the law, nor feel guilt but as they dread pun-
> ishment.

No. 62 is an attack on imprisonment for debt, particularly
in cases where the only fault was that a man went surety for
another who turned out to be incompetent or criminal: "nothing is more inequitable than that one man should suffer for
the crimes of another, for crimes which he neither prompted
nor permitted, which he could neither foresee nor prevent."
It is interesting that Johnson uses in his argument the notion
of a contract without mutual considerations:

> It is, I think, worthy of consideration whether, since no
> wager is binding without a possibility of loss on each side,
> it is not equally reasonable that no contract should be
> valid without reciprocal stipulations; but in this case, and
> others of the same kind, what is stipulated on his side to
> whom the bond is given? He takes advantage of the secur-
> ity, neglects his affairs, omits his duty, suffers timorous
> wickedness to grow daring by degrees, permits appetite to
> call for new gratifications, and, perhaps, secretly longs for
> the time in which he shall have power to seize the for-
> feiture . . . .

Johnson's last reference to the law in the *Adventurer* (No.
102) is a little vignette of a country magistrate, who may be
typical of such men in this period who were at all conscien-
tious: "I once resolved to go through the volumes relating to
the office of justice of the peace, but found them so crabbed
and intricate, that in less than a month I desisted in despair,
and resolved to supply my deficiencies by paying a competent
salary to a skillful clerk."

When in 1747 Johnson wrote the *Plan of an English Dictionary* and promised that it would contain some alien law
terms, because the reader would expect to find them, he probably had no expectation that his law terms would number well

over a thousand, as they do. To be sure, many of these are common English words used with some special significance in the law, but a large number are purely technical, and many alien. For the purposes of this study I have made a rough analysis of the first five letters of the alphabet in Johnson's great work, or just under a third of the *Dictionary* in bulk. No thorough study of the *Dictionary* has ever been made, but I believe the facts here presented will throw light both on that book and on Johnson's legal training.

The famous Preface contains only one comment on the law: "It has been asserted, that for the law to be *known*, is of more importance than to be *right*."[6] This might almost be taken as a text, or an explanation why Johnson included so many legal terms in his work, but one may also remember his long interest in the law, and the excuse or opportunity afforded by the preparation of the *Dictionary* to read books on the law and browse through law dictionaries.

The principal authority used by Johnson is John Cowell, whose law dictionary, *The Interpreter* (1607), was burnt by order of the House of Commons because it so exalted the royal prerogative. (One may doubt whether Johnson found that feature of it objectionable.) Of some 332 definitions in the section I examined, nearly a third were attributed to Cowell, and he was quoted in a few other instances. But as was Johnson's custom in defining technical or scientific terms, he was seldom satisfied with a mere definition, but frequently quoted so extensively as to constitute a short article on the subject. For instance, under *action*, all the following is quoted from Cowell:

> *Actions* are personal, real, and mixed; *action* personal belongs to a man *against* another, by reason of any contract, offence or cause, of like force with a contract or offence made or done by him or some other, for whose fact he is to answer. *Action* real is given to any man *against* another, that possesses the thing required or sued for in his own name, and no other man's. *Action* mixed is that which lies as well *against* or *for* the thing which we seek, as *against* the person that hath it; called *mixed*, because it hath a mixed respect both to the thing and to the person.

6. *Works*, 9. 198

Action is divided into civil, penal, and mixed. *Action* civil is that which tends only to the recovery of that which is due to us; as, a sum of money formerly lent. *Action* penal is that which aims at some penalty or punishment in the party sued, be it corporal or pecuniary: as, in common law, the next friends of a man feloniously slain shall pursue the law *against* the murderer. *Action* mixed is that which seeks both the thing whereof we are deprived, and a penalty also for the unjust detaining of the same.

Action upon the case is an *action* given for redress of wrongs done without force *against* any man, by law not specially provided for.

Action upon the statute is an *action* brought *against* a man upon breach of a statute.

The authority used with the next greatest frequency is John Ayliffe, whose *Parergon juris canonici Anglicani* was in Johnson's library, and which Gilbert Walmsley had purchased at the Lichfield bookstore at a time when the young Johnson was almost certainly working in the shop. Ayliffe's definitions are used some eighteen times and he is quoted in twenty-two other instances under the legal terms in the part of the *Dictionary* under consideration. As with Cowell, Johnson frequently gives a full paragraph in illustration. For example, defining *absence* as "want of appearance, in the legal sense," Johnson then excerpts the following from the *Parergon:*

Absence is of a fourfold kind or species. The first is a necessary *absence*, as in banished persons; this is entirely necessary. A second, necessary and voluntary; as, upon the account of the commonwealth, or in the service of the church. The third kind the civilians call a probable *absence;* as, that of students on the score of study. And the fourth, an *absence* entirely voluntary; as, on the account of trade, merchandise, and the like. Some add a fifth kind of *absence*, which is committed *cum dolo et culpâ*, by a man's non-appearance on a citation; as, in a contumacious person, who, in hatred to his contumacy, is, by the law, in some respects, reputed as a person present.

The works of Bacon are cited with some frequency to illustrate the use of law terms, but not employed for the purposes of definition, though Johnson in some cases may have developed his definitions out of his citations. No other authors were used to an extent comparable with Cowell or Ayliffe, but we find that Ephraim Chambers's dictionary is the source of eight definitions, one of which is of special interest. Under *attorney*, Johnson quotes from Cowell: "Such a person as by consent, commandment, or request, takes heed, fees, and takes upon him the charge of other men's business, in their absence." There is much more, but it does not bring the definition wholly up to the current usage of 1755, so Johnson adds this paragraph from Chambers:

> *Attorneys* in common law are nearly the same with proctors in the civil law, and solicitors in courts of equity. *Attorneys* sue out writs or process, or commence, carry on, and defend actions, or other proceedings, in the name of other persons, in the courts of common law. None are admitted to act without having served a clerkship for five years, taking the proper oath, being enrolled, and examined by the judges. The *attorney general* pleads within the bar. To him come warrants for making out patents, pardons, &c. and he is the principal manager of all law affairs of the crown.

Among his illustrations of the use of the word Johnson permits himself to quote Pope:

> Despairing quacks with curses fled the place,
> And vile *attorneys*, now an useless race.

I think this represents only a general social prejudice against the lowest rank of lawyers, as everyone dislikes shysters, though one's own lawyer is never one: Johnson had several friends who were attorneys, and I do not know of a single one whom he did not respect.

Six definitions were attributed to "Dict.", which is usually Bailey. It may be of some significance that five of these occur in the first letter of the alphabet, and only one in the next four: either Johnson became neglectful of acknowledging his source, or he used it less, preferring to rely on writers of more authority in the law. There is a like number attributed to Thomas Blount, whose law dictionary went into a third edition in 1717. Four definitions come from Phillips's dictionary (Seventh edition, 1720), one each from Calvinus's *Lexicon Juridicum*, which was in Johnson's library, from Coke, from John Harris's *Lexicon Technicum*, 1704, and from Hanmer's edition of Shakespeare. I found no definitions from Sir Matthew Hale, but he is quoted seven times, particularly his *Common*

Law. This is a rather larger list of authorities than one might expect, and though in bulk it is principally confined to two, nevertheless it is clear that Johnson ranged through a rather wide variety of books on the law.

It is somewhat surprising that on such a subject as this, most of Johnson's definitions are his own. It would have been easy to have his amanuenses copy out definitions of such technical matter, but this was not done. To be sure, Johnson may have arrived at many of his definitions by a process of paraphrase or analysis of his illustrative quotations, and in one instance the use of "hath" in a definition suggests the phraseology of some other writer. Nevertheless, Johnson invented many more definitions than he took over from others — 178 as against 154, if the reader wishes figures. This shows something of interest to the student of Johnson's methods of compilation, but it is even more pertinent to our present inquiry. For it is manifestly impossible to go through several books marking paragraphs to be excerpted by a copyist and then devise hundreds of definitions on a subject without acquiring more than a casual acquaintance with it. I cannot estimate quantitatively how much Johnson learned of the law from this work, but I suspect that it was quite as much as many students in the Inns of Court learned by a somewhat similar process.

I shall confine myself to quoting two of Johnson's definitions. The first is uncontroversial, like the great bulk of the *Dictionary:* "Common Law contains those customs and usages which have, by long prescription, obtained in this nation the force of laws. It is distinguished from the statute law, which owes its authority to acts of Parliament." The second, perhaps only on the fringe of the law, is the famous definition of excise: "A hateful tax levied upon commodities, and adjudged not by the common judges of property, but wretches hired by those to whom excise is paid."

In 1756 Johnson contributed a long essay, "The Political State of Great Britain," to *The Literary Magazine,* in which we find a rather restrained comment on the state of international law at the time:

It was, however, understood, by a kind of tacit compact among the commercial powers, that possession of the coast included a right to the inland; and, therefore, the charters granted to the several colonies limit their districts only from north to south, leaving their possessions from east to west unlimited and discretional, supposing that, as the colony increases, they may take lands as they shall want them, the possession of the coasts excluding other navigators, and the unhappy Indians having no right of nature or of nations.7

Johnson's sympathies were with the natives, and it is not surprising to find him defending other natives against their invaders, in this instance the King of Prussia, also in *The Literary Magazine:* "It is hard to find upon what pretence the King of Prussia could treat the Bohemians as criminals, for preparing to defend their native country, or maintain their allegiance to their lawful sovereign against an invader . . . ." (4.572.) In the same essay Johnson makes a point in favor of the possessor of an estate which has since become statutory law:

To every man that knows the state of the feudal countries, the intricacy of their pedigrees, the confusion of their alliances, and the different rules of inheritance that prevail in different places, it will appear evident, that of reviving antiquated claims there can be no end, and that the possession of a century is a better title than can commonly be produced. So long a prescription supposes an acquiescence in the other claimants; and that acquiescence supposes also some reason, perhaps now unknown, for which the claim was forborne. (4.542.)

To preface his epitome of Frederick's plan to reform the courts of Prussia, Johnson makes some pointed comments on such reforms:

It is perhaps impossible to review the laws of any country without discovering many defects and many superfluities. Laws often continue when their reasons have ceased. Laws made for the first state of the society continue unabolished, when the general form of life is changed. Parts of the judicial procedure, which were at first only accidental, become in time essential; and formalities are accumulated on each other, till the art of litigation requires more study than the discovery of right.

The King of Prussia, examining the institutions of his own country, thought them such as could only be amended by a general abrogation and the establishment of a new body of

7. *Works*, 10.179

law. to which he gave the name of the Code Frederique.
which is comprised in one volume of no great bulk, and
must therefore unavoidably contain general positions, to be
accommodated to particular cases by the wisdom and integrity of the courts. To embarrass justice by multiplicity
of laws, or to hazard it by confidence in judges, seem to be
the opposite rocks on which all civil institutions have been
wrecked, and between which legislative wisdom has never
yet found an open passage. (4.550.)

After the epitome, Johnson remarks that the code "affords
one proof more that the right is easily discovered, and that
men do not so often want ability to find, as willingness to
practice it [4.555]."

In the preface to Rolt's *Dictionary*, 1756, Johnson states
that a merchant ought "to examine what kinds of commerce
are unlawful, either as being expressly prohibited, because
detrimental to the manufactures or other interest of his
country, as the exportation of silver to the East Indies,
and the introduction of French commodities; or unlawful in
itself, as the traffic for negroes [9.429]." It may be noted that
the slave trade was not prohibited by Great Britain for many
years after this manly statement.

The *Idler*, like Johnson's earlier periodical essays, contains several references to the law. The first, in No. 5,
merely mentions the Salic law in passing. In No. 10, Johnson
by implication deprecates the strictness of the laws against
papists, when he ridicules a fictitious character who fears
that those laws are not strong enough. In No. 11, attacking
theorists who derive civil institutions from climate, Johnson
remarks: "Laws are often occasional, often capricious, made
always by a few, and sometimes by a single voice." In No.
22, Johnson returns to the subject of imprisonment for debt,
which he had earlier treated in the *Rambler*. His approach is
at the same time economic, humanitarian, and legal, as is
evident almost at once:

    The wisdom and justice of the English laws are, by English-
    men at least, loudly celebrated; but scarcely the most zeal-
    ous admirers of our institutions can think that law wise,
    which, when men are capable of work, obliges them to beg;
    or just, which exposes the liberty of one to the passions
    of another.

He goes on to remark that imprisonment is a loss to the nation of the productive capacity of the one confined, and no gain to the creditor:

> For of the multitudes who are pining in those cells of misery, a very small part is suspected of any fraudulent act by which they retain what belongs to others. The rest are imprisoned by the wantonness of pride, the malignity of revenge, or the acrimony of disappointed expectation.

Johnson is not content with exposing the evils of the system, but suggests a remedy:

> The end of all civil regulations is to secure private happiness from private malignity; to keep individuals from the power of one another; but this end is apparently neglected, when a man, irritated with loss, is allowed to be the judge of his own cause, and to assign the punishment of his own pain; when the distinction between guilt and happiness, between casualty and design, is entrusted to eyes blind with interest, to understandings depraved by resentment.

> Since poverty is punished among us as a crime, it ought at least to be treated with the same lenity as other crimes; the offender ought not to languish at the will of him whom he has offended, but to be allowed some appeal to the justice of his country. There can be no reason why any debtor should be imprisoned, but that he may be compelled to payment; and a term should therefore be fixed, in which the creditor should exhibit his accusation of concealed property. If such property can be discovered, let it be given to the creditor; if the charge is not offered, or cannot be proved, let the prisoner be dismissed.

Then Johnson reverts to a favorite notion, that there may be culpability in the creditor as well as in the debtor:

> Those who made the laws have apparently supposed that every deficiency of payment is the crime of the debtor. But the truth is that the creditor always shares the act, and often more than shares the guilt of improper trust. It seldom happens that any man imprisons another but for debts which he suffered to be contracted in hope of advantage to himself, and for bargains in which he proportioned his profit to his own opinion of the hazard; and there is no reason why one should punish the other for a contract in which both concurred.

Johnson is ready with an answer to the question of how this change would affect trade:

> The motive to credit is the hope of advantage. Commerce can never be at a stop while one man wants what another can supply; and credit will never be denied while it is like-

ly to be repaid with profit. He that trusts one whom he de-
signs to sue, is criminal by the act of trust; the cessation
of such insidious traffic is to be desired, and no reason can
be given why a change of the law should impair any other.

We see nation trade with nation, where no payment can be
compelled. Mutual convenience produces mutual confidence;
and the merchants continue to satisfy the demands of each
other, though they have nothing to dread but the loss of
trade.

And Johnson concludes with a fine peroration:

It is vain to continue an institution which experience shows
to be ineffectual. We have now imprisoned one generation
of debtors after another, but we do not find that their numbers lessen. We have now learned that rashness and impru-
dence will not be deterred from taking credit; let us try
whether fraud and avarice may be more easily restrained
from giving it.

No. 38 is also devoted to imprisonment for debt, but aside
from noting that it contains another plea to change the law, it
need not detain us here.

In No. 65 Johnson complains of the bad editing of a standard book on the law: "How Hale would have borne the muti-
lations which his *Pleas of the Crown* have suffered from the
editor, they who know his character will easily conceive."
This statement indicates a considerable knowledge of the
book, probably from Johnson's use of it in preparing the *Dictionary*.

In No. 71 Dick Shifter, a young law student not unlike his
predecessors in the *Rambler*, who preferred plays, poems, and
romances to "the severity of the law," found, when he took a
holiday in the country, another of Johnson's attorneys,

who told him that unless he made farmer Dobson satisfaction
for trampling his grass, he had orders to indict him. Shifter
was offended, but not terrified; and telling the attorney that
he was himself a lawyer, talked so volubly of pettifoggers
and barraters, that he drove him away.

In No. 85 Johnson quotes in passing the proverb "a corrupt society has many laws," but without indicating agreement or disagreement. In No. 89, he remarks: "Of justice one
of the heathen sages has shown, with great acuteness, that
it was impressed upon mankind only by the inconveniences
which injustice had produced." In the next essay, on oratory,

he shows his low opinion of that art:

> Neither the judges of our laws nor the representatives of
> our people would be much affected by labored gesticulation,
> or believe any man the more because he rolled his eyes,
> of puffed his cheeks, or spread abroad his arms, or stamped
> the ground, or thumped his breast, or turned his eyes some-
> times to the ceiling and sometimes to the floor. Upon men
> intent only upon truth, the arm of an orator has little
> power; a credible testimony, or a cogent argument, will
> overcome all the art of modulation, and all the violence of
> contortion.

Surely Parliament and the English courts have seldom been so
flattered. Johnson adds that in Athens "the arts of mechanical persuasion were banished from the court of supreme judicature." In the following essay, on the riches of the English
language, Johnson comments on the wealth of English legal
literature: "The original law of society, the rights of subjects, and the prerogatives of kings, have been considered
with the utmost nicety, sometimes profoundly investigated,
and sometimes familiarly explained."

With 1760, Johnson's early study of the law may be said to
have concluded. Begun perhaps desultorily with glancing at a
few law books in his father's shop, stimulated by his Lichfield and Oxford acquaintance, put to a test in London when
Cave asked his opinion of the legality of abridgments, temp-
orarily balked when the lack of a degree prevented his admission to practice at Doctors' Commons, resumed with the years
of composing the *Parliamentary Debates* and the dogged preparation of the *Dictionary*, and finding some outlet in the
Rambler, the *Adventurer*, and the *Idler*, Johnson's study had
prepared him with a broad and humane knowledge which was
to bear still more fruit in the future.

Johnson's Study of the Law

In the 'sixties Johnson's interest in the law reached a sort of climax, owing in part to his acquaintance with William Gerard Hamilton, whose brilliant debut in Parliament and subsequent inactivity earned him the name "Single Speech" Hamilton. Johnson knew him from about 1760 onwards,[1] and perhaps owed his acquaintance to Burke, who for the six years ending in 1765 had served as a fact-gatherer for Hamilton. In the spring of 1765 Burke had left in disgust, finding that he had no prospects of advancement. It is possible that Johnson had already performed one service for Hamilton via Burke, for in that same year Jenkinson, later Earl of Liverpool, wrote Johnson asking for the return of "papers concerning the late negotiations for the Peace [of Paris]" which he had lent Johnson two years before. Nothing is known of any use to which Johnson put the papers, but it is just the sort of information which Hamilton constantly sought. At any rate, after Burke's resignation Hamilton sought a successor, "who, in addition to a taste and an understanding of ancient authors, and what generally passes under the name of scholarship, has likewise a share of modern knowledge, and has applied himself in some degree to the study of the law." The stipend would be "an income, which would neither be insufficient for him as a man of letters, or disreputable to him as a gentleman," and later some sort of political post.[2] Chambers was recommended, but probably thought his prospects better at

1. Hamilton, *Parliamentary Logic*, ed. Malone, p. xl.

2. *Life*, 1. 519-20

Oxford as understudy to Blackstone, and in September we find Johnson undertaking the study of law, undoubtedly having come to some sort of agreement with Hamilton.

In his *Prayers and Meditations*, we find, dated Sept. 26, 1765:

Before the Study of Law.

Almighty God, the Giver of wisdom, without whose help resolutions are vain, without whose blessing study is ineffectual, enable me, if it be thy will, to attain such knowledge as may qualify me to direct the doubtful, and instruct the ignorant, to prevent wrongs, and terminate contentions; and grant that I may use that knowledge which I shall attain, to thy glory and my own salvation, for Jesus Christ's sake. Amen.

A few weeks later another prayer shows that his association with Hamilton was beginning:

Engaging in Politics with H--n.

Nov. 1765.

Almighty God, who art the Giver of all wisdom, enlighten my understanding with knowledge of right, and govern my will by thy laws, that no deceit may mislead me, nor temptation corrupt me, that I may always endeavor to do good, and to hinder evil.

It will be observed that both of these prayers show an intention of studying to some serious and important end—not as a mere avocation or pastime. Johnson must have thought of himself as entering upon a new and active career, perhaps one which would, in time, lead him to Parliament. Conversely, it is equally clear that he did not think of himself as a mere drudge for a man almost twenty years his junior, and indeed at this stage of his career, with his pension, his LL.D. from Dublin, and most of his major works accomplished, he would have thought a position of drudgery wholly beneath him. But Hamilton was a man of some distinction, and a vague sort of collaboration with him might be to Johnson's taste. He was an Oxford man, and Malone says of his studies at Lincoln's Inn:

His researches respecting the English Constitution and municipal law, the charters of our great trading companies, the law of nations, and many branches of civil polity, are

so multifarious, that it is believed few students ever took
more pains to become eminent advocates at the Bar than
he did to acquire such stores of political knowledge as
might give him an indisputable claim to the character of a
wise and distinguished statesman.3

What Johnson did in his first year of association with Hamilton is unknown, but in November 1766 he was at work writing
Considerations on the Corn Laws for Hamilton's use. Malone,
who found Johnson's manuscript among Hamilton's papers,
and published it with Hamilton's *Parliamentary Logic*, describes the background of the composition:

> The harvest in that year had been so deficient, and corn had
> risen to so high a price, that in the months of September
> and October there had been many insurrections in the Mid-
> land counties, to which Johnson alludes; and which were of
> so alarming a kind, that it was necessary to repress them
> by military force. In these tumults several persons were
> killed. The Ministry therefore thought it expedient to ac-
> celerate the meeting of Parliament, which was assembled
> in November; and the King's Speech particularly mentions
> the scarcity that had taken place (which had induced his
> Majesty to prevent the further exportation of corn by an
> embargo), and the tumultuous and illegal conduct of the
> lower orders of people in consequence of the dearth.4

We have one important piece of information showing Johnson's care in preparing his *Considerations*. On 19 November
1766, he wrote to his lawyer friend Chambers: "I beg to be
informed, if you know or can enquire what are the reasons for
which Dr. Blackstone thinks the late embargo to be not legal,
as I hear he does. It always seemed legal to me. But I judge
upon mere principles without much knowledge of laws or
facts."5 Johnson is probably recalling the debate on the Corn
Laws which he reported in the *Gentleman's Magazine* many
years earlier, in which the legality of a similar embargo was
not questioned. We do not have Chambers' reply, but he probably reassured Johnson. In the editions of the *Commentaries*
published after this event, Blackstone flatly affirms the legality of the embargo, and cites the relevant statutes.

3. *Op. cit.*, xv.

4. *Ib.*, x-xi

5. Adam, *Catalogue*, 1. 29

The *Considerations* is a closely reasoned statement on the effect of an export bounty on the production of corn. Johnson asserts that the bounty is responsible for the large increase in acreage in recent years, and by making grain plentiful has made it cheap, but that in times of scarcity it is easy to embargo exportation, as had just been done. What could be better than a law which generally produced such good results, and which could be adjusted to changed situations so easily? "It is perhaps impossible for human wisdom to go further than to contrive a law of which the good is certain and uniform, and the evil, though possible in itself, yet always subject to certain and effectual restraints [p. 247]." In opposition to those who thought that the bounty should have been suspended earlier, Johnson says, with his usual good sense: "It may however be considered, that the change of old establishments is always an evil; and that therefore, where the good of the change is not certain and constant, it is better to preserve that reverence and that confidence which is produced by consistency of conduct and permanency of laws." (pp. 251-252.)

As to the advisability of making frequent adjustments in the rate of bounty, he is equally opposed:

> If by a balance of probabilities, in which a grain of dust may turn the scale, — or by a curious scheme of calculation, in which if one postulate in a thousand be erroneous, the deduction which promises plenty may end in famine, — if by a specious mode of uncertain ratiocination, the critical point at which the bounty should stop, might seem to be discovered, I shall continue to believe that it is more safe to trust what we have already tried; and cannot but think bread a product of too much importance to be made the sport of subtilty, and the topic of hypothetical disputation. (pp. 252-253.)

A month after Johnson had written these observations for Hamilton's guidance in Parliament, another subject was under review. The East India Company was having one of its periodical quarrels between the directors, the stockholders, and Parliament as to the size of its annual dividend. The stockholders naturally wanted more money and felt that the directors were paying themselves enormous salaries. The directors were quick to point out that larger dividends would bankrupt

the company. The government, which owed the company a
large sum, considered itself directly concerned in its finan-
cial health. There was a pamphlet war, and Parliament was
expected to set the amount of the dividend in the current
session. In these circumstances Johnson wrote to Chambers
on 11 December 1766: "If you could get me any information
about the East Indian affairs, you may promise that if it is
used at all, it shall be used in favor of the Company."[6] The
phrase "if it is used at all" indicates, I think, that Johnson,
as before, was merely gathering material for Hamilton which
might be used in a speech but would more probably serve only
for his use in casting an intelligent vote.

On 22 January, Johnson was still concerned with the matter,
and again asked Chambers for help:

> The affairs of the East Indies are to come at last before
> the Parliament, and therefore we shall be glad of any in-
> formation about them. We are likewise desirous of the
> papers which have been laid before the House, which can
> no longer be secret, and therefore, I suppose, may be easily
> granted us. We will pay for transcribing if that be any dif-
> ficulty. What other papers shall be put into our hands, shall
> be used if they are used at all, in defence of the Com-
> pany. (Adam, 1.30.)

Johnson's use of the first person plural in this letter is
suggestive. It indicates, I think, that his association with
Hamilton was no secret to Chambers, and it also shows that
Johnson had a feeling of partnership about this work. What
use he made of this information is not known. I suspect that
the answer may be found in the manuscript volumes of *Adver-
saria* written by Hamilton on various political topics, if these
volumes still exist. Malone would have recognized such an
essay if it had been in Johnson's hand, but since he was un-
aware that Johnson had any particular interest in the East
India Company at this time, he might have missed it if it
was present only in a copy by Hamilton.

There is no further evidence of professional association
between Johnson and Hamilton, and it may be assumed that
Johnson found that the work had no future for him. The two
men remained close friends, however; and Johnson remembered

6. Adam, 1. 29

Hamilton in his will with a book of his choice. (He forgot Boswell.)

We may now inquire what books were available to Johnson for his study of law. The best record is the sale catalogue of his library, as it was auctioned off after his death. The list is tantalizing, because, as is usual with such catalogues, many of the books are not named, as in lot 28, which consisted of twelve volumes, "Wood's Laws of England, 2 v., &c." We are left in the dark as to the other ten volumes in the lot. The list, therefore, does not prove that a particular book was not in the library, nor, of course, does it prove that Johnson read any given book listed. It will also be clear that not all of these books were in Johnson's possession at the period under consideration. Some information as to his familiarity with his law books may be derived from Boswell and elsewhere; this I shall indicate in its proper place.

The law of nature and of nations is represented by Grotius' *De jure et belli*, and by John Towers' translation of Cumberland's reply to Hobbes: *A philosophical enquiry into the laws of nature*, Dublin, 1750. In this category might also be included Franciscus Suarez' *Tractatus de legibus ac Deo Legislatore*, 1679. In 1775 Johnson wrote Boswell that the Scots lawyers were "great masters of the law of nations [*Life*, 2.292 ,"] and he later remarked that not all the great writers on the law had been in practice: "Grotius, indeed was; but Pufendorf was not, Burlamaqui was not [2.430]." On another occasion, when Ferguson's book on civil society was about to appear, he said: "Alas! what can he do upon that subject? Aristotle, Polybius, Grotius, Pufendorf, and Burlamaqui have reaped in that field before him."[7] He was well enough acquainted with Pufendorf's writings to cite his opinion of corporal punishment of pupils in a conversation with Boswell.[8]

In the field of foreign law, excluding civil law, Johnson possessed *A Code of Gentoo laws, or ordinations of the Pundits*, 1776. This work of Halhed might have been presented to Johnson by Jones, a member of the Club, and the great

7. *Misc.*, 1.419
8. *Life*, 2. 157

authority on Sanskrit. It was popular enough to go into two
subsequent editions. Johnson also owned *Jus Hebraeorum*, a
quarto not otherwise identified, but perhaps a printer's error
for John Hottinger's *Juris Hebraeorum*, a quarto published in
1655.

As to Johnson's familiarity with foreign law, the reader will
recall his reply to the Dutchman who "inveighed against the
barbarity of putting an accused person to the torture": "Why,
Sir, you do not, I find, understand the law of your own country.
The torture in Holland is considered as a favor to an accused
person; for no man is put to the torture there, unless there is
as much evidence against him as would amount to conviction
in England. An accused person among you, therefore, has one
chance more to escape punishment, than those who are tried
among us." (1.466-467.)

In the field of civil law, Johnson owned the French jurist
Denis Godefroy's *Corpus juris civilis*, Lyons, 1652, and the
French advocate Nicholas Boerius' *Decisiones Burgedalenses*,
Geneva, 1708. His high opinion of the civil law is well known.
In 1763 he wrote to the young Boswell, "I know not how you
will make a better choice, than by studying the civil law
[1.474]," and five years later, when Barnard was going abroad
to purchase books for the King's library, Johnson gave him
this advice:

> The schoolmen and canonists must not be neglected, for
> they are useful to many purposes; nor too anxiously sought,
> for their influence among us is much lessened by the Re-
> formation. Of the canonists at least a few eminent writers
> may be sufficient. The schoolmen are of more general value.
> But the feudal and civil law I cannot but wish to see com-
> plete. The feudal constitution is the original of the law of
> property, over all the civilized part of Europe; and the
> civil law, as it is generally understood to include the law
> of nations, may be called with great propriety a regal
> study.9

The rest of the books may all be classified under English
law, perhaps stretching the definition a little. There are two
dictionaries, Giles Jacob's *New law dictionary*, which had
gone through numerous editions since 1729, and Joannus Calvinus's *Lexicon juridicum*, which Johnson had used in pre-
9. *Letters*, 206

paring the *Dictionary*.

Canon and ecclesiastical law are well represented. John Ayliffe's *Parergon juris canonici Anglicani: or a commentary by way of supplement to the canons and constitutions of the Church of England*, 1726 or 1734, will remind the reader that Johnson's early friend Walmsley had bought "Aliffs Canon and Civill Law" from the Lichfield bookstore of Johnson's father, and that Johnson used this as his principal authority on canon law in the *Dictionary*. This book is followed by Richard Burn's *Ecclesiastical Law*, 2 v., 1763, which was the standard work on the subject. These are supplemented by the canonist Lyndwood's *Provincial Constitutions of England*, Oxford, 1679, and by *De jure ecclesiae*, 1670, which is probably Herbert Thorndike's *De ratione ac jure finiendi controversias Ecclesiae disputatio*, published in that year.

Statutes and reports are numerous. There is an eight-volume *Abridgement of the statutes*, as well as thirty folio volumes of Acts of Parliament, and five more volumes of statutes. Blackstone's edition of *The Great Charter and charter of the forest, with other authentic instruments*, Oxford, 1759, might have been the gift of Blackstone or Chambers. Then there are Henry Rolle's *Abridgement of cases*, 4 v., 1688, Edmund Plowden's *Reports*, Salkeld's *Reports*, and for Scotland John Maclaurin's *Arguments and decisions in remarkable cases, before the High Court of Judiciary, and other supreme courts in Scotland*, Edinburgh, 1774. In 1776 Johnson had read over and approved Maclaurin's plea in the case involving the negro slave Knight, and later dictated to Boswell an argument in his favor. It seems likely that in return Maclaurin sent him this book.

Treatises on the law are also numerous. The earliest is Fortescue's *De laudibus legum Angliae*, probably in the edition of 1738, since it is a folio. Then come Sir Matthew Hale's *Historia placitorum Coronae, or history of the pleas of the Crown*, 2 v., in the edition of 1736, Sir Henry Spelman's *Works*, 1723, Hawkins' *Pleas of the Crown*, 1716, William Ryley's *Placita Parliamentaria*, and another volume merely described as *Pleadings in Parliament*. Among Johnson's contemporaries the first is Thomas Wood's *Institute of the Laws of England*, which went through ten editions in fifty years. Wood is remembered for having anticipated Blackstone in his efforts to have the English law taught in the universities. Then there is William Nelson's *Lex maneriorum, or the laws and customs of England relating to manors*, first published in 1724, which is balanced on the Northern side by George Wallace's *Thoughts on the origin of feudal tenures and the descent of ancient peerages connected with the State of Scotland*, Edinburgh, 1783, a book which amused Boswell and which I suspect he sent to Johnson. Eleven years before this book was published Johnson had urged Boswell to write such a book. A minor general work might be mentioned next, William Smith's *Nature and institution of government, containing an account of the feudal and English polity*, 2 v., 1771. Smith was a prolific hack, whose writings are now wholly forgotten. Blackstone's *Commentaries*, 4 v., is listed among the octavo volumes, which would make the edition that of 1775 or later. It is entirely possible that this was the gift of the author. John Nichols, another friend of Johnson's, probably presented him with his *Collection of royal wills*, 1780. Another book, published anonymously, was not the gift of the author. Boswell tells the story:

> Soon after the Honorable Daines Barrington had published his excellent "Observations on the Statutes," Johnson waited on that worthy and learned gentleman; and, having told him his name, courteously said, "I have read your book, Sir, with great pleasure, and wish to be better known to you." Thus began an acquaintance which was continued with mutual regard as long as Johnson lived. 1

The book was published in 1766, so that Johnson must have read it very near the time we have been considering in this chapter. The book was described by Bentham as "everything apropos of everything." Another book which may have been presented by the author was Henry Ballow's *Treatise of equity*, published anonymously in 1737. This was the only book on equity published in Johnson's lifetime, and according to Sir William Holdsworth bears out Johnson's statement that

1. *Life*, 3. 314

Ballow was a very able man. It will be remembered that Johnson told Boswell that what he knew of law he had learned
chiefly from Ballow (3.22). The two were friends for many
years.

Boswell records a conversation between Johnson and Sir
Alexander Macdonald which may refer to books in Johnson's
library:

> Sir A. "I think, Sir, almost all great lawyers, such at least
> as have written upon law, have known only law, and noth-
> ing else." Johnson. "Why no, Sir; Judge Hale was a great
> lawyer, and wrote upon law; and yet he knew a great many
> other things, and has written upon other things. Selden
> too." Sir A. "Very true, Sir; and Lord Bacon. But was not
> Lord Coke a mere lawyer?" Johnson. "Why, I am afraid he
> was; but he would have taken it very ill if you had told him
> so. He would have prosecuted you for scandal." (2.158.)

The second phase of Johnson's legal education, then, may
be said to have consisted in his study for his work with Hamilton, his consideration of the corn laws and the East India
Company, and no doubt other parliamentary problems, and a
continued immersion in the many law books of his own library,
for which he soon found good use.

Johnson and Chambers

The most remarkable chapter in the history of Johnson's interest in the law is that which concerns his association with Robert Chambers, and his collaboration with Chambers in the Vinerian lectures on the English Law. It is only within the past decade that this collaboration has been made known, and this present chapter is the first attempt to determine the extent and nature of Johnson's contribution. It was a secret well kept, remarkably well, considering that Chambers was intimate with many of the Johnsonian circle, and considering also that that admirable gossip Mrs. Thrale knew the secret — was perhaps the only one who did.

Johnson knew Chambers for thirty years, and as early as 1754, when Chambers was a seventeen-year-old, an exhibitioner of Lincoln College, Oxford, we find Johnson writing to him in terms which do not indicate a recent acquaintance. Chambers, son of an attorney of Newcastle, was destined for the law, and that fact must have made him interesting to Johnson, who, unable to pursue law as a profession, had never lost interest in it. They had a common interest in literature, too, and in 1756 Chambers sent Johnson a biographical article for *The Literary Magazine*, which Johnson was editing. In that same year Blackstone published his *Analysis of the Laws of England*, based on the lectures which he had been giving at Oxford, and a preliminary study for the *Commentaries*. It seems likely that Chambers was already his student. It is certain that he was studying the civil law. In the spring of 1758 the Vinerian statutes were being prepared, and the appointment of Scholars, Fellows, and a Professor of the Common Law contemplated. Chambers, not yet twenty-one, seems to have written Johnson asking his opinion of a career leading to the professorship, and Johnson's help in securing a scholarship. Johnson sent letters of recommendation to be handed by Chambers to Oxford acquaintances of Johnson's,[1] and on April 14 wrote again, commenting on the new professorship:

> I long to hear how you go on in your solicitation, and what hopes you have of success. Of what value do you expect any of these new benefactions to be? The great fault of our constitution is that we have many little things which may support idleness, but scarcely any thing great enough to kindle ambition. So that very few men stay in the houses who are qualified to live elsewhere. A professorship of the common law is at least decent, but I do not expect it to be of much use; it will not be worth the acceptance of any practical Lawyer, and a mere speculatist will have no authority. However, I am glad it is thought on. (1.23.)

On 1 June, Chambers was apparently assured of his scholarship, for Johnson wrote:

> I am extremely glad that you are likely to succeed. The honor is not less that you have one of the Scholarships without opposition, for you have it only because your character makes opposition hopeless. Nothing remains but that you consider how much will be expected from one that begins so well, and that you take care not to break the promise you have made. (1.24.)

In 1762 Chambers was elected Vinerian fellow, and in 1765 occurred a series of events which in all probability brought Johnson and Chambers together again. In the spring of that year Burke, who had long acted as a sort of parliamentary secretary for "Single Speech" Hamilton, left the post, and Hamilton sought the advice of Dr. Warton in filling it. Chambers was recommended, but there is no evidence that he accepted. In September Johnson wrote his "Prayer before the Study of Law," and in November his prayer "Engaging in politics with H——n." The sequence of these events makes certain deductions almost inevitable. Burke had been trained as a lawyer, and a successor with legal training was desired. Chambers had more important irons in the fire, but he and Warton had known each other for more than a decade, and

1. Adam, *Catalogue*, 1. 22

both were intimate with Johnson. Why not suggest Johnson
for the post? Perhaps Chambers recommended a few books for
Johnson to look into, though I scarcely think Johnson would
have needed any such suggestions. Johnson later named
Chambers and Ballow as the two men from whom he had learned
most about the law. It is not unlikely that this is the year in
which the instruction from Chambers began. At any rate, Johnson was soon working for Hamilton. In January, 1766, Johnson
wrote to Lucy Porter saying that he could not well come to
Lichfield during the session of Parliament, and in the following November he wrote his *Considerations on the Corn Laws*
for Hamilton.

Meanwhile, Blackstone had resigned as Vinerian Professor,
and in May, 1766, Chambers was elected his successor. It
was a brilliant post for a man still in his twenties. All that
was necessary was to compose and deliver lectures. This,
indeed, had not always been the case with university pro-
fessorships: the Regius Professorship of Modern History at
Cambridge had at times been almost honorary — Thomas Gray,
as incumbent, knew that he ought to deliver lectures, but
never got round to it. But the Vinerian statutes provided
severe fines for failure to lecture, fines which, in the course
of a year, might equal the whole stipend — if they were enforced. And Chambers showed a lamentable inability to begin,
apparently from a timidity which was to plague him almost
throughout his life. In this situation, the fact that Blackstone
had already published the first volume of his *Commentaries*,
expanded from his own Vinerian lectures, and the further fact
that their success was immediate, probably gave Chambers
pause, for comparison was inevitable. He must have written
Johnson in this perplexity (none of his letters to Johnson
have been preserved), and on 8 October Johnson wrote to him
in terms which suggest that they had already decided on some
sort of collaboration: "I do not design that it [a visit to Ox-
ford] shall be longer than may consist with our necessary
operations. Let me therefore know immediately how soon it
will be necessary for us to be together. If I cannot go with
you to Oxford, you must be content to stay a little while in

London." (1.28.) Accordingly, Johnson spent the end of October and the first week of November in Oxford, and there the first series of lectures was probably outlined. The statutes provided that a public lecture was to be given at the beginning of each term, with a penalty of £20 for each failure to deliver such a lecture. But whatever planning or outlining may have been done, no lecture was delivered, as is clear from Johnson's next letter to Chambers, on 11 December: "I suppose you are dining and supping, and lying in bed. Come up to town, and lock yourself up from all but me, and I doubt not but Lectures will be produced. You must not miss another term." (1.29.) He adds, "Come up and work, and I will try to help you. You asked me what amends you could make me. You shall always be my friend." Chambers complied, for six weeks later Johnson wrote, "I hope you are soon to come again, and go to the old business, for which I shall expect abundance of materials, and to sit very close, and then there will be no danger, and needs to be no fear." (1.29.)

These three letters, and particularly the last, suggest with some definiteness the nature of the collaboration. Chambers was to bring his notes — he had been Vinerian Fellow under Blackstone for four years, it will be remembered — and probably such law books as might be needed, though Johnson had, at least later, many in his own library. Then they would plot out the course of a series of lectures, and finally Johnson would dictate a paragraph or so to get Chambers started. To be sure, this is partly conjecture, but it is paralleled by what is known about Johnson's dictation of briefs to Boswell, and Johnson had preferred dictation to writing for over thirty years. The evidence of the lectures themselves, to be examined later, also bears this out. It was not necessary to provide exact citations: these could be inserted at leisure. Lastly, it is to be assumed that Johnson would be interested most in general propositions, especially those with a historical, political, or constitutional bearing, and that Chambers would be expected to develop particular points of law, with which he was naturally far more familiar than Johnson.

The "danger" and "fear" which Johnson deprecated in the

last letter quoted probably refer to Chambers' nervousness
about receiving any help, for fear it might be discovered, and
not, as I once thought, to the danger that lectures might not
be produced. After all, the Vinerian Professor was required
to be "at least a Master of Arts or a bachelor of civil law,
by Oxford University degree, who has completed ten years from
the time of his matriculation, and is also an advocate in the
law of England . . . who has numbered four years from his
admission to the pleading of causes."[2] For such a one to require help from a layman whose whole college career had
been limited to thirteen months would have been humiliating,
if publicly known. And the secret was carefully kept. Boswell did not suspect it, and though Mrs. Thrale knew, she did
not tell. She could not help hinting of it in her *Anecdotes:*
"Dr. Johnson was liberal enough in granting literary assistance to others, I think; and innumerable are the prefaces,
sermons, lectures, and dedications which he used to make
for people who begged of him." No other lectures are known
in which Johnson had a hand, and this remark must have made
Chambers start if he read the *Anecdotes,* or the *Life of Johnson,* where it is quoted (4.344). In the unpublished Mainwar-
ing Piozziana Mrs. Thrale recorded a suspicion that Johnson
had written the lectures, and added that Johnson "used to
visit the University at *Critical Times,* . . . or I thought
so." (1.118.) In *Thraliana,* recently published, she listed the
lectures among Johnson's works (p. 204). Chambers was a
frequent visitor at the Thrales, and was highly thought of
there — so highly that the Thrales commissioned Joshua
Reynolds to paint his portrait for them.

Presumably Chambers came to London and went seriously
to work with Johnson, for on 21 February an announcement
appeared in *Jackson's Oxford Journal* that the Vinerian lectures would begin on 17 March. During Johnson's famous interview with George III in this same February, "His Majesty
enquired if he was then writing anything. He answered, he was
not, for he had pretty well told the world what he knew, and

2. *Oxford Statutes,* 1845, 1. 300

must now read to acquire more knowledge."[3] He did not add
that he was reading law books. Soon he was back in Oxford
at work on the lectures, and on 9 April he recorded in an unpublished diary in the possession of Mr. Donald F. Hyde,
"I returned from helping Chambers at Oxford." The entry is
heavily scored out, and perhaps Boswell, who once had the
diary, merely skipped the item. It is significant that Johnson
made the notation more than three weeks after the lectures
were to begin. According to the statute, sixty lectures, not
counting the four public ones, were to be delivered each year,
not more than four a week. There is no evidence that Chambers ever gave that many (fifty-six survive), and one may doubt
whether a full course was given during the first year. However,
Johnson could have heard a dozen of the lectures before he
returned to London. There is some slight internal evidence
of date in the lectures which survived. The Introduction and
Part I (The Public Law of England) comprise sixteen lectures, and contain a sort of conclusion, which I shall discuss below. It is possible that only these were delivered
the first year.

The next year, 1768, the lectures were announced to begin
on 20 February, and Johnson, who was in Oxford at least
as early as 29 February and remained till 30 April, may at
this time have helped to put Part II (Criminal Law, fourteen
lectures) into shape. In the following December he was in
Oxford again, staying with Chambers in New Inn Hall, of
which Chambers was Principal. On 10 December the lectures
were announced for the next month, and on the 14th Johnson
wrote to Mrs. Thrale:

> Chambers has no heart, so I shall have the pleasure of see-
> ing you on Saturday, and next week will be the end of the
> course [i.e.] we shall have finished writing it. If he had
> courage I think it might have been done by Wednesday.[4]

As I interpret this, the third and last part of the lectures
(Private Law, twenty-two lectures), was completed, or virtually completed, at this time. This section of the work con-

3. *Life*, 2. 35
4. *Letters* 211. 1

tains two dates in hypothetical cases, which indicate that
Chambers was working on them at about this time, and not
in the two earlier years: in Lecture XIV, "24 Dec. 1768,"
and in Lecture XIX, "25th day of March . . . 1769." This is
the sort of thing lecturers still do to give their students a
sense of contemporaneity.

In February Johnson was in Oxford for a few days with
Percy, who noted in his diary that he heard Chambers lecture, as Johnson may have also. And in May he made still
another visit. Boswell remarked on this occasion that Johnson "appeared to be deeply engaged in some literary work,"[5]—
but he did not guess what it was. One may assume that by
this time Johnson's help was finished; at any rate, there is
no later evidence of collaboration.

We are now confronted with the necessity of differentiation,
as far as possible, between Johnson's style and Chambers',
in order to disentangle their respective contributions to this
work. Chambers published only two short works in his lifetime, a speech as President of the Asiatic Society in 1798,
and a *Letter to the Governour General and Council: containing an account of the former government of Chinsura under the
Dutch, and of Chandernagur under the French, with his proposals respecting the future administration of justice and
police in those settlements* (1781). Neither bears much
resemblance to Johnson's style. In addition to these, there
exist in manuscript in the British Museum an abstract of
Chambers' plan relative to the future government of Bengal,
"Observations on Mr. Hastings' Plan for the Administration
of Justice in Bengal," a legal opinion of the case of Cámall á
Deen Ally Khan, and some forty-two letters, many of great
length. These form a body of writings sufficiently extensive
and varied to enable one to come to fairly definite conclusions concerning Chambers' style. (I exclude from consideration the posthumously published *Collection of Orders, made
and passed by the Supreme Court of Judicature at Fort William,*
ed. Smoult, since it is a mixture of Chambers and his fellow-
justice Hyde, and also the *Treatise on Estates and Tenures,*

5. *Life,* 2. 68

since it is an excerpt from the lectures now under consideration.)

Generally speaking, none of the writings mentioned could
possibly be mistaken for Johnson's. The major fault in
Chambers is long-windedness. He is rarely able to make a
point succinctly. At times there is a trace of Johnsonian
balance and periodicity, but it is the form without the substance. Habitual readers of Johnson will recall that his style
never seems mechanical or contrived: however formal, it is
his natural manner of speech. Moreover, when Johnson
generalizes, he never leads the reader for long through a
cloud of abstractions: at frequent intervals an apt illustration,
a simple example, lights the way. So also with his latinity
of vocabulary, which has been much exaggerated. He seldom
unless he is being jocular, uses more than a few learned
words without some blunt Anglo-Saxon to set them off. The
reader will not need examples, since I have quoted extensively from Johnson throughout this book. Finally, there is
evident in all of Johnson's writings, in his letters no less
than in works intended for publication, a constant display of
mind—clear, assured, impatient of cant.

Two quotations from Chambers, which include examples of
his somewhat rare periodicity of style, will serve for comparison with Johnson. The first is taken from the legal opinion
mentioned above:

> That unanimity, where judges happen to be unanimous, must
> give weight to their determinations, and satisfaction to the
> public, is evident to every man of observation and exper-
> ience. It is also evident that the advantages of unanimity
> are proportionate to the importance of the subjects, and to
> the number of cases on which the decision is likely to
> operate. But while laws are made and interpreted by men,
> and partake of the nature of all other human things, unan-
> imous judgments cannot be always expected.6

I submit that while this is a reasonably satisfactory sample
of the periodic style, the substance is so platitudinous as to
be wholly foreign to Johnson's manner. The second example
is a postscript of a letter addressed to Hastings and the
Council at Fort William:

6. B.M., Add. MS. 38400, F. 69

I feel myself too much interested in that part of the foregoing Letter which relates to my brother to suppose that I
can be a competent and impartial judge of the subject there
discussed. His obligations to you and to the Court of which
I have the honor to be a member render it irksome to me to
say anything on the present occasion; but where neither
affection nor interest can intervene, where neither bias nor
the appearance of bias can be objected to my judgment
silence would be criminal and I must declare with respect
to the fees and salaries of the other officers of our Court
I entirely assent to the opinions and concur in the arguments delivered by the Chief Justice and the rest of my
Brethren.7

The verbose and rambling character of these sentences needs
no comment.

It will be obvious, on a moment's consideration, that it is
impossible to analyze all of the 1600 pages of which Chambers' Vinerian lectures consist and divide them exactly into
those parts which are of Johnson's composition and those
which are Chambers'. Many are of a neutral sort, and many
are mere paraphrases of authorities cited, in which the language of the original authority is so closely followed as to be
almost a quotation. (This is also true of Blackstone's *Commentaries.)* What in my opinion is required is to identify those
passages which are unmistakably Johnson's, since we are
concerned primarily with Johnson and the law, and not with
Chambers except as his writings are concerned with Johnson.
This I believe is possible.

It appears to me most likely that Johnson had something to
do with the overall plan of the lectures. At the outset, Chambers must have realized that to follow the plan used by Blackstone, which had already been published as the *Analysis,*
would be too servile a procedure, and would indeed give him
little or no scope to show his own powers. Furthermore,
Blackstone's plan was by no means perfect, and his second
Book, "Rights of Things," was particularly awkward. Hence
a new plan, though covering much the same subject-matter,
was desirable. Whoever was initially responsible for Chambers' plan, it may be taken for granted that he and Johnson
discussed it together and finally agreed upon it. It is better

7. B.M., Add. MS. 16265, F. 17

than Blackstone's, more logical and, as it happens, more in
accord with modern practice. Each begins with four introductory lectures, parallel in subject:

Blackstone:

1. The study of the law.
2. The nature of laws in general.
3. The grounds and foundations of the laws of England.
4. The countries subject to those laws.

Chambers:

1. The law of nature, the revealed law, and the law of nations,
   the primary sources of the law of England.
2. The origin of feudal government, and of the Anglo-Saxon
   government and laws.
3. The feudal law strictly so called, and the effects of the
   law on our constitution and government.
4. The general division of the laws of England.

The first book proper of Chambers corresponds roughly to
most of the similar book in Blackstone, despite the total and
rather misleading difference in title. Blackstone's heads are
those given in his *Analysis*, which were subdivided and somewhat rearranged when he revised his lectures for publication
as his *Commentaries*. Since the *Analysis* represents the lectures as delivered, it is better for the purpose of comparison
with Chambers than are the chapter-headings of the *Commentaries*.

Blackstone: I. The Rights of Persons.

1. The absolute rights of individuals.
2. Parliament.
3. The King, his title and dignity.
4. The King's duties, councils, and Royal Family.
5. The King's prerogative.
6. The King's ordinary revenue.
7. The King's extraordinary revenue.

8. Subordinate magistrates.
9. The people, whether aliens, denizens, or natives; the clergy.
10. The civil, military, and maritime states.
11. Master and servant; husband and wife.
12. Parent and child; guardian and ward.
13. Corporations.

Chambers: I. The Public Law.

1. The origins and different forms of Parliament.
2. The present constitution of Parliaments.
3. The King and his coronation oath.
4. The King's prerogative, and first his prerogative of power and exemption.
5. The King's prerogative of possession or his ancient and established revenue.
6. The Royal Family, and the House of Lords.
7. The House of Commons.
8. The Privy Council and officers of state.
9. Courts of justice, and first general courts of common law and equity.
10. Courts whose judgments are directed by the civil, canon, and maritime law; and courts of private jurisdiction.
11. The civil divisions of England and territorial magistrates.
12. Civil rank, order, and precedence.
13. The rights of ambassadors.
14. Aliens, and the incorporation of England with Wales and its Union with Scotland.
15. The government of Ireland and the American provinces.
16. Corporations.

It will be observed that Chambers omits the relations of master, husband, parent, guardian and their counterparts as having no basic connection with the mainly constitutional questions of public law. He treats them incidentally under either criminal law or private law, where they seem to be more appropriate. On the other hand, he has expanded considerably Blackstone's rather summary consideration of historical back-

ground. Johnson's known interest in antiquarian and historical
questions may have been the deciding factor in this expansion.
Finally, Chambers has given fuller treatment to the courts at
this point, whereas Blackstone saved them for his third book,
"Private Wrongs."

Part II of Chambers corresponds to Book IV of Blackstone:

Blackstone: Public Wrongs, or Crimes and Misdemeanors.

1. The general nature of crimes and punishment.
2. The persons capable of committing crimes, and their several degrees of guilt.
3. The several crimes (with their punishments) against the Divine Law, and the law of nations.
4. Crimes against the municipal law: high treason.
5. Felonies against the prerogative; praemunire; misprisions and contempts.
6. Offences against public justice and public peace.
7. Offences against public trade, health, and economy.
8. Homicide.
9. Other corporal injuries, and crimes against personal liberty.
10. Crimes against habitations and property.
11. The means of prevention, by security for the peace and for good behavior; the methods of punishment and the several courts of criminal jurisdiction.
12. Proceedings: summary, regular; arrest, commitment, bail; prosecution.
13. Process, arraignment, plea, and issue.
14. Trial and conviction; clergy.
15. Judgment and attainder; avoider of judgment; execution.

Chambers: The Criminal Law

1. The general nature of punishment.
2. The history of punishment.
3. Exemption from punishment; incapacity to commit crimes.
4. Benefit of clergy.
5. Offences against the government; high treason (Stat. Edw. III).

6. High treason (subsequent statutes).
7. Felonies immediately against the Crown; lesser offences against the Crown (praemunire, misprision, contempt).
8. Offences against the general duties of citizens; homicide.
9. Acts of injurious violence.
10. Offences against property.
11. Larceny.
12. Offences against the commonwealth; against the established religion.
13. Offences against public justice, tranquility, and order.
14. The different imputation of crimes to agents and accomplices.

The fourteen lectures of Chambers which make up this series correspond with some closeness in subject matter to the first eleven lectures of Blackstone in the like series, but Chambers does not follow through the proceedings of arrest and trial, feeling perhaps that these were things better learned through attendance on the courts. It will be noted that Blackstone's subtitle for this section, "Crimes and Misdemeanors," is better than his title, "Public Wrongs" (it is also closer to Chambers); this subtitle he later dropped, in order, I think, to provide a parallel with his third book, "Private Wrongs," the subtitle of which, "Civil Injuries," was dropped at the same time.

The subject of the third and last part of Chambers' lectures, private law, corresponds with Books II and III of Blackstone:

Blackstone: II. The Rights of Things

1. Property in general; real property: corporeal hereditaments.
2. Incorporeal hereditaments.
3. The feudal system and ancient English tenures.
4. Modern English tenures.
5. Freehold estates, of inheritance.
6. Freeholds, not of inheritance.
7. Estates less than freehold.

8. Estates in possession, remainder, and reversion.
9. Estates in severalty, joint-tenancy, coparcenary, and common.
10. Title to things real.
11. Title by descent and by purchase.
12. Title by occupancy, prescription, and escheat.
13. Title by forfeiture and bankruptcy.
14. Title by alienation; deeds in general.
15. The several species of deeds.
16. Alienation by matter of record.
17. Alienation by special custom and by devise.
18. Things personal, and property in them.
19. Title by occupancy, prerogative, and succession.
20. Title by custom, marriage, forfeiture, and judgment.
21. Title by grant and contract.
22. Title by bankruptcy.
23. Title by testament and administration.

Blackstone: III. Private Wrongs, or Civil Injuries.

1. Redress by the mere act of the parties; by the mere operation of law.
2. Courts in general; courts of common law and equity.
3. Ecclesiastical, military, and maritime courts, and courts of special jurisdiction.
4. The cognizance of private wrongs.
5. Wrongs and their remedies, respecting the rights of persons.
6. Injuries to personal property.
7. Injuries to real property: dispossession or ouster of the freehold.
8. Dispossession of chattels real.
9. Trespass, nuisance, waste.
10. Subtraction and disturbance.
11. Pursuit of remedies by action; the original writ and process.
12. Pleadings, issue, and demurrer.
13. The several species of trial.
14. Trial by jury

15. Judgment, appeal, and execution.
16. Proceedings in the courts of equity.

Chambers: III. Private Law.

1. The personal rights of men and the injuries affecting them absolutely as individuals.
2. Economical and private civil relations.
3. The several species of real estates; fee simple.
'4. Fee-tail.
5. A mere freehold, after possibility of issue extinct; by courtesy, by dower, or for life.
6. Chattels real.
7. Customary estate.
8. The conditions annexed to real estates; tenures and their implied conditions.
9. Conditional estates.
10. Possession of estates by parceners, joint tenants, and tenants in common.
11. Purchase or acquisition of real property without inheritance.
12. Alienation by common assurance.
13. Injuries affecting real property and their remedies.
14. Injuries such as dispossess the proprietor.
15. The several species of chattels; original means of acquiring personal property.
16. Derivative means of acquiring personal property, without the consent of the former owner.
17. Acquiring personal property with the consent of the former owner.
18. Injuries affecting personal property and their remedies.
19. Private rights as protected by courts of equity in cases of securities for money lent.
20. In cases of contract.
21. In cases of fiduciary property.
22. In cases where legal evidence or trial would be insufficient; in cases where there is no legal remedy, or where a legal remedy would be dilatory or inadequate. On the

study of the laws of England.

The obvious change made by Chambers in Blackstone's
arrangement was dictated by the elementary consideration
that private rights and private wrongs are the obverse and re-
verse of the same medal. It will be observed that virtually
all of Book II of Blackstone, which we might call property
rights, is covered, and in somewhat the same order, in Chambers' Part III. (It was later felt, by Chambers' executors, that
the two were sufficiently different to warrant the publication
of twelve lectures from this section, for which see below.)
Blackstone's Book III has no exact counterpart in Chambers:
Lectures 2-4, on the courts, had been covered by Chambers
in Part I, under public law; Lectures 5-10, on wrongs to property, are treated by Chambers in the present section, Part
III; and the last lectures, on proceedings in the courts, he
omitted, as he had done with similar matter under public law,
and probably for the same reason, as being more satisfactorily
learned by attendance on the courts themselves than in aca-
demic exercises. It may be mentioned in this connection, that
Chambers shows no evidence of attempting to make a "com-
pleat lawyer" in sixty easy lectures. I am not sure that
Blackstone did not so desire: one may recall his attempt to
persuade Oxford to set up a school of English law, with himself at the head; and the detail with which he enters into procedure, as well as his appendices of sample legal documents
may lead one to suspect that he was in danger of forgetting
that the stated purpose of the course was to give a general
knowledge of law its proper place in a liberal education of
gentlemen, and not primarily to train lawyers for their profession.

It will be noted that the plan of Chambers' lectures de-
parts more freely from Blackstone in Part II than in Part I,
and still more so in Part III. The reason, I think, was that
the first part was composed in a hurry, almost to meet a dead-
line, and it must have been felt by both Johnson and Chambers that it was more important to produce lectures of some
sort than to strike out a new method of organization. There

is some evidence of this, which I shall explain later. When, therefore, the first part had been composed and perhaps delivered, a successful accomplishment must have made the authors more confident of their powers, and the remaining parts showed a progressive freedom of movement.

We may now delve into the lectures themselves. I shall reproduce all passages which I think are unquestionably Johnson's—passages which bear the hallmark of his style and thinking. I am confident that Johnsonians will not quarrel with most of these passages. I shall not, on the other hand, quote sections which in part seem to me to be Johnson's; it is conceivable that in many instances Chambers revised what Johnson dictated, or that Johnson revised what Chambers wrote, so that there is a mixture of styles.

As one might expect who remembers the numerous prefaces and dedications written by Johnson for the use of his friends, the graceful introductory paragraphs of the first lecture are Johnson's:

> If I commence with diffidence and timidity the employment to which I am now advanced, it is not merely because I consider the law, which I am to profess, as by its extent difficult to be comprehended or by its variety difficult to be methodized; for obstacles like these must be encountered in all studies, must be encountered with vigor and surmounted by diligence.
>
> My fears proceed from discouragements peculiar to myself. Professors like princes are exposed to censure not only by their own defects, but by the virtues of their predecessors. I am to read and explain the laws of England, from a place just vacated by a man equally eminent for extent of knowledge and elegance of diction, for strength of comprehension and clearness of explanation. That by the choice of this learned University I am called into his office, as it depresses my hopes, must excite my diligence. Abilities no man has the power of conferring on himself, but fidelity and industry are always attainable. I hope to erect such a fabric of juridical knowledge as may stand firm by its solidity, though it should not please by its elegance, and shall think it sufficient to mould those materials into strength, which only the genius of a Blackstone could polish into lustre.8

8. B.M. Kings MS. 80, ff. 2-4

One is led to speculate that these must have been in substance Johnson's words to Chambers, encouragement, sturdy advice. Such advice Johnson frequently gave to Boswell: for "Obstacles like these must be encountered in all studies, must be encountered with vigor and surmounted by diligence." A few paragraphs on law in general follow, and then Johnson resumes his dictation, on revealed law:

> By the laws of his Creator howsoever promulgated, man as a created being is naturally and necessarily bound, and as an imperfect being he is the proper subject of their direction. For to say nothing of the corruption of human nature by the fall of our first parents, every man, I believe, is conscious that he is not what he might be and would wish to be, that he is, to speak with the schoolmen, *potentially* more perfect and more happy than he is *in reality*. And since perfection and happiness are unquestionably most desirable, he who believes God to be the author and giver of these, cannot but wish to *know* his will, and unless seduced by sensual appetites or inordinate desires, cannot but choose to follow it. The will of God cannot be known but by revelation or by the light of reason. Of revelation the greatest part of the ancient world had either no knowledge at all, or only obscure and corrupt traditions; they must therefore have had recourse to reason to discover the will of those whom they believed to be gods. (ff. 9-10.)

After an elaboration of this theme, Johnson turns to that "other parent of right," human institutions:

> In what way, or by what means the patriarchal dominion of the first ages was actually exchanged for civil government, since even the most ancient and authentic of all histories, the Sacred Books of Moses, do not with precision inform us, we must be content to conjecture. It is pretty certain, however, that in a matter of will and discretion all men would not choose or think alike, and we may reasonably enough suppose that this was in some cases effected by the express or tacit consent of children on the death of their common parent and governor, in others by the union of several families, combined either by compact or by long accidental cohabitation, and most frequently perhaps, especially in the formation of larger governments, by conquest . . . . But by whatever means political bodies were first *framed*, they are clearly *supported* by these two foundations: 1. a desire of social life, to which both reason and instinct (if I may be allowed the expression) incline men; and 2. a certain rule of obedience established in every State, to which every member of it chooses rather silently to submit than to exchange the protection and pleasures of society for the solitude and horrors of a desert.

Society implies in its nature an interest common to many
individuals, a pursuit of the highest degree of happiness
that can be obtained and enjoyed by any number, great or
small, which that society comprises. To the happiness of
the whole, it will be frequently necessary to sacrifice the
happiness of a part, and as no man is naturally willing that
his happiness should be diminished to increase another's,
or that the profit should be divided among many when the
labor or the danger is all his own, it is apparent that some
public authority must be necessary to overrule single opinion or private interest. Nothing is more evident from daily
experience than that in every undertaking in which many
are employed there must be one presiding and superintend-
ent mind. Some will want diligence and some skill; and men
equally skillful and equally diligent, if they are all left to
their own direction, will counteract one another. There is
therefore a necessity of some *governing* power, by which
those who are inclined to be happy at the cost of others
may be compelled to their part of the general task,—and
of *a public wisdom*, by which private judgment shall be directed and controlled. Those to whom this power is entrusted, and this wisdom is imputed, are the governors of
society; the first care therefore of every new society must
be to select and establish governors, and its first law
must constitute the power by which future laws are to be
made. (ff. 15-19.)

Chambers then proceeds to discuss the legislative power,
the division of law into its public, criminal, and private aspects, the natural law of nations, and the conventional and
the customary laws of nations. At this point Johnson takes up
the argument again:

The *customary* differs from the natural law of nations as
depending more on choice and less on necessity. That
which partakes more of necessity must be more general,
that which partakes more of choice must be more confined.
The chief intercourse between one nation and another is by
the means of public messengers whom we call ambassadors.
That law by which the person of an ambassador is secured
from violation we find observed amidst the fiercest hostility by all nations in the least acquainted with social duties;
it is universally observed because universal reason has
demonstrated that of war there could be no end unless some
man might safely propound terms of peace, and that of
mutual wants there could be no supply unless some man
might safely offer articles of commerce. But all the privileges of ambassadors that pass beyond personal security
are different in different nations, as they excel each other
in elegance, which makes more things necessary, or as
they have been obliged to pay more court to each other
and solicit friendship by mutual courtesy. Thus in France
the lady of an ambassador is a public person, in many
countries the *house* of an ambassador is considered as an
asylum, but in England the retainers to an ambassador were

not exempted by the positive law of the state either from criminal or civil actions till their privileges were enlarged, or at least legally secured to them by an act of the 7th Anne c. 12. To the customary law of nations must likewise be referred many of the laws by which *war* is regulated. Men incited by injuries and heated by oppositions, if resigned to the violence of their own passions without regard to compacts or to precedents, would think only by what possible means they might destroy or injure one another. But there are laws by which the rage of *war* is mitigated, where civility prevails. Thus it is forborne on either side to destroy a general by the treachery of his followers. The use of poison is universally forborne. It is generally agreed on both sides to do no injury to those who are not in arms. And those who in the field of battle were yesterday pointing their swords at one another are today friends and companions in a neutral city.

In all transactions between nation and nation, each is, by all other nations, supposed to be in the right—supposed, not perhaps in reason and speculation, but in practice and external conduct. Thus in time of war both armies are supplied with provisions by merchants of the same country, and ships armed for the destruction of each other are equally sheltered and refitted in a neutral port. Moreover, during the actual exercise of mutual hostility each of the, nations at war forbears to treat the other with the utmost rigor, which the natural right of self-defense and of punishment might perhaps allow. Some writers, particularly Wolfius and Vattel, have found themselves so little able to refer these practices to any of the former heads that they have constituted a fourth law and termed this appearance of approbation and this forbearance of rigor the *Voluntary Law of Nations*—a distinction of which I cannot discover the reality, since nothing is plainer than that whatever is, without any ground of necessity, observed between nation and nation must be observed by *stipulation* or by *custom*. But the truth is that of all laws this is least *voluntary*— the impartiality of neutral states being founded on natural justice, and the forbearance of hostile powers on self-preservation. We are not entitled by natural justice to make ourselves the universal arbiters of mankind, to punish those who have never injured us and for whose conduct we are not responsible, to vindicate laws which we never gave, or to guard the boundaries which we did not fix. The mildness of hostility proceeds only from the fear of establishing a precedent which may in time become fatal to ourselves. If any state were to treat its public enemies as pirates and robbers, it must expect the same treatment in its own turn; and every battle would become a massacre, since it would on either side be more fatal to yield than to resist. And since the vicissitude of human affairs puts every nation in danger of feeling some time the miseries of unsuccessful war, every nation has an interest in providing that those miseries may be mitigated and softened. As all government is the power of the few over the many, all government subsists upon opinion. It is therefore the interest of the supreme power to preserve some degree of reverence for all powers equally supreme and to treat those who act under sovereign authority as performing a lawful duty, though they are sent to execute commands oppressive and unjust. This practice is therefore not voluntary but necessary, so necessary that its neglect would make the world a desert, and the nation that should violate it first would probably be extirpated by a general confederacy of mankind against it. (ff. 32-38.)

Chambers concludes the first lecture with two paragraphs. About two-fifths of the lecture was dictated by Johnson, in my analysis, and there is little doubt that the two men discussed the whole with great care, not only because of the importance of the subjects covered but because a successful introductory lecture would pave the way for a successful series.

The second lecture, "The Origin of Feudal Government, and of the Anglo-Saxon Government and Laws," was opened by Chambers with a brief denial that the common law of England is derived from the laws of the ancient Britons before the Roman occupation. Johnson then intervenes with arguments which will remind the reader of his comments on the likelihood of survival of Ossianic epics among the illiterate Highlanders:

Of a system of laws taught by recitation, and retained by memory, nothing but a few gross and necessary customs could be diffused among the people. The customs requisite to regulate a life vagrant and barbarous could be but few, and those few would be gradually worn away as civility was introduced by intercourse with the Romans. Such must have been the fate of the British laws, upon the most favorable supposition that they had a system of laws amongst them. But of any such system there is no proof; and it is more probable that, as controversies could be but few and the violations of right for the most part gross and open, all complaints were summarily redressed and all disputes decided according to the present opinion of the present judge.

But by what laws soever the Britons were governed before the arrival of those German tribes whom we generally call by the name of Saxons, the subsequent expulsion of the Britons themselves by those northern invaders must undoubtedly have been attended with the expulsion of their laws. Hardly any conquest was ever followed by such fatal consequences to the conquered, or any change so total ever produced as those which were effected by that ferocious people.

By a gradual introduction of knowledge and civility, and a consequential change of the manners of the world, a system of life is now established to which migration is so opposite that nothing less than the united testimony of history could now persuade us that it was ever frequent. And few questions are more difficult to be solved than that which inquires for what reason a nation should rise as a single man and thousands and myriads determine together to quit their habitations and possessions; to abandon known and certain means of life and transport themselves, their wives, and their children into countries, in that state of universal ignorance, utterly unknown; where whenever they settled they must obtain their settlement by violence, after a contest with nations of whose numbers or disposition they had never been informed.

It was natural to suppose that an event so contrary to all moral principles and civil institutions could only be the effect of physical necessity. It has therefore been generally supposed that at a certain period of time the regions of the north were overstocked with inhabitants, and Temple denominates the Gothic invasions *the swarming of the northern hive*. But this cause has always appeared to me to be assumed without proof, only because no other could be found. It may be doubted whether there is not now room in Scandinavia and Sarmatia for all their present inhabitants and all the other nations of Europe put together. Ingenuity, however, will always find some method of supporting an hypothesis. The northern countries have been supposed not properly to have been scanty in themselves, but to have been insufficient for their inhabitants from want of tillage. We must, however, suppose mankind to be differently disposed from the present race, if they would not rather learn agriculture than deliver up themselves and posterity to chance; if they could willingly leave all that possession made certain, and that custom had made pleasing, to plunge at once into the miseries of war, with no other hope than that of finding, what the world does not afford, a country that would feed them without cultivation. It may be suspected with greater probability that the nations who burst upon the south and west of Europe, fled before some nation fiercer than themselves that issued from the deeper and more horrid recesses of the north. (ff. 45-50.)

After a brief excursion into Tacitus and Plutarch on the invasions of the Cimbri and Teutones, which might have been written by either Johnson or Chambers, Johnson continues:

When such bodies of men transplanted themselves from Sarmatia or Scythia into Germany and Scandinavia, they must, to make room for themselves, have driven out the former inhabitants of those countries, who would of necessity therefore endeavor to obtain new territories by the expulsion of their more polite and more effeminate neighbors, or at least by conquering them and intermixing with them. And this perhaps was the cause of that extraordinary

change which happened in the state of Europe in the fifth,
sixth, and seventh centuries, when many various flights of
northern barbarians invaded those countries which had
been first conquered, then civilized, and at last deserted
by the Romans. It must, however, be confessed that of these
successive irruptions, by which barbarian power was driven
into Europe as one wave urges on another, we have no such
historical testimony as can enforce our credit; and as these
expulsive invasions must be rare and sudden, they seem
not adequate and sufficient causes of a practice so constant and continued. It therefore remains to be inquired
whether they had not some other motives of regular influence and perpetual cogency.

The superstitious opinions of the northern nations were
such as disposed them to hazard and adventure. Peace was
regarded by them as sluggish, effeminate, and inglorious,
and they considered the man who suffered himself to waste
away with the pains of sickness or languor of age, not only
as neglecting his *fame* but his *duty*. They held that in some
future state the happiness of heroes would be proportioned
to the numbers whom they had slain in battle, and that they
who had attained the highest rank by violence and slaughter
would be received into the Hall of Odin, or the Place of
Souls, where they should feast and drink ale in the skulls
of their enemies. When men were once persuaded that to
slaughter was the highest honor, and that to be slaughtered
at last the highest happiness, we need no longer inquire
why they engaged themselves in unnecessary wars. Battle
was *to them* its own reward—they might gain something
by conquest and they lost nothing by defeat. Their civil
constitution seems likewise to have been such as cooperat-
ing with such superstition would naturally produce pirates,
adventurers, and invaders. As far backward as we can trace
their constitution we find every tribe or nation broken from
time to time into petty sovereignties. A patrimony was
equally divided among all the sons, who had all the same
rank and title with their father and with each other. It will
easily be conceived that after a few descents, the possession always growing less and the rank continuing the same,
nobility and indigence would generate adventure; that men
born to the obedience of others and taught from their infancy to think highly of themselves, led by hope and stimulated by necessity, would endeavor to gain dominions equal
to their merit. Some of these from time to time erected a
standard, proclaimed a design to migrate, and promised
their companions shares of their acquisitions. These were
followed by more or fewer according to the difference of
interest or reputation, or as any accidental cause had made
more or fewer discontented with their present state . . . .
A single chief was perhaps contented to commit piracies
on the sea or plunder villages on the coast. But if many
united together and formed a great army, they marched on-
ward with avowed hostility till they were destroyed by repeated opposition or till weariness disposed them to rest
in some fruitful country. But whatever was the cause of it,
certain it is that the Gothic and Teutonic nations, in their

several irruptions on more southern countries, did not in general, like other conquerors, either content themselves with plunder or endeavor to annex their new acquisitions to their ancient territories, but settled themselves with their families on the lands of the conquered and established new governments of a peculiar form, from which (though after many and great alterations) the present constitutions of most of the states in Europe are derived. (ff. 51-56.)

Chambers now takes up the narrative, on the military constitution of the state set up in England by the Saxon invaders, and the body of laws promulgated by Ethelbert. The introduction of Christianity and consequent spread of learning were subjects irresistible to Johnson, and accordingly we find that the next paragraph is his:

When Christianity was received by the Saxons it necessarily introduced some degree of literature, and literature would soon be employed in settling some system of written law. But the learning of savage nations newly converted must necessarily for a long time reside among the clergy. And that the clergy were the first authors of the Saxon laws we have reason to believe, because we find them chiefly formed *for the regulation of ecclesiastical discipline* which would be the *first* consideration amongst the clergy, whose chief care must be the establishment of proper subordination amongst themselves, and *for the punishment of crimes*, which would claim the *second* attention of those who were to reform and superintend the manners of the people. The modifications and adjustment of civil property, in which they had less interest and less skill, were deferred to an age in which by the diffusion of knowledge those who were possessed of riches and power became able to think and write for themselves, to discover the causes of their own distresses and the means by which they might be prevented or removed. That the first preachers of our religion were likewise the first authors of our laws is yet further evident because our laws and our religion are drawn alike from the volumes of revelation; the first forty-nine laws in the Code of Alfred are transcribed from the Mosaic institutions. It can be no objection to this hypothesis that there are in the same Code other laws peculiar to that time and to that people, for he professes to collect the laws of former times, and those that were found convenient he had no reason to abrogate. Of the laws which have given so much renown to the name of Alfred, it will naturally be expected that something should be said. So far as we can judge of his Code by the fragments which time has left us, it seems to be the effort of benevolent power endeavoring to rescue a people yet unformed from the insecurity and unhappiness of savage license. He seems to have it more in his thoughts to avert evil than to procure good. His institutions are such as the sense of present inconvenience would naturally dictate; but the nation had not then experience or knowledge sufficient to open prospects into remote futurity, to fix the exact bounds of civil rights, or regulate with nice adjustment the distributions of property and evolutions of succession. (ff. 65-68.)

Chambers concludes the lecture with a few paragraphs on the Code of Edward the Confessor and the coming of the Normans. The proportion of Johnson's contributions to Chambers' is about the same as in the first lecture, and again we see Johnson choosing general and historical topics on which to elaborate, and leaving more technical matters to Chambers. The ellipsis above, on page 87 indicates my omission of a citation from Caesar's *Gallic War;* one may perhaps suggest that Johnson reminded Chambers that he might appropriately quote Caesar here, and that Chambers found and inserted it, with the page reference.

Lecture III, "The Feudal Law strictly so called, and the Effects of that Law on our Constitution and Government," is almost wholly Chambers'. There are occasional phrases in the introduction which seem eminently Johnsonian; the barbarian invaders of Rome were "possessed of that martial and free spirit which had formerly raised Rome from a nest of outlaws to the state and grandeur of mistress of the world;" and he speaks of men "raised to the imperial dignity remarkable only for their weakness and wickedness [ff. 78-79]." But for several pages of summary of the continental codes of feudal law, Chambers holds the pen. When, however, a general view of these laws is forthcoming, it is Johnson's:

Their general character is this, that being formed for nations in which private quiet was more endangered by violence than subtilty, they have chiefly endeavored to restrain crimes, and have made very few provisions for ascertaining property or deciding disputes. It may be supposed that when they first occupied the lands of conquered nations, according to a distribution publicly made, while every man's title was recent, it was undisputed; and that for some time whoever desired more than he had, found it easier to take it from an old inhabitant than a fellow soldier. By degrees, however, military violence began to subside, and the strangers coalesced into one system of government with the original people. At this time, or rather as this time was advancing, it became necessary to protect the Romans

from the outrages of their conquerors and therefore many
laws were made *ne fortior omnia posset*. By degrees, as
they had no enemies to oppose, they would naturally form
claims upon one another; and as intermarriages diffused
relation, the order of inheritance would be more perplexed.
We may *then* reasonably suppose that the rules of descent,
which had been preserved hitherto by custom and tradition,
were first deduced into regular subordination; and in the
decrees of emperors, registered in the later laws of the
Lombards, may plainly be discovered the first rudiments
of feudal tenures. (ff. 89-91.)

Chambers then proceeds to a brief discussion of the four
periods of feudal law, and introduces the student to feudal
tenures. Johnson interjects a short and characteristic comment:

In the endless variety of claims and jurisdictions which,
after all the reformations of our law, yet remain amongst us,
there is sufficient evidence that the feudal system in its
subordinate parts and particular tenures, complied very
freely with custom, with caprice, with private passions, or
private conveniences. As all these are causes uncertain in
their operations, their effects admit of no regular distribution; many claims admitted and now admit of no other proof
than custom or prescription, and suits could be decided only
by evidence of old writings or old inhabitants. But the great
and essential parts, having their foundation in solid principles, grew up into stated rules and regular practice and
may be reduced to a few heads which will afford a compre-
hensive view of feudal tenure. (ff. 106-107.)

The discussion of feudal tenures continues, and leads to a
consideration of the power of a feudal king, where Johnson
contributes another paragraph:

The king was maintained in times of peace, not by taxes
or imposts, but by the profits of his own lands, which in
reigns of luxury and negligence were diminished by wanton
grants, or profuse alienations, and in times of contest or
tyranny, were increased by seizures and forfeitures. As he
subsisted upon his own revenues, he had very little de-
pendence upon his people. But in a time of war, whether incited by ambition or enforced by necessity, he was compelled to summon his feudatory lords, whose greatness was
such that when they combined against him he had scarcely
power to compel their attendance. In later times, it was
found necessary to levy subsidies for the payment of the
army, and as subsidies could not regularly be levied but by
concurrence of the great men, these were the times at which
they stipulated for redress of grievances and reformation
of government. (ff. 114-115.)

Chambers concludes the lecture with a short comment on
the power of the barons.

The fourth lecture, and the last of the introductory series, is entitled "The General Division of the Laws of England." Of this, only two brief paragraphs can be assigned to Johnson with any certainty. Nevertheless, his help in plotting out the lecture may have been considerable. Chambers begins by dividing law according to its form, into general and particular, and subdividing general into common and statutory law. Johnson opens the discussion:

> The *unwritten* or *common law*, being begun by necessity, amidst the darkness of barbarous ages and the tumults of fluctuating dominion, when we have pursued it as far as history will guide our search, ends, like the nation that received it, in fable and uncertainty. Some sources may, however, be discovered from which it may with great probability be derived. (ff. 120-121.)

After two paragraphs, probably by Chambers, on the relation of common law to the divine law and to the law of nature and of nations, Johnson resumes:

> The common law, *in its strict acceptation*, consists of customs derived from immemorial tradition, and of maxims established by immemorial practice. Of these, whether they were derived from the Saxons or the Normans or were common to both nations, it is for the most part vain to inquire. When there is a resemblance in the great principles of government, it may be supposed that there was some likeness in subordinate institutions and that therefore the Norman and Saxon law easily coalesced. But of their resemblances and differences, if much is known, much likewise is forgotten. (ff. 123-124.)

The rest of the lecture comprises a short discussion of the early English authorities on the common law, the concept of statute law, particular statutes, the applicability of civil and canon law, and maritime law. The conclusion consists of a summary of the lectures to follow on public law.

Part I, the Public Law, begins with a lecture on the origin and different forms of Parliament. To this Johnson contributed relatively little. One short paragraph is highly characteristic, showing as it does his caution and skepticism in dealing with remote periods of history:

> In surveying the confusion of remote and obscure ages, we must be often content with slight hints and uncertain

conjectures; and great care is to be taken that no man too hastily improve hints into systems, or imagine himself to know what he only guesses. Of the small information that laws and histories afford us, the dubiousness and darkness is sufficiently proved by remarking that they have been advanced in defense of opposite opinions, and that those who write in contradiction to each other can make a specious use of the same authority. (81. 10-11.)

A few pages farther on, Johnson elaborates upon these notions, with his usual sturdy common sense:

It may not be improper in this place to caution young inquirers into the origin of our government against too great confidence in systematical writers or modern historians, of whom it may justly be suspected that they often deceive themselves and their readers when they attempt to explain by reason that which happened by chance, when they search for profound policy and subtle refinement in temporary expedients, capricious propositions, and stipulations offered with violence and admitted by compulsion and therefore broken and disregarded when that violence ceased by which they were enforced. Our political historians too often forget the state of the age they are endeavoring to describe — an age of tyranny, darkness, and violence, in which perhaps few of the barons, to whom the contrivance of this wonderful system of government is ascribed, were able to sign their names to their own treaties, and in which therefore there could be little foresight of the future because there was little knowledge of the past. When they thought themselves oppressed by the regal power, they endeavored to set themselves free as a horse unbroken shakes off his rider; but when they had obtained a present relief, they went back to their castles and their tenants and contrived little for themselves and nothing for posterity. (ff. 22-24.)

Finally, there is a short observation by Johnson on the sending of members to Parliament in earlier times:

By what rule the choice was made of boroughs to be represented in Parliament, or by what power they were compelled to send their representatives, the inquiries of the learned have not yet decided. This much is indubitably certain, that what is now boasted as a privilege was then avoided as a burden; and the records yet remain of exemptions granted to some boroughs upon complaints of inability to maintain their deputies. (ff. 26-27.)

The second lecture, on the present constitution of Parliaments, contains little or nothing certainly Johnsonian. One may assume that Johnson criticised and discussed it with Chambers, but if he dictated any of it, his signature has been

largely obliterated in the process of revision. The third
lecture, "The King and his Coronation Oath," is illumined,
as Boswell might have said, with many rays of Johnson's
genius, particularly in the part concerning the coronation
oath, which is almost wholly of Johnson's composition:

It will be found by observation that when countries emerge
from barbarity, the first approaches to elegance and civility
are made by public celebrities and formal magnificence.
While men are gross and ignorant, unskilled in the arts of
reasoning, and enjoying few opportunities of information
and instruction, they are much influenced by unusual and
splendid ceremonies which strongly affect the imagination
and leave deep impressions on the memory. Nations as well
as individuals have their childhood, and the mind, unformed
by reflection and unoccupied by knowledge, must receive
its whole intelligence immediately from the senses. When
coronations therefore were first contrived they were probably of great use. As they procured veneration to the
person of the king, they at least *confirmed* his authority
though they did not *give* it.

In those times when very few could read, when all the
intelligence which one part of the kingdom received of
things transacted, from another, was derived from the uncertain and unskillful reports of vagrants and of pilgrims,
some method was necessary to give *notoriety* as well as
legality to the powers of government. At every devolution,
therefore, of the regal power the great men were called together from all parts of the kingdom, who were seldom so
universally assembled on any other occasion; and the
people were invited from all parts by exhibitions of rude
magnificence and by every allurement of barbarous recrea-
tion. They were caressed, feasted, and delighted, and
returning to their own habitations, related in distant provinces the grandeur of their king.

In that age of prejudice and ignorance, when the civil
institutions were yet few, and the securities of legal
obligation were very weak, both because offences against
the law were often unpunished and because the law itself
could be but little known, it was necessary to invest the
king with something of a sacred character that might secure
obedience by reverence and more effectually preserve his
person from danger of violation. For this reason it was
necessary to interpose the clerical authority, that the crown
being imposed by a holy hand might communicate some
sanctity to him that wore it. And, accordingly, the inaugura-
tion of a king is by our ancient historians termed conse-
cration; and the writings, both fabulous and historical, of
the middle ages connect with royalty some supernatural
privileges and powers. (ff. 84-88.)

After a paragraph by Chambers telling of the coronation of William the Conqueror, Johnson continues:

It may not be unreasonably conjectured that to this necessity of the clerical benediction, we are now indebted for the Coronation Oath. Such an oath could be required by no civil power because all civil power was subordinate to the king. But, in the opinion of our superstitious ancestors, the ecclesiastics might impose it by the rights of the priesthood which kings do not give and cannot take away.

Nihil prodest Jura condere (says Bracton Lib: 2. C: 24) *nisi sit qui Jura tueatur.* It had been vain for the civil power to impose an oath of which it could not exact the performance, nor punish the violation. But the clergy, having the sword of excommunication in their hands, could easily provide that what had once been granted should not afterwards be revoked.

Thus coronation in ancient times procured to the king the homage of his nobles, with a public acknowledgment of his right, gave notoriety to his accession and conferred sacredness on his person. What are its effects at present it is not so easy to determine. It is perhaps now to the nation the regular and legal notification of their sovereign. It is provided by the statute of the eleventh Henry the seventh C: 1. that the king, reigning by whatever title, may so far legitimate the actions of those who carry his commission that though he should be afterwards deposed, no man can be punished for having acted under him.

If we suppose two rival princes exercising regal power within the kingdom at the same time in opposition to each other, and both without any rightful claim, they cannot both impart to their followers the protection of this statute because the kingdom can have but one king. Under whom then must we suppose that the subject can act with safety? It is, I think, probable that he who is crowned first may give protection to his own party and put the penal laws in force against the other. For the people must have some means of knowing their king, and where other tokens of royalty are equal, perhaps coronation must decide the question.

As the king of England is, instantly on the demise of the crown, invested with all the rights and powers of royalty, he must necessarily be bound from the same instant to the performance of those duties for the sake of which his rights and his powers are conferred on him by the public and constitutional laws of the kingdom. By the Coronation Oath, therefore, he only adds a religious to a moral obligation; and as an oath is a direct appeal to the Supreme Being, by whom perjury will undoubtedly be avenged, a promissory oath can be in no case more proper than when the highest of all trusts is received and the most important of all duties are undertaken. (ff. 89-92.)

The fourth lecture, "Of the King's Prerogative, and first of his Prerogative of Power and of Exemption," allows Johnson to expatiate on one of his favorite subjects, trade:

That part of the subjects might know where to vend their superfluities, and the other part where to supply their wants, it was necessary to fix places of commercial concourse in which assemblies were held at stated times, either ordinarily, and for common purposes, called markets, or more rarely for commodities of greater bulk and value, which were distinguished by the name of fairs.

In the present age when every village is stored with shops and every road encumbered with carriages, and all the necessaries and luxuries of life solicit us to purchase them at our own doors, we do not readily comprehend the great importance of fairs and markets. To know, therefore, how much they contributed to plenty and convenience, we must place ourselves in an age when there was no post by which one man could make his wants known at a distance to another; when by the want of intercourse the state of few men's fortune was known, and therefore very little credit could be given; when there was not money sufficient to fill up by its circulation all the wants of life, and a great part of the nation lived upon the immediate produce of the earth, fixed, either by physical or legal necessity, to the turf on which they labored. We are told by Pontoppidan, in his natural history of Norway, that all the utensils in the house of a Norwegian peasant are produced by the labor of his own hands. This account may assist us in forming some idea of the modes of living among our early ancestors. They had little at home but what was the effect of manual labor; but as even in this state everyone would have too little of something and too much of something else, they went to the *weekly market* to carry on their petty traffic, and even those who lived at manor houses and at castles waited impatiently for the *fair*, at which they were to fill their stores with every kind of exotic delicacy and to supply themselves with finery and ornaments, which if they should miss they could never buy till the next fair.

The modes of common life when they are once changed are easily forgotten, for no man records that which when he records it is already known to all mankind. We have, therefore, no distinct view of the methods by which the internal commerce of the country was transacted, and a distribution made of manufactures and commodities. It is believed that when a fair was held at any seaport or large town, the petty traders from smaller places gathered up the horses of the country and purchased commodities at the fair for their respective shops, in such quantities as they expected to be sufficient till the same opportunity of purchase should return. They were probably accommodated on their journey at religious houses, for as men in those days travelled but little, few inns could be maintained. (ff. 109-113.)

A few paragraphs later Johnson injects another characteristic comment, on the power of the king:

> He that has wealth has necessarily power; and therefore the general influence of the crown must be always great, since the king, by having in his hands the disposal of all military offices, all the great ecclesiastical preferments, the nomination of officers of justice and officers of the revenue, and the appointment of all those who compose the state of his court or serve him as his counsellors or agents in the administration of government, has in his hands a very considerable part of the public riches and has respect and adherence secured to him by the gratitude of possessors and ambition of expectants. (ff. 116-117.)

The maxim that the king can do no wrong prompted Johnson to one more paragraph of remark:

> That this maxim may be morally and physically false it is not difficult to discover. But in the legal sense it is generally true, for the king cannot be supposed to do much but by previous advice and subsequent ministration, and the peace of the world is sufficiently secured by the power which the law always retains of vindicating itself from violation by the punishment of evil counsellors and evil ministers. Of this maxim, so magnificent in sound, the true sense is only this: that when wrong is done it is not to be charged on the king, who being the original of all criminal jurisdiction cannot be supposed accountable to himself. The blame must therefore be thrown where punishment can be inflicted, and falls, not only legally but justly, upon those who if not the original authors must, almost in all cases where wrong is done, be the immediate agents. (ff. 117-118.)

In the fifth lecture, on the king's revenue, Johnson makes one of his frequent comments on the unreliability of the older English authors:

> By the paucity of books every age was ignorant of what was past, and every country of what was distant; and as ignorance naturally produces credulity, the writers of those times were naturally fond of wonders, and filled their books with all that rumor brought to their ears, and with all that could delight a solitary fancy. (82. 9-10.)

Toward the end of the lecture, in discussing the forfeiture of estates to the crown in cases of treason, Johnson makes some interesting remarks on the justice and propriety of this punishment:

> It has appeared to many hard, and to some unreasonable, that the son should be impoverished by the father's crimes,

which he perhaps neither abetted nor approved. But no man ought rashly to censure this regulation till he has considered the multifarious relations of civil life, the different modes by which artificial property is acquired, and the different principles upon which it is possessed. It must be remembered that, though a man may have some natural claim to possession, yet he has no natural right to be protected in the exercise of those claims or vindicated from their violation, that the obligation of one man to defend another arises merely from mutual compact, that a compact implies conditions, and that of the conditions on which any society shall unite, that society must be judge. Different societies, indeed, judge differently, and we may therefore suppose some of them to judge amiss. But if we consider how many ages and nations, ages in which knowledge has been most diffused and nations in which legislation has been most cultivated, have concurred in appointing this punishment of treason, we shall be inclined to believe these securities of public peace salutary to mankind; and as rebellions and civil wars are the greatest evils that can happen to a people, will think that people most happy in which as they are most severely punished they are most effectually prevented. (ff. 32-34.)

Johnson made no identifiable contribution to the sixth lecture, on the Royal Family and the House of Lords, but the seventh, on the House of Commons, opens with several pages in his best vein:

The original of the House of Commons, as I had occasion to observe in my first lecture upon Parliament, is very obscure. Whether they had or had not a seat from the earliest ages in our legislative assemblies is a question once agitated with so much ardor that it became a kind of test by which principles were tried; and every man was considered as a flatterer of despotism or friend of liberty as he held one opinion or the other. The world is either now grown wiser or its follies have taken another mode; we are content to enjoy our present plenitude of liberty without inquiring into the condition of ancient times with our former solicitude, and it has been generally held, since no man has had any interest to deny it, that the Commons for several reigns after the conquest had no part in the legislature. Mr. Barrington, no enemy to the rights of the people, in his observations upon the ancient statutes (p. 59), affirms that in the transactions of the earlier reigns no man shall find any reason to believe that the House of Commons subsisted, who does not read with the desire of finding it.

We now live at a time when by diffusion of civility and circulation of intelligence the manners of the whole nation are uniform, when by determinations of acknowledged authority the limits of all jurisdictions are fixed; when a long course of records and precedents has furnished models for almost every civil transaction, and experience has supplied what reason wanted in the art of government. To us, therefore, it is natural to think that former ages glided on with, the same regular and uniform tranquility. But when we search into early times this idea must be carefully driven from our minds. We must remember that in every compound the proportion of the components must be settled by successive trials; that there was a time when every thing polished was rough, when every thing artificial was rude; that the first law was made without law, and the first precedent established without precedent; that the essays of a new government were experimental; that the public affairs were at first conducted by extemporaneous prudence and regulated by such expedients as opportunity supplied and necessity enforced; that authority was more connected with personal than political characters; that power was undefined, and practice unsettled.

From these considerations it will follow that it is improper to pay too great regard to particular clauses of records or particular passages of history. The transaction of one year was no rule for the next, the style of one writing was changed in another. Formularies were not yet adjusted, and the same words were used with different meanings. From these causes it proceeds that those who hold contrary opinions can support them by quotations from records, and from history. The contrariety of evidence proves little more than the uncertainty of practice.

Of the authors by whom this controversy is discussed, who call themselves with whatever reason writers for the crown or writers for the people, though we should suppose their zeal to be so much overpowered by their honesty as that they are not guilty of quotations intentionally false, yet it is, I fear, the invariable practice to consider themselves as advocates rather than as witnesses; if they tell the *truth*, they are not careful to tell the whole *truth*, and give only the records which favor their own prejudices.

To suppose them always to preserve integrity of intention is indeed sufficiently difficult. Sir Robert Cotton, to gratify his desire of adding something to the grandeur of the House of Commons, has more than once translated "Prelates, Comtes, Barons et *Grantz*," "the Prelates, Earls, Barons and *Commons*" which Prynne has detected without severity by only placing in his margin the original word. See Cotton's abridgment of the records, 6th Edward the 3d. Sess: 1. No: 5 and 6.

This is not the only question which makes it necessary to be remembered that our constitution like all others was once irregular and chaotic, a consideration by which much labor may be spared, which will otherwise be lost in searches that must end at last without conviction. The next degree of satisfaction to the attainment of certainty is the knowledge that certainty cannot be attained.

There are, however, many antiquaries whose curiosity cannot without injustice be censured, and whose labors cannot without ingratitude be depreciated. These are the men to whom we must always be indebted for the ·complete knowledge of our institutions. Few laws have ever been received that were not expedient and reasonable when they were first enacted, though the law sometimes continues when the reason is forgot, and, when the intention of the legislator is no longer understood, may be easily misinterpreted or misapplied. These dangers can be obviated only by tracing institutions to their first principles, and by knowing the state of things to which they owe their establishment. Thus the different tenures yet subsisting among us appear nothing but a wild mass of caprice, absurdity, and oppression to a mind unacquainted with the feudal system of subordination. And in the account which is now to be given of the House of Commons it will be shown that the mode of representation, which now appears so unequal and unreasonable, is such as the ancient constitution of the kingdom naturally produced. It is, therefore, not by searching into past times but by searching superficially and deciding hastily that just censure is incurred. Knowledge is always promoted by inquisitive industry, and almost always retarded by systematic dogmatism. To these studies may be eminently applied that important axiom *"Qui pauca considerat facile pronunciat,"* and of antiquaries, as of other scholars, I suppose it will be found that often as their knowledge increases their confidence grows less.

In treating of the House of Commons it will be necessary to consider both its ancient and present constitution—as the one is exhibited in daily practice, and the other discovered by conjectural investigation (ff. 92-99.)

One should note in passing Johnson's citation of his friend Barrington's *Observations on the Statutes*, mentioned in an earlier chapter. After a few paragraphs by Chambers, Johnson contributes another paragraph, in which he mentions one of his favorite notions, the changing value of currency, and the difficulty with which its real value is computed for any past period:

The time has not long been over when unwilling deputies were sent to Parliament by grudging constituents. It is well known that the seat which was once avoided by excuses is now sought with all the art of intrigue and all the rage of contest; and as it is apparent that what is so much desired will sometimes be sought by other means than those of virtue, provision has been made with great appearance of vigilance against the malignant operations of bribery. Every elector is obliged to swear at the requisition of either candidate, that he has not by himself or by another taken a price for his vote. The qualifications of electors derived from their external condition are various. He that

votes for knights of the shire must have freehold in the
county to the annual value of forty shillings; this proportion of wealth was settled in the year 1430, by the 8th of
Henry the 6th, c. 7, at a time when forty shillings were
equivalent to at least twenty pounds of our present money.
It is one of the defects of civil knowledge that property is
yet only estimated by denominations of money, which have
not the same ultimate meaning in two places or in two
years. Money is in some sense only the shadow of property
and is, like the shadow, always varying its proportion to
the substance. By this mode of computation quit-rents are
almost annihilated, and ecclesiastical revenues are very
much impaired. The time will perhaps come when the law
that qualifies candidates shall depart as far from the original intention as that which now qualifies electors. But to
compute by pecuniary notation is most easy and most in-
telligible at the present time; every age provides for itself, and is content to leave the same obligation on posterity. (ff. 116-118.)

To the eighth lecture, "The Privy Council and Officers of
State," after a short introduction by Chambers, Johnson contributed the following paragraphs:

There can be no doubt but that a Privy Council, though
perhaps in different ages differently constituted, is of the
same antiquity with monarchy itself. No man however diligent could ever understand the whole system of government, and no man however confident could trust wholly to
his own understanding, waylaid on every side, as a king
must be, by artifice and interest. A king must at all times
have felt the necessity of some to inform and some to advise him, some to show him what were the wants or distresses of his people, and some to tell him how wants might
be supplied and distresses remedied.

The impossibility of conducting great affairs and adjusting
the different motions of government, otherwise than by the
united power of associated understandings, is so generally
confessed that the despotic monarchs of the East are always surrounded by their viziers, and assemble their divans
for frequent consultation. And the wild rovers of the American continent, who pass the common course of their lives
in the fishery or chase, almost without intercommunity of
intelligence, yet call their old men and their chiefs together
when there is fear of common danger or prospect of common
advantage. (83. 3-5.)

The ninth lecture, on general courts of common law and
equity, gave Johnson an opportunity to remark on the general
question of equity, a subject to which he returned in the final
lecture of the course:

It has appeared to some a question difficult of decision
what is the use of a court of equity if our laws are right,
and what is the use of laws if they are wrong. This question supposes in human institutions a degree of excellence
which they never have attained. No human law was ever
perfect; it has always equity for its object, but it sometimes
misses of its end. The imperfections of our criminal law are
therefore remedied by the mercy of the king, and those of
our civil institutions by the equity of the chancery. Yet law
is not unnecessary; by laws against crimes wickedness is
restrained, by laws relating to property commerce is regulated and possession is secured. The subject has, in the
law, a rule of action always safe, and commonly right; and
where it happens to be wrong a remedy is provided.
(ff. 59-60.)

To the tenth lecture, on courts employing civil, canon, and
maritime law, and courts of private jurisdiction, Johnson contributed nothing which can be identified with certainty, but
the eleventh, "Of the Civil Division of England and of Territorial Magistrates," has these comments, after a short introduction by Chambers:

The necessity of local magistracy is apparent at the first
view. The punishment of *crimes* always requires a sudden
and extemporaneous process, for a criminal will not stay to
be apprehended by an officer deputed from a distant power.
And if in *civil* cases no recourse could be had to prompt
and domestic justice, much wrong would necessarily be
done and suffered, relief would to the poor be utterly in-
accessible, and where the matter litigated was not of great
value, oppression would be always more supportable than
redress. For this reason the wisdom of our ancestors has
distributed the kingdom into many portions, has appointed
petty courts for petty causes, and stationed magistrates as
public sentinels to oppose in many cases the approach of
evil, and in all cases to hinder its progress and to punish
its authors.

The first and principal division of the kingdom is that which
distributes it into shires or counties. *County* or *comitatus*
signifies, as has been observed in a former lecture, the territory subject to the jurisdiction of a *comes* or earl. *Shire*
is a Saxon word, signifying simply portion or division, and
means only part of a whole without any further reference or
allusion. When the first counties were cantoned out or
erected, we have no certain information. It is probable that
as policy advanced and government was established, the
number of counties was gradually increased till in the time
of Alfred the whole kingdom was finally distributed. "Totius
Angliae Pagos et Provincias (says Ingulphus) in Comitatus
primus omnium Alfredus commutavit." This assertion Selden thinks himself able totally to overthrow, by instances
of some counties that appear to have subsisted before Al-

fred's reign. (Seld: Tit: Hon: P: 2. C: 5. S: 3) But such are
the words of Ingulphus that both assertions may easily be
true, for he affirms, not that Alfred created the first counties
but that he first extended this form of partition through the
whole kingdom. And it is likely that Alfred not only cast
into shires, or counties, that part of the country which had
no such denomination but that he was the author of that
system which unites all the shires under one general jurisdiction. The exact idea of a county as it existed before the
regulations of King Alfred cannot easily be settled; and
perhaps in those ages of confusion, when occasional and
local institutions were very frequent, the administration of
one county differed very much from that of another. Selden
supposes counties to have been originally of two kinds, in
one of which the alderman or earl was both proprietor and
governor; in counties of this kind, the government was naturally hereditary. The counties of the other kind were governed by an alderman upon no other right than deputation
from the king, and were therefore committed to different
hands as influence or favor might happen to prevail. But
it is supposed that the jurisdiction over each county was
separate and exclusive, with very little reference to any
general authority, and probably very nearly resembling that
which after the conquest prevailed for a long time in the
counties Palatine.

In contemplating the kingdom thus distributed, it seems
impossible to avoid some remarks on the apparent capri-
ciousness and irregularity of division, which, however, has
been hitherto very little observed, nor appears to have
alarmed the curiosity of either antiquaries or historians. It
is apparent that no proportion is observed in the magnitude
of different shires, that they are divided upon no principles
of geography or art of mensuration, and that no regard has
been had to natural boundaries whether rivers or mountains.
It is vain to seek the boundaries of counties in any general
system, political or physical. They must, therefore, be referred to partial and local causes, and perhaps were commonly determined by the particular convenience of private
men, who, having their chief seats in any county, procured
their whole estates to be appended to it, or, having their
estates in a county, obtained that by a little extension it
might include their seats. (84. 32-37.)

The twelfth lecture, on civil rank, order, and precedence,
allowed Johnson to expatiate on one of his favorite subjects,
and in his best manner:

Political society is that state of man in which some govern
and others are governed; it therefore necessarily implies
subordination, and ranks those of which it is composed in
different degrees. In a speculative system of government the
mind may satisfy itself with temporary subordination and
suppose that part to be governed at one time which governs
at another. But as experience immediately shows that but
a very small number of any society are qualified to regulate

manners or superintend the interest of the rest, and that
these qualifications must be the effect of study and inquiry
not easily made consistent with manual labor or the constant solicitudes of husbandry or trade, almost every civilized nation has distributed its inhabitants into different
orders and, by conferring established precedence and hereditary honors, has in some sense designated from the birth
a certain number to public cares and liberal employments.

Riches long continued in a family constitute a kind of
nobility without any positive designation, and where the
rank of nobles is established by an edict of the sovereign
authority riches have always been considered as a motive
to preference. Of all kinds of superiority that of riches is
most notorious and least disputable. It has been alleged by
modern politicians, and alleged with reason, that rich men
ought to be more trusted than others by the public because
they have more to lose by bad administration. We are not,
however, too readily to imagine that the institutions of our
savage ancestors were founded in deep research or refined
ratiocination. Riches always obtained honor, because riches
always comprised the power of benefaction. Those who had
less than they wanted adhered naturally to those who had
more. But there is likewise another reason; wealth is the
only superiority that can be successively transmitted. The
son of a rich man will be rich, but the son of a wise man
will not always be wise. Wealth is therefore perhaps the
only ground of hereditary greatness.

No constitution of which history gives us any intelligence
produced such regular and natural subordination as the
feudal system, which ranged a people in successive gradations from the king or general proprietor, till a long train of
tenures and subinfeudations ended in the churl who gleaned
his bread from the land of another.

The ranks into which the Saxon laity were generally divided
seem to have been *thanes*, *middle thanes*, and *churls*, of
which the first held immediately from the king, the second
held from the first, and the third lived only at the mercy of
the former. The title of thane continued in some families,
though we know not exactly with what civil rank, for several reigns after the conquest. In a record of the thirteenth
year of Henry the Third, quoted by Madox, mention is made
of the knights, *thanes*, and free tenants in the king's forest
of the Honor of Lancaster. (Madox's *Firma Burgi*: p. 85.
Note y.) In general, however, these names seem to have
been changed by the Normans to those of barons, vavasours,
and villains. But as civility increased and political institutions were multiplied, each of these denominations was
subdivided. The nobles were distinguished by different
titles, the vavasours became knights, esquires, and gentlemen, and the villains rose often to the dignity of copyholders.

As peace and security produced leisure to study, luxuries
for the great, and conveniencies for all, manual occupations

were multiplied and commerce was extended; the burgess began to grow rich, and perhaps the enfranchised villain often became a burgess. These changes in the form of life were for many ages in continual progress, till in the reign of Queen Elizabeth, Sir Thomas Smith, then Secretary of State, taking a survey of the community (in his *Commonwealth of England*, Part 1) divides it into four classes, of which the first comprehends the greater nobility or Lords of Parliament, the second contains the lesser nobility, the knights, and gentlemen, the third comprises citizens, burgesses, and yeomen, and in the fourth are thrown together all those who bear no rule or, which in his conception is the same, have no free land. Among these he reckons copyholders, merchants, retailers, and artificers. This division is followed by Camden and, except that the last order is omitted, by Lord Coke. 2 Inst: 666. But though in its comprehension adequate to the subject, it is become, by changes in the modes of property, uncertain and delusive— the quantity of free land in each man's possession being no longer the rule by which his rank or importance in the community is to be measured. It seems, therefore, better to follow the division of the law, and distinguish the nation into Lords and Commons. (ff. 86-93.)

Toward the end of the lecture, Johnson added a summary comment on some practical aspects of precedence:

The doctrine of precedence is in our time very little studied. In a country of commerce and an age of action, every man is more diligent to press on those that go before him than to turn back and stop the encroachments of those that follow him. And precedence, or, what is of more importance, that respect which precedence is intended to imply, will be proportioned to every man's riches or usefulness, to his acknowledged power of benefitting others or his supposed abilities to acquire it. (ff. 115-116.)

On the rights of ambassadors, the subject of the thirteenth lecture, Johnson apparently had nothing to say, but it is not surprising to find that he was tempted to comment on Scotland in the fourteenth, "Of Aliens, and of the Incorporation of England with Wales and its Union with Scotland:"

By this union which had been long wished and often projected, Scotland gained an immediate admission to that commerce which had been established over the world by English industry and English power, and became entitled to the benefits of trade in its advanced state, without partaking the dangers or suffering the losses of the first adventurers. They have since gained likewise an increase of liberty, and a deliverance from the oppression of old feudal establishments and of incommodious and vexatious tenures. The advantage to England is, that the whole island is united in one interest and can act upon all occasions with its full

power, that the government is consolidated into one system,
that intestine ravages are now at an end, and that no enemy
of our king can now weaken or embarrass him by inciting
one part of his subjects against the other. (85. 78-79.)

It is to be hoped that there were no Scots in Chambers'
audience.

To the next lecture, the fifteenth, on the government of Ireland and the American provinces, Johnson contributed the
closing pages. These may be taken as a preliminary and sober
study for the violent political pamphlet, *Taxation No Tyranny*,
which Johnson was to write on the question a few years later.
Several of his later arguments, particularly that of virtual
representation, are here adumbrated:

That the colonies are bound by all those statutes of the
British Legislature in which the colonies are particularly
or generally named, I have already shown to be the opinion
of the most learned lawyers, and their opinion has been
sanctioned both by the practice of Parliament and its solemn
declarations. But a question has been lately raised and
agitated, for some reason or other, with uncommon warmth,
whether our colonies are bound by statutes of taxation, or
whether any part of the public expense shall be required
from them. The *moral* part of this question is in my opinion
easily decided: No man has a right to any good without
partaking of the evil by which that good is necessarily produced; no man has a right to security by another's danger,
nor to plenty by another's labor, but as he gives something
of his own which he who meets the danger or undergoes the
labor considers as equivalent; no man has a right to the
security of government without bearing his share of its inconveniences. Those who increase the expenses of the
public ought to supply their proportion of the expenses increased. The payment of fleets and armies may be justly
required from those for whose protection fleets and armies
are employed. No state intends to place its colonies in a
condition superior to its own, to afford protection without
the return of obedience, or to be satisfied with obedience so
easy and unexpensive as every man suffered to be his own
judge would prescribe to himself. If by forsaking our native
country we could carry away all its happiness and leave
its evils behind, what human being would not wish for
exile? If the name of a colonist conferred a right to live in
plenty and security at the expense and hazards of the mother
country, to refuse all contribution to the necessities of the
public, or to proportion his share by his own interest or
humor, a colonist would then obtain more than sovereignty.
He would obtain sovereignty exempt from the care of its
own preservation. In such a state it never was yet the intention of one man to place another, and to this state,
therefore, our colonies can have no reasonable claim.

9. MS: "case"

The whole difficulty, therefore, of this question must arise from *positive institutions;* and it has been objected that our colonies cannot legally be taxed, because every subject of this kingdom is taxed by the consent of his representative. That the British Empire in general is represented by the British Parliament, the law uniformly supposes, but if we attempt to subdivide this representation and consider what proportion the representing powers bear to the numbers represented, we shall find nothing but deficiency, vacuity, and confusion—small villages with two representatives, the greatest city in the world with only four, and many large and opulent towns to which, having risen since the original regulation, no representatives have been ever granted. Our House of Commons, therefore, with whatever observance of proportion it was instituted at first, can now be considered only as a body of men summoned to consult the general interest of the community with very little or no reference of particular men to particular places. The value of pecuniary property is now known by the weight of taxes to bear no small proportion to the value of our land; but 130 millions, now circulating in our funds, have no representative assigned them, nor confer the right of a single vote. Surely it cannot be charged as injustice that we do not for our colonies what we do not for ourselves, that we content ourselves with the ancient mode of election, notwithstanding the changes that have been made amongst us by commerce and by time. If we are content that the owners of land should tax those whose possessions are in money, if we do not permit our trading companies to delegate to the Great Council any particular guardians of their interests, if we allow equal authority to the voice of him who represents half the inhabitants of a village almost uninhabited as to him who is deputed by a fourth part of the inhabitants of London, it may surely be allowed us to include our colonies in this extensive legislation and commit them to the care of the Parliament on the same terms as we commit ourselves.

If it be argued that on these principles the colonies may be taxed without due attention or full knowledge of their abilities, the same argument might be used by the trading companies. If it shall be said that they may be taxed wantonly, because the legislators pay no part of the taxes imposed upon them, it must be considered that if they are useful and beneficial to their mother country it can never be our interest to diminish their usefulness or obstruct the benefits that we receive ourselves. We have the same interest in their preservation and their happiness as a representative of Cornwall can have in the trade or prosperity of Leeds or Manchester. We shall be restrained from oppression by that great principle which holds all empires together, "that the happiness of the whole is the happiness of its parts." It appears, therefore, reasonable to conclude that all colonies may be taxed by that state on which they depend for support, and to which they fly for protection, and that English colonies may (whenever it shall be found necessary or expedient) be taxed by the English legislature, on prin-

ciples equally reasonable and just with those on which the
public expenses are levied on the greater part of their
fellow subjects. (86. 35-42.)

The sixteenth and last lecture of Part I, on corporations,
contains nothing particularly Johnsonian.

Part II, The Criminal Law, opens with a lecture on the
general nature of punishment. After a few introductory paragraphs, Johnson takes up the argument, which proceeds in a
most amusing fashion. He begins with a magnificent sentence
in his best style, rolling, periodic, grandiose. To balance
this in the next paragraph, he quotes a little story from Montaigne, whose style is so different, in his own translation—
"rioting in superfluities" is a Johnsonian hallmark. Finally
he closes in his own manner.

When we consider in abstracted speculation the unequal
distribution of the pleasures of life, when we observe that
pride, the most general of all human passions, is gratified
in one order of men only because it is ungratified in another and that the great pleasure of many possessions
arises from the reflection that the possessor enjoys what
multitudes desire, when it is apparent that many want the
necessaries of nature, and many more the comforts and
conveniences of life, that the idle live at ease by the
fatigues of the diligent and the luxurious are pampered
with delicacies untasted by those who supply them, when
to him that glitters with jewels and slumbers in a palace
multitudes may say what was said to Pompey, *Nostrâ
miseriâ tu es magnus*, when the greater number must always
want what the smaller are enjoying and squandering, enjoying often without merit and squandering without use, it
seems impossible to conceive that the peace of society
can long subsist; it were natural to expect that no man
would be left long in possession of superfluous enjoyments
while such numbers are destitute of real necessaries, but
that the wardrobe of Lucullus should be rifled by the naked
and the dainties of Apicius dispersed among the hungry,
that almost every man should attempt to regulate that distribution which he thinks injurious to himself and supply
his wants from the common stock.

An ingenious but whimsical French author gives us a very
remarkable account of the opinions entertained on this subject by three savage American chieftains who came to Roan
at the time that Charles the Ninth of France was there.
"The king (says he) discoursed a long time with them,
They were shown our manner of living, our pomp, and the
several beauties of that great city. Some time after, a gentleman asked what it was that struck them most among the
various objects they had seen. They answered three things

(the last of which to my great regret I have forgot, but the other two I remember): First, they thought it very strange that so many tall men wearing beards, armed and standing round the king, should submit voluntarily to a child, and that they did not rather choose one of those tall men to govern them; secondly, that they had observed there were among us, men who seemed rioting in superfluities of every kind, whilst their other half (a phrase used in their language) stood begging at their doors, quite pale and mortified through hunger and misery. Now they wondered extremely that this necessitous half should submit to such great injustice, and that they did not take the other half by the throat, or set fire to their houses." *Montaigne's Essays, p. 169 of the 8 vo Ed. printed at Paris, 1604.* Such are naturally the first thoughts of an uninstructed mind concerning the unequal distribution of external goods; but the experience of many ages has taught every civilized nation that as in the physical disposition of the universe every planet is detained in its orbit by an exact equipoise of contrary tendencies, so in the economy of the moral world contrary passions debilitate each other. Every man desires to retain his own in proportion as he desires to seize what is another's, and no man can be allowed to rob, where none are are willing to be robbed. We, therefore, mutually agree to protect and be protected, and every invader of property is opposed by the whole community, at least by all that part of it which has anything to lose.

The same account may be given of the means by which the *irascible* passions are restrained. Every man would at some time be willing to hurt another but that he is afraid of being hurt himself. Of Achilles it was natural to expect that *Jura neget sibi nata*, because the consequences of unlimited violence would be probably in his favor, but the rest of mankind would combine against him, and supply by their united power what was wanting to particular persons. Thus we permit anger and revenge to be restrained by law, because if they were once let loose upon mankind one mischief would forever beget another, and he that had been oftenest conqueror would at last be conquered. (87. 5-10.)

After a brief interruption by Chambers, Johnson continues:

In explaining the formation of things, matter is often considered as acting by its own properties, even among those philosophers who acknowledge creation to be the work of omnipotence. So in the foregoing speculation society has been considered, not as modelled by any superior direction but as forming itself by successive experiments and raising order by slow degrees out of confusion. This, however, was not the real opinion of Plato or of Socrates; and to us who have the advantage of sacred history it must seem more probable that no society was thus formed. The laws of God revealed to Adam and to Noah were undoubtedly propagated through their descendants. Accordingly, civil life may be traced backwards to the East; the laws of the

Egyptians were borrowed by the Cretans, by them transmitted into Greece, and from Greece adopted by the Romans.
There are indeed some nations in the world lawless and
barbarous. In every society one class of men will be more
ignorant than another and the poor commonly more ignorant
than the rich; nothing is more evident than that those who
have least to lose will be most adventurous, and those
most inclined to migrate who leave nothing behind them; it
is, therefore, easy to conceive how a nation of regulated
polity might send out a colony or drive out a troop very
little qualified to retain or transmit civility. The knowledge
of the first ages was not registered in books; the vulgar had
little leisure to receive oral instruction and the little which
they knew would easily be lost amidst the labors and
distresses of a new settlement, in which every day was to
struggle for itself without respect to the past or anticipation of the future. They that went out ignorant became
quickly savage, and I know not that history furnishes an
example of any savage race that was ever able to recover
the maxims and practice of civil life, but as they were subdued by foreign power or enlightened by foreign information.
Had mankind received no original instructions from a superior being, they would probably have continued through all
ages *mutum et turpe pecus,* fattening in the summer and
starving in the winter, worrying the kid and flying from the
tiger. Such are the solitary savages sometimes caught on
the borders of Poland and Russia, supposed to have been
dropped there, when young, by flying Tartars; such was
likewise Peter, the wild youth caught in a forest in Hanover
and sent over to England as a present to King George the
First. See *Salmon's Modern History, etc.*

If it be inquired what is the use of supposing a state of
life which is confessed never to have subsisted, it may be
answered that in moral as in natural disquistions objects
must be magnified that they may be more clearly perceived.
What would be true in its whole extent of savages becoming
civil, is true to a certain degree of the imperfect rudiments
of every society. The desire of greater and greater security
makes successive improvements in all political institutions. This first collected under chieftains the scattered
tribes of our Gothic ancestors, ranged them by degrees in
feudal subordination, by applying military authority to civil
life, and has at last, partly by refinement of manners and
partly by positive institutions, melted down the feudal
system into equal laws and community of right.

While mankind continued in the state of gross barbarity in
which all were eager to do wrong and all unwilling to
suffer, it is apparent that every man's fear would be greater
than his hope; for an individual, thinking himself at liberty
to act merely for his own interest, would consider every
other individual as his enemy who acted only by the same
principle. When they came to deliberate how they should
escape what many had felt and all dreaded, they would soon
find that safety was only to be obtained by setting interest
on the side of innocence, by such a scheme of regulation

as should give every man a prospect of living more happily
by forbearing than by usurping the property of another, and
which should repress the passions of anger and revenge by
making their gratification the cause of immediate misery.

This was the *first principle* of *penal laws.* Pleasure is forborne only for fear of pain, and to the imagination impor-
tuned by inordinate desires it is necessary to represent
the terrific images of misery and death. While in a nation of
nomads, or wandering inhabitants, no other idea is present
to the mind but that he who lessens his neighbor's flock
shall increase his own, most men would be strongly instigated to secret theft or to open violence. But when law has
determined that he who diminishes another's flock shall
not only restore what he has stolen but add to it a double
number of his own cattle, he then finds it safer to grow rich
by natural increase than injurious invasion. This disposition to peace will be more and more increased as the forfeiture is doubled or trebled or made tenfold, or as corporal
punishment is superadded, or as the fact is to be followed
by exile or by death.

The great strength of human laws arises from the constitution of things ordained by Providence, by which man is so
formed and disposed that he can suffer more than he can
enjoy. If the evil of penalty could not exceed the advantage
of wickedness, the mind, so far as it is influenced merely
by the laws of man, could never pass beyond an equipoise
of passion, and the nearer good would generally outweigh
the remoter evil. But such is the frame of man that the
dread of evil may be always made more powerful than the
appetite of good. He that possessing a hundred sheep shall
steal a hundred more, will by no means gain such a degree of
happiness as he will lose if his own hundred be taken away.
Even the *Lex Talionis* has upon this principle a very powerful operation, for no man can have as much pleasure in
pulling out the eyes of another as he will suffer pain from
the pulling out of his own.

To this principle, which is easily discovered, society owes
all its power over individuals. It was soon found that pain
would be too powerful for pleasure, and the question then
remaining was, on what occasions and in what proportions
pain should be applied. (ff. 11-19.)

After these extended contributions to the first lecture,
Johnson seems to have let Chambers do the second, on the
history of punishment, and the third, "Exemption from Punishment, wherein of Incapacity to commit Crimes." In the
fourth, on benefit of clergy, Johnson comments on the clergy
as preservers of civilization in the Dark Ages:

In those times of ferocious barbarity which succeeded the
first establishment of feudal power, when there was yet no
regular distribution of civil justice, when the laws, *yet few*

in number, were unequal to the exigencies of life, when
those laws (imperfect as they were) were unknown to the
greatest part of the people and, for want of a gradual subordination of power, were violated by every chieftain who
was stronger than his opponent, it was natural for the oppressed and the timorous to fly for shelter to the ministers
of religion, whose character restrained them at least from
open violence and *avowed* contempt of reason and of justice.

In those days almost every man who was not a clergyman
was a soldier, habituated to tumult and outrage and accustomed to think nothing wrong which he had strength to defend. They in whose hands the power of government was
placed were feudal lords, ignorant and savage, insolent
with habitual superiority, and too little acquainted with
argument and distinction to control by reason their passions
and their interests. The priest was naturally a lover of
peace because he suffered many of the calamities of war
and had no hope of plunder or of honor. He was by his cel-
ibacy much disengaged from the prejudices of alliance,
which are known to be in feudal countries the great sources
of corruption and injustice. As he held his estate only for
life, his power and riches, whatever they were, were regarded with less jealousy; and his person being considered
as inviolable, he was in less danger of revenge from those
whom his decision might disappoint and offend.

To these arguments of propriety was added what may be
almost termed a reason of necessity for the weight and
authority of ecclesiastics. The clergy were chiefly employed in all cases where a cultivated understanding was
required, because all learning was confined to the clerical
order. The learning here intended is not restrained to difficult speculations, for the clergy were necessarily called
if there was a record to be read or a contract to be written,
because the clergy were almost the only men that in those
days could read and write.

The accounts occasionally transmitted to us of the gross-
ness and ignorance of the feudal ages make it evident that,
without some order of men devoted to literature, the business of life could scarce have been transacted; and perhaps in the long continuance of that state of violence this
literary order could scarcely have subsisted without the
security of religious reverence. (88. 10-12.)

In the fifth and sixth lectures, both on high treason, there
is nothing which can be definitely attributed to Johnson. In
the seventh, on felonies and lesser offences against the
Crown, we find a Johnsonian introduction on the obscure
origins of law:

It might be reasonably imagined that words and things of
most frequent use should be most accurately understood;

yet it happens in almost all cases that frequency abates curiosity, and that of what has been long in use the original is forgotten. Few make inquiry about that which never struck them with novelty. We enjoy domestic conveniences without knowing or caring to know by what arts they are produced, we observe established customs without examination of their first institution, and we speak our native language for the most part with little knowledge of its derivation.

What happens in all other cases happens likewise in the law; much is done and much is said by prescription, that is, with no other reason than that the practice and the terms are of immemorial establishment. (ff. 117-118.)

Later on in the same lecture Johnson's interest in commerce gave him an opportunity for some remarks on the laws against exportation of currency:

Laws to retain the precious metals where they once come into possession are made in almost every country and are in all countries ineffectual. An offence which being only political does not much alarm the conscience, and which requiring little participation or confidence is not capable of detection, will be always committed when it is excited by the hope of profit. That which the merchant is sure of selling to large profit, if he cannot buy it with commodities he will buy with money, and with money of his own country if no other can easily be had. To this practice it must be imputed that crown pieces have almost vanished from among us, and that half crowns seem to follow them. The oath required at the exportation of silver is a restraint intended indeed to operate in secret, but long experience has too well informed us that the contest is unequal between oaths and interest, and that they vitiate morals without regulating trade. (ff. 132-133.)

There are no Johnsonian passages in the eighth and ninth lectures, on offences against the subjects of other states, and against the persons of fellow subjects. The mid-point of the whole course of lectures had now been reached, and Chambers must have required less help as he dealt with specific crimes, in the discussion of which he was certainly competent. In the tenth lecture, however, on offences against property, Johnson's interest was aroused by the crime of forgery and its danger to a commercial nation to comment as follows:

Forgery is one of the most dangerous and extensive evils to which men are subjected by the combinations of society and the regulations of civil life. One of the great advan-

tages of a common weal is that every man lives under the
protection of all the rest, that every claim is publicly decided, and every considerable transaction publicly attested.
But if records and testimonies be forged or falsified the
whole power of society is turned *against the right*. If there
were no written testimonies, truth would stand at least
upon equal ground with falsehood, but if there be any art
by which falsehood can arm itself with the securities of
truth, the invention of those securities would be an evil.

Thus it is one of the great advantages of a regular government that a man can leave his acquisitions by his will, to
those whom he best loves or to whom he is most nearly related, but if wills were easily forged it were more happy
that all property should descend by some settled rule or
perhaps that it should be picked up, as derelict, by chance,
for into what hands can it fall so bad as into those that
are practiced in forgery?

This, as was before hinted, is a crime which the present
state of the commercial world makes particularly dangerous.
The greater part of all movable property is now wandering
in bills, round land and sea, and stands wholly upon the
faith of paper. If this faith should by frequent and successful forgery become suspicious and uncertain the traffic of
mankind must stop, and the wealth of thousands be annihilated. (89. 79-80.)

Chambers then cited the three statutes in force against forgery, which had been made a capital crime in the time of
George II, and Johnson added a concluding remark: "Upon
these acts many have been tried and many have been executed,
yet it may be feared that more will be tempted from time to time
to practice a mode of deceit so easy in the attempt and so gain-
ful if it succeeds." (f. 82.) Johnson must have remembered
his comment a few years later, when, despite the most valiant
efforts, he failed to save the popular preacher Dr. Dodd from
hanging for this crime.

Johnson made no contributions to the last four lectures of
Part II, on larceny, crimes against the commonwealth, and
the different imputation of crimes to agents and accomplices.

Part III, The Private Law, begins with a lecture on the
personal rights of men and the injuries affecting them absolutely as individuals. I find nothing Johnsonian in this, but
in the second, on the rights of men in economical relations
and in private civil relations, Johnson comments at some
length on the problem of divorce:

All concord in the married state arises from the reflection that discord must produce unhappiness. In connubial contests the motive to compliance and reconciliation is that those who *must* live together will live *best* in *peace*. Without this principle marriage would be like any other temporary league of interest or pleasure of which we see scarcely any to be of long duration, because no two are always of a mind, and of those that can part at pleasure neither will suffer the mortification of yielding to the other.

In the present state of matrimonial life the parties are *forced* to agree because they know that they *must* live together, and duty is supported by interest; but if irreconcilable discord were allowed to be a sufficient cause of separation, whoever desired to be parted would very easily find a cause of discord; every slight provocation would be returned with unextinguishable resentment, every casual disgust would be indulged, sometimes injuries would be committed only to excite anger, and sometimes anger would be excited when very small injuries afforded opportunity.

The nature and merits of the question are not altered by saying that "to *justify separation the desire of separation must be mutual;*" for if either desires to part and knows that by petulance and malignity this desire may be gratified, the power of giving offence is always at hand, and they that are weary of their partners may soon make their partners weary of them.

Those who suppose that by the education of children the ends of marriage are completed, and that therefore the obligation ceases, consider only one of the ends of marriage and forget that confidence and friendship are necessary to the happiness of life, and particularly of those declining years which they have selected for the time of separation. If this were to be allowed, the married pair could live on together to *trust* and to *love* less and less; and as the children must belong either to the father or the mother, that parent which had least interest would have least attention. Those who loved each other would see with regret the improvement of their children as lessening the stability of their own happiness, and those who longed for permission to part would have little regard to those whom they intended to desert, and still less as the hour of desertion made its approaches, so that the fabric of domestic happiness, which has nothing to fear but from the mutability of those who compose it, would either never be framed or would be subject to destruction from gusts of petulance or schemes of malice.

For these reasons, and probably for a thousand more which human wisdom will never fully discover, marriage is by our religion made indissoluble; and, therefore, Christian nations have universally appointed it to be solemnized with such rites as shall make it a contract, sacred as well as civil, and superadd to the legal obligation the sanction of a vow. (91. 58-61.)

Lectures 3 to 7 inclusive, "The Several Species of Real Estates," are a commentary on the first book of Littleton's *Tenures*, and as such required no assistance from Johnson until the seventh, when the subject of villenage attracted his attention and brought forth this finely typical example of his style:

The progress of feuds may be traced backwards till it exhibits all the appearances of an incipient polity, and shows a nation of savages newly reduced from lawless wildness to imperfect order and uncertain government. The first act by which polity begins is appropriation of lands, a division of territory into *meum* and *tuum*, by which the builder is enabled to inhabit his house, and the tiller to reap the product of his seed. As mankind were never all equally wise or equally powerful, property never subsisted amongst them in equal shares. In the division of feudal property, however it was made, very little regard appears to have been paid to philosophic notions of original equality, for the chiefs, by whatever title they attained their authority, shared the land amongst them, and the benefits of nature were no longer common. When the accommodations of life were few, but few arts were necessary to produce them; one man was therefore less necessary to another, and the numerous wants and ready supplies by which the system of polished life is held together were not yet known in the world. Men held commerce with men but as givers and receivers; where there was little traffic there was little money, and all the products of the earth which are now circulated through a wide range of buyers and sellers, then passed immediately, if they passed at all, from him that raised to him that consumed them. He only was rich who was the owner of land, and he that had no land was necessarily poor: And the poverty of those days was not want of splendor but want of food.

We that see the world in motion by the power of artificial riches, and receive all that the bounties of nature can give or the diligence of art can fabricate, in exchange for gold and silver, that devour at every meal the product of every[2] quarter of the globe and enjoy in every humble habitation[2] the labor of a thousand artificers, cannot easily conceive a state in which almost every man was sufficient for himself, in which families, then called splendid and opulent, provided in the house almost everything that life was then supposed to require. Yet this was undoubtedly the state of the first feudal communities, of which the traces still remain in some parts of the world. What then must have been the condition of the unhappy man that had no land? We all live upon the fruits of the earth and every man, therefore, must buy or raise them. To buy could be in the power of

1. MS: "wild"
2. MS: "habitations"

few, where there were so few wants and so little money. To raise them was impossible to him that had no land, unless he might be permitted to cultivate the land of another, and this permission he must purchase on any terms which the lord or tyrant of the district, as he was more or less benevolent, should happen to prescribe. If it be objected that land is of no use to the owner but as it is tilled and that, therefore, he would willingly feed all that would labor, it must be remembered that while men are satisfied with the products of the earth very little improved by art or manufacture, many will be sustained by the labor of a few, a single shepherd can tend a numerous flock, a few plows will till a spacious farm; and as there was then no commerce by which superfluities might be turned to profit, the lord could desire to raise no more than he consumed. Thus land was more necessary to the laborer than the laborer to the land. Many petitioned to be fed whose work was not wanted by him that fed them. They were, therefore, reduced to the hard choice of servitude or hunger and accepted small portions of land on the cruel terms of becoming in some sense the cattle of their lord, a property appendant to the soil by which they were sustained. This is the *natural* and, therefore, probably the *true* original of villenage. And such, with accidental differences of mode, will be inevitably the state of every nation where lands are appropriated and arts are few. One part must live wholly at the mercy of the other, and where there is no reciprocation of benefits the conditions of life will always be unequal. (93. 15-21.)

Chambers inserted a paragraph of citations from Bracton and Littleton at this point, and then Johnson continued:

As peace softened manners and religion rectified opinions, the inequalities of life were gradually levelled and the rigors of inferiority imperceptibly mollified. That one Christian should be held in bondage by another was considered by the clergy as contrary to that mercy which religion dictates, and by lawyers as inconsistent with that justice which is the end of legal institutions. It is, therefore, probable that many were emancipated by the piety of their lords, and some enfranchised by subtleties of law. The villain might become a free tenant in villenage and the tenant in villenage rise to a copyholder. That this was the gradation by which base tenures were brought to their present state is very probable. (f. 23.)

No clearly Johnsonian passages appear in the next four lectures, on the conditions annexed to real estates, joint possession of estates, and acquisition of estates by occupancy, prescription, forfeiture, escheat, and bankruptcy. In the twelfth lecture, however, on alienation by common assurance, Johnson discusses recoveries:

There was an age when the ignorance of mankind exposed them to be dazzled by forms and entangled in labyrinths of tedious processes, when all that was solemn was thought important, and all that was obscure was considered as wise. In this age, and in the reign of Edward the Fourth, the judges, supposing that entails obstructed the public prosperity, found out or admitted that method of stopping them which is called a recovery.

What were the evils of entails which required and justified a remedy at once so laborious and so fraudulent, we perhaps do not at this distance sufficiently discern. It is, however, apparent that if all land be devolved by entails through a settled and necessary succession, no land can be sold, and none therefore can be bought; no new families therefore can be raised, the future proprietors of the country can only be the heirs of the present. The great motive to adventure and industry would be taken away, few would have the hopes of growing rich, and those whom skill in trade or any other ability had enabled to accumulate money would be tempted to remove their wealth to some other country where they might obtain possessions permanent and secure.

This would be a sufficient reason why the law of a commercial nation should abhor a perpetuity, but it may be doubted whether this was the reason that first incited the artifice of recoveries. This nation had then little trade, and those who were not born to lands were seldom able to purchase them with money. It appears more probable that as the feudal combinations of interest began to be relaxed, and tranquility and safety gave the mind leisure to extend its views and multiply its desires, men grew weary of having estates which they (in effect) held only for life and which, being determined to a certain course of succession, gave them no power to raise hope or fear, nor enable them to reward kindness or to punish neglect. Every man naturally loves dominion and favors that scheme by which his power is advanced; those who at first were desirous to secure estates to their families grew in time willing to have them wholly to themselves. (94. 86-88.)

The thirteenth lecture, on injuries to real property, contains nothing Johnsonian, but the fourteenth, "Injuries such as dispossess the proprietor," has one paragraph:

But it is necessary that these writs for the recovery of possession be brought within a certain and limited time, for the peace of society requires that there should be a period for which succession should be certain and property secure. In times of tumult and civil contentions (and in such times were most of our ancient statutes enacted and all our common or customary law had its original), the memory of transactions between particular persons was quickly lost, conveyances were often oral and ceremonial (as by verbal feoffment with livery of seizin), of which the natural mortal-

ity of man in a short time destroyed the remembrance; and
writings, when writings *had* intervened, were easily lost
when houses were plundered, or their proprietors fled for
their lives. At all times it must inevitably happen that evidence of things not influencing the general state of the
world will grow weaker by time, and therefore there is in
most countries a period fixed when presumption and prescription may supply its place. (95. 50-52.)

Johnson did not contribute to the next three lectures, on
chattels, but in the eighteenth, on injuries affecting personal
property, he has some sound advice on the use of books by a
law student:

Precedents thus necessarily established are necessary to
be learned, but they must be learned only from books, for
there could be no use of reciting in a lecture a long form
which by its exactness is inevitably too long for the memory
and too minute for the attention of the hearer, and which
the lecturer, having no power to alter or contract, can only
transcribe from a book in which any of his auditors can read
it for himself.

The course and order of this legal process or the reciprocal
transactions of a suit might be generally deduced and described, but of such accounts the use would probably not
equal the expectation of the hearer because it is useless to
be told of that which may every day be seen, and a judicial
process like everything else is learned with less danger of
error or forgetfulness, by practice and observation than by
precept and description. To know forms it is necessary to
read precedents, and to learn practice it is requisite to frequent the courts, not neglecting to excite observation and
to confirm experience by the use of such books as the great
masters of legal proceedings have given us for our direction.
(96. 89-90.)

The nineteenth lecture, the first of the five concluding lectures of the course, all on equity, contains three passages by
Johnson, which are expansions of his earlier remarks in the
ninth lecture of Part I. He begins:

To deduce the history of the courts of justice and fix the
time of their institution is very difficult, for most things
at their beginning are small and what is small is necessarily obscure.

The methods of government and processes of jurisdiction
have not been devised at once, or described and established by any positive law, but have grown up by slow and
imperceptible degrees, as experience improved and necessity enforced them; and what is known of them in early
times has been gathered not from any distinct and positive

narrations of history but deduced by inference and conjecture from rolls and registers, from obscure hints and incidental circumstances. (97.2.)

After a few paragraphs by Chambers, Johnson resumes:

To explain the difference between law and equity and to enumerate the occasions on which equity is, in a well regulated state, to prevail over law, or in which law is to operate without exception or mitigation is very difficult. "Omnis definitio in jure civili periculosa est," say the Roman lawyers (Digest Lib: 50. Tit. 17. Lege 202), and there is perhaps no question in which definition is less practicable than when law and equity require to be contradistinguished. It is indeed to this difficulty that *judicial equity* owes its existence, for if all cases in which law requires the interposition of equity could be defined, they could all have been foreseen; and if they could have been foreseen the law would have been framed with such enumeration of particulars as might have comprehended them. (f.7.)

There is a brief interruption, and Johnson concludes:

The end of all law is *suum cuique tribuere*, to give to every man that which he may justly claim, and the design of all juridical maxims and institutions is to adjust and satisfy the various degrees of right which may arise in the devolutions of succession, the reciprocations of contracts, the terms or conditions of credit and of partnerships, and the various combinations of accident or commerce. These combinations, being indefinitely variable and increasing every day as new schemes of action produce new relations among men, could never be all foreseen by any legislator, and therefore cannot have been all comprehended in any law. It will therefore sometimes happen that those rules which were made to secure right would if they were closely observed establish wrong, because they would operate in a manner not foreseen when they were made. Upon these occasions the aid of equity is solicited, not properly to control or supersede the law, but so to regulate its operation that it may produce the effect which the law always intends. The decisions of equity as contradistinguished from those of law are not *contra legem* but *preter legem*, they do nothing which the law forbids, they do only what the law desires but cannot perform. Equity supplies the deficiencies of law, but cannot correct the errors of the legislator. Where the will of the lawgiver is known it must be obeyed, at whatever hazard and with whatever inconvenience. In cases which the legislator did not foresee, equity endeavors to do what he would have done if the question had been before him, but in cases for which the law is apparently and expressly made, whoever may be oppressed, equity can give no relief. It may be a doubt says Grotius (in his little treatise *de A Equitate*) whether a law be equitable, but there can be no doubt whether law ought to be obeyed. It is with respect to laws, as to a testament, for he that makes a will is a lawgiver with respect to the disposition of those possessions which are in his power. If a will be obscure, the chancellor can explain it, and he will explain it according to equity, because he will suppose the testator meant to do right. But if a will be unequal or unkind and it appears that such inequality or unkindness was intended by the testator, the chancellor cannot redress it; for though the will be unequitable, it is yet equitable that men should make their wills at their own discretion. (ff. 9-12.)

At the end of the last lecture of Part I, there is a curious and perplexing statement: "Having now, gentlemen, finished my account of public law, I shall proceed to the law criminal, which will give my auditors better entertainment, as for want of time and leisure, I have been obliged to borrow some unpublished lectures from my learned predecessor." (86. 71.72.) It will be observed that Chambers does not specify which lectures or how many he borrowed. One may point out that there are no Johnsonian passages in five lectures of Part I: perhaps these are the ones where he used manuscript material given him by Blackstone. It is impossible, I believe, to mistake Blackstone's style for Johnson's, but it is conceivable that some notes of Blackstone's were used here and there in the other lectures. I may add that the manuscript lectures by Blackstone in the King's Library (British Museum) are trial versions of those published in the *Commentaries*, and are not those which Chambers says he used.

The ineptitude of Chambers' remark, and its unintentional reflection on Blackstone, were perhaps merely the result of his timidity, of which we have already seen ample evidence; the remark is an amateurish attempt to forestall criticism, and I think it should not be taken too seriously. Dr. Johnson cannot have seen or approved it.

The subsequent history of the lectures must detain us for a short time. After Chambers had delivered the series seven times, he was appointed to the Supreme Court of Bengal, but did not at once resign his professorship, intending to return if the climate proved unfavorable. Before he sailed, however, he had a copy of the lectures prepared, at the request of the King, through his librarian. This he presented in person, and it is from that copy that I have taken the quotations printed in this chapter. The King's librarian was Barnard, the friend

of Johnson who had arranged the famous interview with George
the Third in February, 1767, the very time when Johnson was
most actively engaged in helping Chambers, Johnson had
assisted Barnard in selecting books for the royal library,
and it appears highly probable that he suggested that Barnard
request a copy. It passed to the British Museum when George
IV sold his father's books to that institution. The copy is
hurried work, by several amanuenses, abounds in verbal errors,
and has few corrections.

Chambers did not return to England until shortly before his
death in 1803. In his will he left to his wife "the copyright of
my lectures formerly read before the University of Oxford,
and all my notebooks concerning the same, requesting however that she will not publish them without good advice."[3]
Whether Chambers remembered his statement that some of the
lectures in Part I were by Blackstone, one cannot guess, but
that might be one reason for advising caution about publication. Lady Chambers turned over at least part of the materials to her nephew, Sir Charles H. Chambers, himself a lawyer, who in 1824 published twelve lectures from Part II as
A Treatise on Estates and Tenures. It may be that the manuscript was thereupon destroyed as of no further use. At any
rate, it is not mentioned in Lady Chambers' will, and present
representatives of the family are able to give no information
about the matter. If it exists, I doubt that it would throw much
light on the present inquiry. Although it might bear an occasional correction in Johnson's hand, his contributions were
certainly dictated.

The Vinerian Lectures, then, include Dr. Johnson's major
contribution to legal literature and to legal education. The
range of subjects which he touched on is highly characteristic—revealed law and human, customary law, the disappear-
ance of ancient British law, origins of feudalism, the codes
of Alfred and Edward the Confessor, the general character of
feudal law and of common law, scepticism a requisite for historical inquiry, the implications of the coronation oath, royal

3. Chambers, *Catalogue of the Sanskrit MSS.*, p. 27

power and medieval trade, the maxim that the king can do no wrong, forfeiture of estates for treason, the origins of the Commons and the Privy Council, courts of equity, local magistracy, civil rank and precedence, the Union with Scotland, taxation of colonies, the general nature of punishment, the medieval clergy as preservers of civilization, the laws against exportation of specie, forgery, divorce, villenage, recoveries, and the use of books by a law student. It is an amazing list, one which illustrates the breadth of Johnson's interests, the curiosity of his wide-ranging mind. It is almost superfluous to add that we should be the duller without the flashes of wit with which he illuminates these topics.

Johnson Advises Boswell on the Law

When Boswell met Johnson in 1763 the young man had un-willingly given up his romantic dreams of a brilliant career in the footguards, and had deferred to his father's wishes that he study the law. He was about to set out for Utrecht "to hear the lectures of an excellent Civilian in that University"[1] as an introduction to that Roman law on which Scots law was based. He asked Johnson for a plan of study, and he reports that Johnson advised him to read five hours a day, as inclina-tion prompted him. They had other conversations on the sub-ject which give no further details. This was perhaps the way in which Johnson had studied the law, and might be considered surprising advice. But it should be recalled that Boswell was still unwilling to study the law at all, and it may be that Johnson felt that desultory reading was more likely to awaken an interest than a strictly prescribed course, which might cause a final revolt. During one of these discussions Boswell remarked that he was afraid that his father would force him to be a lawyer. Johnson replied,

> Sir, you need not be afraid of his forcing you to be a labor-ious practicing lawyer; that is not in his power. For as the proverb says, "One man may lead a horse to the water, but twenty cannot make him drink." He may be displeased that you are not what he wishes you to be, but that displeasure will not go far. If he insists only on your having as much law as is necessary for a man of property, and then endeav-ors to get you into Parliament, he is quite in the right. (1.427.)

A few months later, after Boswell had reached Utrecht, John-son wrote him a strong letter urging him to study civil law and to pursue his studies daily (1.474).

1. *Life*, 1. 400

On Boswell's return to England he sought out Johnson again, and almost at once brought up the subject of his profession, saying that a "gay friend" had advised him against being a lawyer because he would be excelled by "plodding blockheads." Johnson replied, moderately enough, "Why, Sir, in the formulary and statutory part of law, a plodding blockhead may excel; but in the ingenious and rational part of it a plodding blockhead can never excel [2.10]." So Boswell returned to Scotland and in a few months sent Johnson a copy of his inaugural thesis in civil law, on the publication of which he had been admitted advocate at Edinburgh. Johnson, after criticising his Latin, sent a word of encouragement:

> The study of the law is what you very justly term it, copious and generous; and in adding your name to its professors, you have done exactly what I always wished, when I wished you best. I hope that you will continue to pursue it vigorously and constantly. You gain, at least, what is no small advantage, security from those troublesome and wearisome discontents, which are always obtruding themselves upon a mind vacant, unemployed, and undetermined. (2.21.)

Next spring Boswell was in London again, this time with scruples as to whether the practice of the law did not, in some degree, "hurt the nice feeling of honesty." One may be permitted thinking that he merely wished to draw Johnson.

Johnson: Why, no, Sir, if you act properly. You are not to deceive your clients with false representations of your opinion: you are not to tell lies to a judge.

Boswell: But what do you think of supporting a cause which you know to be bad?

Johnson: Sir, you do not know it to be good or bad till the judge determines it. I have said that you are to state facts fairly; so that your thinking, or what you call knowing, a cause to be bad, must be from reasoning, must be from your supposing your arguments to be weak and inconclusive. But, Sir, that is not enough. An argument which does not convince yourself, may convince the judge to whom you urge it: and if it does convince him, why, then, Sir, you are wrong, and he is right. It is his business to judge; and you are not to be confident in your own opinion that a cause is bad, but to say all you can for your client, and then hear the judge's opinion.

Boswell: But, Sir, does not affecting a warmth when you have no warmth, and appearing to be clearly of one opinion

when you are in reality of another opinion, does not such
dissimulation impair one's honesty? Is there not some
danger that a lawyer may put on the same mask in common
life, in the intercourse with his friends?

Johnson: Why no, Sir. Everybody knows you are paid for
affecting warmth for your client; and it is, therefore, properly no dissimulation: the moment you come from the bar you
resume your usual behavior. (2. 47.)

Johnson's refreshing common sense did not permanently
satisfy Boswell, for he reintroduced the subject a few years
later by reading to Johnson a passage from Laud's diary in
which the archbishop reported that Prince Charles had said
that he could not be a lawyer, since he could not "defend a
bad, nor yield in a good cause." Johnson disposed of this
briefly: "Sir, this is false reasoning; because every cause
has a bad side: and a lawyer is not overcome, though the
cause which he has endeavored to support be determined
against him [2.214]." With such a disposition, Charles might
have kept his throne.

A few months later, at Edinburgh, the subject came up
again, introduced, I suspect, by Boswell. Forbes, himself a
lawyer, gave his opinion against undertaking a cause which
one was satisfied was not just. Johnson demurred:

Sir, a lawyer has no business with the justice or injustice
of the cause which he undertakes, unless his client asks
his opinion, and then he is bound to give it honestly. The
justice or injustice of the cause is to be decided by the
judge. Consider, Sir: what is the purpose of courts of justice? It is that every man may have his cause fairly tried, by
men appointed to try causes. A lawyer is not to tell what he
knows to be a lie: he is not to produce what he knows to be
a false deed; but he is not to usurp the province of the jury
and of the judge, and determine what shall be the effect of
evidence, —— what shall be the result of legal argument. As
it rarely happens that a man is fit to plead his own cause,
lawyers are a class of the community, who, by study and
experience, have acquired the art and power of arranging
evidence, and of applying to the points at issue what the
law has settled. A lawyer is to do for his client all that his
client might fairly do for himself, if he could. If, by a superiority of attention, of knowledge, of skill, and a better
method of communication, he has the advantage of his
adversary, it is an advantage to which he is entitled. There
must always be some advantage, on one side or other; and
it is better that advantage should be had by talents than by

chance. If lawyers were to undertake no causes till they were sure they were just, a man might be precluded altogether from a trial of his claim, though were it judicially examined, it might be found a very just claim. (5.26-27.)

Boswell appears finally to have been convinced, for he used these arguments a few days later, when the subject was discussed at St. Andrews.

Another question of legal ethics arose some years later, when Boswell held that it was no more improper for a lawyer to solicit employment than for a politician to solicit votes.

Johnson: Sir, it is wrong to stir up law-suits; but when once it is certain that a law-suit is to go on, there is nothing wrong in a lawyer's endeavoring that he shall have the benefit, rather than another.

Boswell: You would not solicit employment, Sir, if you were a lawyer.

Johnson: No, Sir; but not because I should think it wrong, but because I should disdain it. . . . However, I would not have a lawyer to be wanting to himself in using fair means. I would have him to inject a little hint now and then, to prevent his being overlooked. (2. 430-431.)

Besides discussing these general legal questions with Johnson, Boswell consulted him, from time to time, on particular cases in which he was involved. The first of these occurred before Boswell went to Utrecht to study, and before he was familiar with English law. His landlord had been rude to him (had Boswell been drunk and noisy?), and he had been informed by the magistrate to whom he had complained that upon proof of the landlord's bad behavior he might break his lease without obligation. Johnson commented:

Why, Sir, I suppose this must be the law, since you have been told so in Bow Street. But, if your landlord could hold you to your bargain, and the lodgings should be yours for a year, you may certainly use them as you think fit. So, Sir, you may quarter two life-guardmen upon him; or you may send the greatest scoundrel you can find into your apartments; or you may say that you want to make some experiments in natural philosophy, and may burn a large quantity of assafoetida in his house. (1. 423.)

I think that all Johnson meant by this amusing outburst was that if a landlord could hold his tenant to a lease regardless of his own behavior, the tenant could do likewise.

About a year after being admitted to the bar, Boswell became interested in the Douglas Cause, a case which aroused the Scots to passion and even mob violence. The question was whether Archibald Douglas was the son of Lady Jane Douglas, in which case he would inherit large estates, or whether he was an imposter, in which case the property would go to the Duke of Hamilton. The Court of Session had, by the margin of one vote, decided in favor of the Duke, the plaintiff, but had been reversed by the Lords. Boswell had thrown himself into the case with vehemence, writing on behalf of Douglas in the newspapers, editing Lady Jane's *Letters*, and publishing a novel, a ballad, and a pamphlet on the dispute. But he was unable to get Johnson to show much interest in the matter. I suspect that Johnson thought Boswell's activities indiscreet for a new and young advocate, and he may have felt that the Duke's family was more entitled to belief than one which indulged in secret marriages abroad and other un-British practices. At any rate, Boswell did extract a few remarks on the case from time to time.

In 1768 Johnson said of it:

I am of opinion that positive proof of fraud should not be required of the plaintiff, but that the Judges should decide according as probability shall appear to preponderate, granting to the defendant the presumption of filiation to be strong in his favor. And I think, too, that a good deal of weight should be allowed to the dying-declarations, because they were spontaneous. There is a great difference between what is said without our being urged to it, and what is said from a kind of compulsion. (2. 50-51.)

Some years later, when the case, though determined, was still a matter of controversy, Johnson remarked that the close division of the Court of Session showed that the case was not "of easy decision," and commented on the subsequent reversal: "No, Sir, a more dubious determination of any ques-

tion cannot be imagined [2.230] ." Boswell was piqued because Johnson refused to read his pamphlet on the case, and
Johnson was no doubt bored with Boswell's enthusiasm. When
they visited the Douglas estate later in the year, Johnson
twitted Boswell about Douglas: for once Boswell was rude,
and told Johnson he knew nothing about the case. Where we
may leave the matter.

In the spring of 1772 Boswell asked for help in the case of
Hastie, a schoolmaster of Campbelltown, who had been deprived of his office "for being somewhat severe in the chas-
tisement of his scholars [2.144] ." Boswell had represented
him as counsel before the Court of Session, which had restored him to his position, and was to appear before the House
of Lords in the appeal. As he explained to Johnson, the
question was general, and not a point of particular law. He
also indicated the nature of his argument before the Scots
court — that it was "dangerous to the interest of learning
and education, to lessen the dignity of teachers, and make
them afraid of too indulgent parents, instigated by the complaints of their children [2.145] ." Johnson replied that the
ejection "appears very cruel, unreasonable, and oppressive."
He later added, "Why, Sir, till you can fix the degree of
obstinacy and negligence of the scholars, you cannot fix the
degree of severity of the master. Severity must be continued
until obstinacy be subdued, and negligence be cured [2.146] ."
(This characteristic attitude toward authority may be the key
to Johnson's attacks on the Americans.) A few days later
Johnson, who had been mulling the matter over and had read
the papers in the case, developed his argument a little:

Sir, (said he), the government of a schoolmaster is somewhat of the nature of military government; that is to say,
it must be arbitrary, it must be exercised by the will of one
man, according to particular circumstances. You must show
some learning upon this occasion. You must show that a
schoolmaster has a prescriptive right to beat; and that an
action of assault and battery cannot be admitted against
him, unless there is some great excess, some barbarity.
This man has maimed none of his boys. They are all left
with the full exercise of their corporeal faculties. In our

schools in England, many boys have been maimed; yet I
never heard of an action against a schoolmaster on that
account. Pufendorf, I think, maintains the right of a schoolmaster to beat his scholars. (2.157.)

Pufendorf and Grotius, two of the best known continental
writers on the law, agreed to the "moderate use of gentle
discipline," but the question was on the point of moderation.
In the argument which Johnson dictated to Boswell a fortnight later, he tried to meet this issue at the outset:

The charge is, that he has used immoderate and cruel correction. Correction, in itself, is not cruel; children, being
not reasonable, can be governed only by fear. To impress
this fear is, therefore, one of the first duties of those who
have the care of children. It is the duty of a parent; and
has never been thought inconsistent with parental tenderness. It is the duty of a master, who is in his highest exaltation when he is *loco parentis.* Yet, as good things become evil by excess, correction, by being immoderate, may
become cruel. But when is correction immoderate? When it
is more frequent or more severe than is required *ad monen-
dum et docendum,* for reformation and instruction. No severity is cruel which obstinacy makes necessary; for the greatest cruelty would be to desist, and leave the scholar too
careless for instruction and too much hardened for reproof.
Locke, in his treatise of Education, mentions a mother, with
applause, who whipped an infant eight times before she subdued it, for had she stopped at the seventh act of correction,
her daughter, says he, would have been ruined. The degrees
of obstinacy in young minds are very different; as different must be the degrees of persevering severity. A stubborn
scholar must be corrected till he is subdued. The discipline of a school is military. There must be either unbounded
licence or absolute authority. The master, who punishes,
not only consults the future happiness of him who is the
immediate subject of correction but he propagates obedience through the whole school; and establishes regularity
by exemplary justice. The victorious obstinacy of a single
boy would make his future endeavors of reformation or instruction totally ineffectual. Obstinacy, therefore, must
never be victorious. Yet, it is well known that there sometimes occurs a sullen and hardy resolution that laughs at
all common punishment and bids defiance to all common degrees of pain. Correction must be proportioned to occasions. The flexible will be reformed by gentle discipline,
and the refractory must be subdued by harsher methods. The
degrees of scholastic, as of military punishment, no stated
rules can ascertain. It must be enforced till it overpowers
temptation; till stubbornness becomes flexible, and perverseness regular. Custom and reason have, indeed, set
some bounds to scholastic penalties. The schoolmaster
inflicts no capital punishments, nor enforces his edicts by
either death or mutilation. The civil law has wisely deter-

mined that a master who strikes at a scholar's eye shall
be considered as criminal. But punishments, however severe, that produce no lasting evil, may be just and reasonable because they may be necessary. Such have been the
punishments used by the respondent. No scholar has gone
from him either blind or lame, or with any of his limbs or
powers injured or impaired. They were irregular, and he
punished them: they were obstinate, and he enforced his
punishment. But, however provoked, he never exceeded the
limits of moderation, for he inflicted nothing beyond present
pain; and how much of that was required, no man is so little
able to determine as those who have determined against
him—the parents of the offenders. It has been said that he
used unprecedented and improper instruments of correction.
Of this accusation the meaning is not very easy to be found.
No instrument of correction is more proper than another but
as it is better adapted to produce present pain without lasting mischief. Whatever were his instruments, no lasting mischief has ensued; and therefore, however unusual, in hands
so cautious they were proper. It has been objected that the
respondent admits the charge of cruelty by producing no
evidence to confute it. Let it be considered, that his scholars are either dispersed at large in the world, or continue
to inhabit the place in which they were bred. Those who are
dispersed cannot be found; those who remain are the sons
of his persecutors, and are not likely to support a man to
whom their fathers are enemies. If it be supposed that the
enmity of their fathers proves the justice of the charge, it
must be considered how often experience shows us that men
who are angry on one ground will accuse on another; with
how little kindness, in a town of low trade, a man who
lives by learning is regarded; and how implicitly, where
the inhabitants are not very rich, a rich man is hearkened
to and followed. In a place like Campbelltown, it is easy
for one of the principal inhabitants to make a party. It is
easy for that party to heat themselves with imaginary grievances. It is easy for them to oppress a man poorer than
themselves; and natural to assert the dignity of riches, by
persisting in oppression. The argument which attempts to
prove the impropriety of restoring him to his school, by al-
leging that he has lost the confidence of the people, is not
the subject of juridical consideration; for he is to suffer, if
he must suffer, not for their judgment but for his own actions. It may be convenient for them to have another master;
but it is a convenience of their own making. It would be
likewise convenient for him to find another school; but this
convenience he cannot obtain. The question is not what is
now convenient, but what is generally right. If the people
of Campbelltown be distressed by the restoration of the respondent, they are distressed only by their own fault; by
turbulent passions and unreasonable desires; by tyranny,
which law has defeated, and by malice, which virtue has
surmounted. (2. 183-185.)

Two or three points in this argument deserve mention. It
will be noted that Johnson has elaborated the parallel with

military law which he had remarked on earlier. He does not cite Pufendorf, but merely refers to the civil law, which was of particular relevance as the basis of Scots law. He takes pains to dispose of the charge that the instruments of correction were unprecedented—they were described in the court as "wooden squares." And finally he builds up with great effect the picture of a poor schoolmaster in a town which despises learning. This shows an ability to put himself in the place of his client which would have been of great use to him pleading in a court, and is also of interest to a biographer because it may be a bitter reflection of Johnson's own experience as a schoolteacher in a small town many years before.

Boswell lost the case, apparently because the Lords were impressed that Hastie was exceptionally brutal, even for those days, and that his position was a public office from which he was liable to be dismissed for just cause. That Johnson did not have a closed mind on the subject is indicated by two subsequent remarks. Boswell read him a sentence from Lord Mansfield's speech: "My Lords, severity is not the way to govern either boys or men." "Nay, (said Johnson,) it is the way to *govern* them. I know not whether it be the way to *mend* them." (2.186.) And afterwards he wrote Boswell: "I am glad if you got credit by your cause, and am yet of opinion that our cause was good and that the determination ought to have been in your favor. Poor Hastie, I think, had but his deserts [2.202] ." To paraphrase: abstractly considered, you should have won the case, and yet Hastie was a brutal man.

While Boswell was in London on the Hastie case, he consulted Johnson on what he calls "a question purely of Scotch law." It had formerly been held that "whoever intermeddled with the effects of a person deceased, without the interposition of legal authority to guard against embezzlement, should be subjected to pay all the debts of the deceased, as having been guilty of what was technically called *vicious intromission* [2.196] ." But the courts had of late relaxed the strictness of this when the intermeddling was minor. Boswell had petitioned the court for a strict interpretation in the case of Wilson vs. Smith and Armour, and had been rejected. As he wished to apply for a "revision and alteration of the judgment," he asked Johnson for help. Johnson dictated to him as follows:

> This, we are told, is a law which has its force only from the long practice of the Court: and may, therefore, be suspended or modified as the Court shall think proper.
>
> Concerning the power of the Court to make or suspend a law, we have no intention to inquire. It is sufficient for our purpose that every just law is dictated by reason, and that the practice of every legal Court is regulated by equity. It is the quality of reason to be invariable and constant; and of equity, to give to one man what, in the same case, is given to another. The advantage which humanity derives from law is this: that the law gives every man a rule of action, and prescribes a mode of conduct which shall entitle him to the support and protection of society. That the law may be a rule of action, it is necessary that it be known; it is necessary that it be permanent and stable. The law is the measure of civil right; but if the measure be changeable, the extent of the thing measured never can be settled.
>
> To permit a law to be modified at discretion is to leave the community without law. It is to withdraw the direction of that public wisdom by which the deficiencies of private understanding are to be supplied. It is to suffer the rash and ignorant to act at discretion, and then to depend for the legality of that action on the sentence of the Judge. He that is thus governed, lives not by law but by opinion: not by a certain rule to which he can apply his intention before he acts, but by an uncertain and variable opinion which he can never know but after he has committed the act on which that opinion shall be passed. He lives by a law, (if a law it be,) which he can never know before he has offended it. To this case may be justly applied that important principle, *misera est servitus ubi jus est aut incognitum aut vagum*. If Intromission be not criminal till it exceeds a certain point, and that point be unsettled, and consequently different in different minds, the right of Intromission, and the right of the creditor arising from it, are all *jura vaga*, and by consequence, are *jura incognita;* and the result can be no other than a *misera servitus*, an uncertainty concerning the event of action, a servile dependence on private opinion.
>
> It may be urged, and with great plausibility, that there may be Intromission without fraud; which, however true, will by no means justify an occasional and arbitrary relaxation of the law. The end of law is protection as well as vengeance. Indeed, vengeance is never used but to strengthen protection. That society only is well governed where life is freed from danger and from suspicion, where possession is so sheltered by salutary prohibitions that violation is prevented more frequently than punished. Such a prohibition was this, while it operated with its original force. The cred-

itor of the deceased was not only without loss, but without fear. He was not to seek a remedy for an injury suffered, for injury was warded off.

As the law has been sometimes administered it lays us open to wounds, because it is imagined to have the power of healing. To punish fraud when it is detected is the proper act of vindictive justice; but to prevent frauds, and make punishment unnecessary, is the great employment of legislative wisdom. To permit Intromission, and to punish fraud, is to make law no better than a pitfall. To tread upon the brink is safe, but to come a step further is destruction. But, surely, it is better to enclose the gulf, and hinder all access, than by encouraging us to advance a little, to entice us afterwards a little further, and let us perceive our folly only by our destruction.

As law supplies the weak with adventitious strength, it likewise enlightens the ignorant with extrinsic understanding. Law teaches us to know when we commit injury, and when we suffer it. It fixes certain marks upon actions, by which we are admonished to do or to forbear them. *Qui sibi bene temperat in licitis,* says one of the fathers, *nunquam cadet in illicita.* He who never intromits at all, will never intromit with fraudulent intentions.

The relaxation of the law against vicious intromission has been very favorably represented by a great master of jurisprudence, whose words have been exhibited with unnecessary pomp and seem to be considered as irresistibly decisive. The great moment of his authority makes it necessary to examine his position. "Some ages ago, (says he,) before the ferocity of the inhabitants of this part of the island was subdued, the utmost severity of the civil law was necessary to restrain individuals from plundering each other. Thus the man who intermeddled irregularly with the moveables of a person deceased was subjected to all the debts of the deceased without limitation. This makes a branch of the law of Scotland, known by the name of *vicious intromission;* and so rigidly was this regulation applied in our Courts of Law that the most trifling moveable abstracted *malâ fide* subjected the intermeddler to the foregoing consequences, which proved in many instances a most rigorous punishment. But this severity was necessary in order to subdue the undisciplined nature of our people. It is extremely remarkable that in proportion to our improvement in manners, this regulation has been gradually softened, and applied by our sovereign Court with a sparing hand."

I find myself under a necessity of observing that this learned and judicious writer has not accurately distinguished the deficiencies and demands of the different conditions of human life, which, from a degree of savageness and independence in which all laws are vain, passes or may pass, by innumerable gradations, to a state of reciprocal benignity in which laws shall be no longer necessary. Men are first wild and unsocial, living each man to himself, taking from the weak and losing to the strong. In their first coalitions of society, much of this original savageness is retained. Of general happiness, the product of general confidence, there is yet no thought. Men continue to prosecute their own advantages by the nearest way; and the utmost severity of the civil law is necessary to restrain individuals from plundering each other. The restraints then necessary, are restraints from plunder, from acts of public violence and undisguised oppression. The ferocity of our ancestors, as of all other nations, produced not fraud but rapine. They had not yet learned to cheat, and attempted only to rob. As manners grow more polished, with the knowledge of good, men attain likewise dexterity in evil. Open rapine becomes less frequent, and violence gives way to cunning. Those who before invaded pastures and stormed houses, now begin to enrich themselves by unequal contracts and fraudulent intromissions. It is not against the violence of ferocity but the circumventions of deceit that this law was framed; and I am afraid the increase of commerce, and the incessant struggle for riches which commerce excites, gives us no prospect of an end speedily to be expected of artifice and fraud. It therefore seems to be no very conclusive reasoning which connects those two propositions — "the nation is become less ferocious and therefore the laws against fraud and *covin* shall be relaxed."

Whatever reason may have influenced the Judges to a relaxation of the law, it was not that the nation was grown less fierce; and, I am afraid, it cannot be affirmed that it is grown less fraudulent.

Since this law has been represented as rigorously and unreasonably penal, it seems not improper to consider what are the conditions and qualities that make the justice or propriety of a penal law.

To make a penal law reasonable and just, two conditions are necessary, and two proper. It is necessary that the law should be adequate to its end; that, if it be observed, it shall prevent the evil against which it is directed. It is, secondly, necessary that the end of the law be of such importance as to deserve the security of a penal sanction. The other conditions of a penal law, which though not absolutely necessary are to a very high degree fit, are that to the moral violation of the law there are many temptations and that of the physical observance there is great facility.

All these conditions apparently concur to justify the law which we are now considering. Its end is the security of property, and property very often of great value. The method by which it effects the security is efficacious because it admits, in its original rigor, no gradations of injury, but keeps guilt and innocence apart by a distinct and definite limitation. He that intromits, is criminal; he that intromits not, is innocent. Of the two secondary considerations it cannot be denied that both are in our favor. The temptation to intromit is frequent and strong, so strong and so frequent as to require the utmost activity of justice, and vigilance of caution, to withstand its prevalence; and the method by which a man may entitle himself to legal intromission is so open and so facile that to neglect it is a proof of fraudulent intention: for why should a man omit to do (but for reasons which he will not confess,) that which he can do so easily and that which he knows to be required by the law? If temptation were rare, a penal law might be deemed unnecessary. If the duty enjoined by the law were of difficult performance, omission, though it could not be justified, might be pitied. But in the present case neither equity nor compassion operate [sic] against it. A useful, a necessary law is broken, not only without a reasonable motive but with all the inducements to obedience that can be derived from safety and facility.

I therefore return to my original position, that a law, to have its effect, must be permanent and stable. It may be said, in the language of the schools, *Lex non recipit majus et minus,* — we may have a law or we may have no law, but we cannot have half a law. We must either have a rule of action or be permitted to act by discretion and by chance. Deviations from the law must be uniformly punished, or no man can be certain when he shall be safe.

That from the rigor of the original institution this Court has sometimes departed cannot be denied. But as it is evident that such deviations, as they make law uncertain, make life unsafe, I hope that of departing from it there will now be an end; that the wisdom of our ancestors will be treated with due reverence; and that consistent and steady decisions will furnish the people with a rule of action and leave fraud and fraudulent intromission no future hope of impunity or escape. (2. 196-200.)

Several points in this fine analysis demand comment. In the first place, Johnson's attack on judge-made law is of perennial interest, although he omits consideration of the constitutional question of whether law-making is a proper function of the judicial branch. The security of society and of the individual are with him primary considerations, and security of property, while always of interest to Johnson, is not made dominant over the others. Next, whatever his prejudice against the Scots, he pays a handsome compliment to that "learned and judicious writer," Lord Kames, — "a great master of jurisprudence," — from whose *Historical Law Tracts* he quotes. He appears to be aware, as Boswell seems not to have been, that the principle underlying the question of vicious intromission was a common matter of civil law, and not limited to Scotland. In opposing Kames, Johnson airs one of his favorite notions, that in the present state of civilization protection against fraud is of much greater importance than protection against violence. Finally one may note in passing the admirable lucidity of the brief paragraph in which Johnson states the proper and necessary conditions to make a penal law reasonable and just.

Boswell's comment (2.200) that Johnson here treated "a subject altogether new to him, without any other preparation than my having stated to him the arguments which had been used on either side" is naive, to say the least. Later he wrote to Johnson that the paper was "a noble proof of what you can do even in Scotch law [3.102]." But Johnson had been reading books on the civil law for years, and may well have been aware of the passage in Blackstone's *Commentaries*, which he owned, where a similar situation is discussed:

> If a stranger takes upon him to act as executor, without any just authority (as by intermeddling with the goods of the deceased, and many other transactions) he is called in law an executor of his own wrong, *de son tort*, and is liable to all the trouble of an executorship, without any of the profits or advantages.... Such a one cannot bring an action in right of the deceased, but actions may be brought against him. [2]

Boswell prepared this paper in the form of a petition, with a few verbal changes, and presented it to the court, but was again unsuccessful. Johnson wrote him that he was sorry for the result, "because I yet think the arguments on your side unanswerable." But he was well aware of the casual character of Boswell's legal knowledge, for in the same letter he urged him "to consolidate in your mind a firm and regular system of law, instead of picking up occasional fragments."[3]

That Johnson had looked over the papers in this case with some care may be inferred from a remark which he made to Boswell a few weeks later:

> The English reports, in general, are very poor: only the half of what has been said is taken down; and of that half, much

2. Ed. 1775, 2. 507
3. *Life*, 2. 206

is mistaken. Whereas, in Scotland, the arguments on each side are deliberately put in writing, to be considered by the Court. I think a collection of your cases upon subjects of importance, with the opinions of the Judges upon them, would be valuable. (2.220.)

The criticism of the English reports indicates both some familiarity with them and some acquaintance with the cases on which they were based.

A fortnight later Boswell proposed a hypothetical question, supposing it to be pleaded before the General Assembly of the Church of Scotland: "Whether the claim of lay-patrons to present ministers to parishes be well founded; and supposing it to be well founded, whether it ought to be exercised without the concurrence of the people [2.242]?"The question was not wholly hypothetical, since the Laird of Auchinleck had the power to present the living of his parish. Johnson referred Boswell to Wharton's *Defence of Pluralities* for a good treatment of the subject, and remarked that he himself thought the right to be clear, though he "thought that a patron should exercise his right with tenderness to the inclinations of the people of a parish." He then dictated the following argument:

Against the right of patrons is commonly opposed, by the inferior judicatures, the plea of conscience. Their conscience tells them that the people ought to choose their pastor; their conscience tells them that they ought not to impose upon a congregation a minister ungrateful and unacceptable to his auditors. Conscience is nothing more than a conviction felt by ourselves of something to be done, or something to be avoided; and, in questions of simple unperplexed morality, conscience is very often a guide that may be trusted. But before conscience can determine, the state of the question is supposed to be completely known. In questions of law, or of fact, conscience is very often confounded with opinion. No man's conscience can tell him the rights of another man; they must be known by rational investigation or historical enquiry. Opinion, which he that holds it may call his conscience, may teach some men that religion would be promoted, and quiet preserved, by granting to the people universally the choice of their ministers. But it is a conscience very ill informed that violates the rights of one man for the convenience of another. Religion cannot be promoted by injustice: and it was never yet found that a popular election was very quietly transacted.

That justice would be violated by transferring to the people the right of patronage, is apparent to all who know whence that right had its original. The right of patronage was not

at first a privilege torn by power from unresisting poverty.
It is not an authority at first usurped in times of ignorance,
and established only by succession and by precedents. It
is not a grant capriciously made from a higher tyrant to a
lower. It is a right dearly purchased by the first possessors, and justly inherited by those that succeeded them. When
Christianity was established in this island, a regular mode
of public worship was prescribed. Public worship requires
a public place; and the proprietors of lands, as they were
converted, built churches for their families and their vas-
sals. For the maintenance of ministers, they settled a certain portion of their lands; and a district, through which
each minister was required to extend his care, was, by that
circumscription, constituted a parish. This is a position so
generally received in England that the extent of a manor and
of a parish are regularly received for each other. The
churches which the proprietors of lands had thus built and
thus endowed, they justly thought themselves entitled to
provide with ministers; and where the episcopal government
prevails, the Bishop has no power to reject a man nomi-
nated by the patron, but for some crime that might exclude
him from the priesthood. For the endowment of the church
being the gift of the landlord, he was consequently at liberty to give it according to his choice to any man capable
of performing the holy offices. The people did not choose
him, because the people did not pay him.

We hear it sometimes urged that this original right is passed
out of memory, and is obliterated and obscured by many
translations of property and changes of government; that
scarce any church is now in the hands of the heirs of the
builders; and that the present persons have entered sub-
sequently upon the pretended rights by a thousand accidental and unknown causes. Much of this, perhaps, is true.
But how is the right of patronage extinguished? If the right
followed the lands, it is possessed by the same equity by
which the lands are possessed. It is, in effect, part of the
manor, and protected by the same laws with every other
privilege. Let us suppose an estate forfeited by treason,
and granted by the Crown to a new family. With the lands
were forfeited all the rights appendant to those lands; by
the same power that grants the lands, the rights also are
granted. The right lost to the patron falls not to the people,
but is either retained by the Crown, or, what to the people
is the same thing, is by the Crown given away. Let it change
hands ever so often, it is possessed by him that receives
it with the same right as it was conveyed. It may, indeed,
like all our possessions, be forcibly seized or fraudulently
obtained. But no injury is still done to the people; for what
they never had, they have never lost. Caius may usurp the
right of Titius; but neither Caius nor Titius injure the
people; and no man's conscience, however tender or however active, can prompt him to restore what may be proved
to have been never taken away. Supposing, what I think
cannot be proved, that a popular election of ministers were
to be desired, our desires are not the measure of equity. It

were to be desired that power should be only in the hands of the merciful, and riches in the possession of the generous; but the law must leave both riches and power where it finds them: and must often leave riches with the covetous, and power with the cruel. Convenience may be a rule in little things, where no other rule has been established. But as the great end of government is to give every man his own, no inconvenience is greater than that of making right uncertain. Nor is any man more an enemy to public peace than he who fills weak heads with imaginary claims, and breaks the series of civil subordination by inciting the lower classes of mankind to encroach upon the higher.

Having thus shown that the right of patronage, being originally purchased, may be legally transferred, and that it is now in the hands of lawful possessors, at least as certainly as any other right, — we have left to the advocates of the people no other plea than that of convenience. Let us, therefore, now consider what the people would really gain by a general abolition of the right of patronage. What is most to be desired by such a change is, that the country should be supplied with better ministers. But why should we suppose that the parish will make a wiser choice than the patron? If we suppose mankind actuated by interest, the patron is more likely to choose with caution, because he will suffer more by choosing wrong. By the deficiencies of his minister, or by his vices, he is equally offended with the rest of the congregation; but he will have this reason more to lament them, that they will be imputed to his absurdity or corruption. The qualifications of a minister are well known to be learning and piety. Of his learning the patron is probably the only judge in the parish, and of his piety not less a judge than others; and is more likely to enquire minutely and diligently before he gives a presentation, than one of the parochial rabble, who can give nothing but a vote. It may be urged that though the parish might not choose better ministers, they would at least choose ministers whom they like better, and who would therefore officiate with greater efficacy. That ignorance and perverseness should always obtain what they like was never considered as the end of government, of which it is the great and standing benefit that the wise see for the simple and the regular act for the capricious. But that this argument supposes the people capable of judging, and resolute to act according to their best judgments, though this be sufficiently absurd, is not all its absurdity. It supposes not only wisdom but unanimity in those who upon no other occasions are unanimous or wise. If by some strange concurrence all the voices of a parish should unite in the choice of any single man, though I could not charge the patron with injustice for presenting a minister, I should censure him as unkind and injudicious. But it is evident that as in all other popular elections there will be contrariety of judgment and acrimony of passion, a parish upon every vacancy would break into factions, and the contest for the choice of a minister would set neighbors at variance, and bring discord into families. The minister would be taught all the arts of a candidate, would flatter some and bribe others; and the electors, as in all other cases, would call for holidays and ale, and break the heads of each other during the jollity of the canvass. The time must, however, come at last, when one of the factions must prevail and one of the ministers get possession of the church. On what terms does he enter upon his ministry but those of enmity with half his parish? By what prudence or what diligence can he hope to concil- iate the affections of that party by whose defeat he has obtained his living? Every man who voted against him will enter the church with hanging head and downcast eyes, afraid to encounter that neighbor by whose vote and influ- ence he has been overpowered. He will hate his neighbor for opposing him, and his minister for having prospered by the opposition; and, as he will never see him but with pain, he will never see him but with hatred. Of a minister pre- sented by the patron, the parish has seldom anything worse to say than that they do not know him. Of a minister chosen by a popular contest, all those who do not favor him have nursed up in their bosoms principles of hatred and reasons of rejection. Anger is excited principally by pride. The pride of a common man is very little exasperated by the supposed usurpation of an acknowledged superior. He bears only his little share of a general evil, and suffers in common with the whole parish; but when the contest is be- tween equals, the defeat has many aggravations; and he that is defeated by his next neighbor is seldom satisfied without some revenge: and it is hard to say what bitterness of malignity would prevail in a parish where these elec- tions should happen to be frequent, and the enmity of opposition should be rekindled before it had cooled. (2. 242-246.)

It is interesting that Johnson goes back to feudal times, when "the extent of a manor and of a parish" were the same, and decides from historical grounds that the right of patronage is clear. But more interesting, perhaps, is his picture of the turmoil which would result from popular choice of a minister. In some quarters, this would be cited as evidence of John- son's distrust of the people: it may equally well be said to show his usual good common sense. One may note in passing that Caius and Titius are the civilian's terms for John Doe and Richard Roe. Johnson used them naturally in dealing with a question common in ecclesiastical law. Twenty-one years later (26 Feb. 1793) Boswell was called upon to present the living of Auchinleck, and, doubtless recalling Johnson's remarks, wrote characteristically to his friend Temple: "The choice of a minister of a worthy parish is a matter of very

great importance, and I cannot be sure of the real wishes of
the people without being present. Only think, Temple, how
serious a duty I am about to discharge!''

Early in 1775 Boswell asked Johnson's help in a rather
absurd case in which he was defending The Royal Infirmary
of Aberdeen:

> In a translation of the charter of the Infirmary from Latin
> into English, made under the authority of the managers, the
> same phrase in the original is in one place rendered *Physi-
> cian*, but when applied to Dr. Memis is rendered *Doctor of
> Medicine*. Dr. Memis complained of this before the translation
> was printed, but was not indulged with having it altered;
> and he has brought an action for damages, on account of a
> supposed injury, as if the designation given to him were an
> inferior one, tending to make it be supposed he is *not a
> Physician*, and, consequently, to hurt his practice. My
> father has dismissed the action as groundless, and now he
> has appealed to the whole Court. (2. 291.)

Johnson replied: "I have no facts but what are against us,
nor any principles on which to reason. It is vain to try to
write thus without materials [2.294]." Ten days later, having
received no help from Boswell, Johnson consulted Dr. Lawrence, president of the London College of Physicians, as to
whether M.D. was not a legitimate title, and whether it might
be considered a disadvantageous distinction. Lawrence said
that "with us, *Doctor of Physic* (we do not say *Doctor of
Medicine)* is the highest title that a practicer of physic can
have; that *Doctor* implies not only *Physician* but teacher of
physic; that every *Doctor* is legally a *Physician;* but no man
not a *Doctor* can *practice physic* but by *license* particularly
granted. The Doctorate is a license of itself." (2.297.)

With this support, Johnson was encouraged to say: "It
seems to us a very slender cause of prosecution." Three
months later, when Boswell was in London, Johnson dictated
to him the following argument:

> There are but two reasons for which a physician can de-
> cline the title of *Doctor of Medicine*, because he supposes
> himself disgraced by the doctorship, or supposes the
> doctorship disgraced by himself. To be disgraced by a
> title which he shares in common with every illustrious
> name of his profession, with Boerhaave, with Arbuthnot,
> and with Cullen, can surely diminish no man's reputation.
> It is, I suppose, to the doctorate, from which he shrinks,

that he owes his right of practicing physic. A Doctor of Medicine is a physician under the protection of the laws, and by the stamp of authority. The physician who is not a Doctor, usurps a profession, and is authorized only by himself to decide upon health and sickness, and life and death. That this gentleman is a Doctor, his diploma makes evident — a diploma not obtruded upon him, but obtained by solicitation, and for which fees were paid. With what countenance any man can refuse the title which he has either begged or bought, is not easily discovered.

All verbal injury must comprise in it either some false position, or some unnecessary declaration of defamatory truth. That in calling him Doctor, a false appellation was given him, he himself will not pretend, who at the same time that he complains of the title, would be offended if we supposed him to be not a Doctor. If the title of Doctor be a defamatory truth, it is time to dissolve our colleges; for why should the public give salaries to men whose approbation is reproach? It may likewise deserve the notice of the public to consider what help can be given to the professors of physic, who all share with this unhappy gentleman the ignominious appellation, and of whom the very boys in the street are not afraid to say, *There goes the Doctor.*

What is implied by the term Doctor is well known. It distinguishes him to whom it is granted, as a man who has attained such knowledge of his profession as qualifies him to instruct others. A Doctor of Laws is a man who can form lawyers by his precepts. A Doctor of Medicine is a man who can teach the art of curing diseases. There is an old axiom which no man has yet thought fit to deny, *Nil dat quod non habet.* Upon this principle to be Doctor implies skill, for *nemo docet quod non didicit.* In England, whoever practices physic, not being a Doctor, must practice by a license: but the doctorate conveys a license in itself.

By what accident it happened that he and the other physicians were mentioned in different terms, where the terms themselves were equivalent, or where in effect that which was applied to him was the more honorable, perhaps they who wrote the paper cannot now remember. Had they expected a lawsuit to have been the consequence of such petty variation, I hope they would have avoided it. But, probably, as they meant no ill, they suspected no danger, and, therefore, consulted only what appeared to them propriety or convenience. (2.372-373.)

In the last paragraph Johnson may have been more kind to the Infirmary than the facts warranted. Memis had complained about the term before the charter was printed, but was not humored. We are not informed that this was mere negligence, and indeed one may suspect that the corporation wished to be annoying to a man who appears rather pompous. Some eighteen months later Boswell had not informed Johnson of the outcome of the case, and he delayed still longer to answer Johnson's inquiry. Finally he said that Memis had lost, with £40 costs. Boswell was not pleased, though he had won the case: "My own opinion is, that our court has judged wrong. The defendants were *in malâ fide*, to persist in naming him in a way that he disliked.... The difficulty is, whether an action should be allowed on such petty wrongs. *De minimis non curat lex*." (3.101.) What a perverse man! His quotation of the principle *de minimis* is very apt: one wonders whether he used it in the case itself. In a somewhat similar question a few years later, the Society of Solicitors vs. Robertson, Johnson did use it. It has had some fame in the United States in recent years.

While the Memis case was in progress, Boswell was interested in another, and consulted Johnson upon it — Paterson *et al*. vs. Alexander *et al*. The Court of Session had determined that the Corporation of Stirling was corrupt, and had set aside the election of some of its officers on the ground that "three of the leading men who influenced the majority, had entered into an unjustifiable compact, of which, however, the majority were ignorant [2.373]." Johnson, "after a little consideration," dictated a few remarks on the question of the innocent members of the majority suffering with the guilty:

There is a difference between majority and superiority; majority is applied to number, and superiority to power; and power, like many other things, is to be estimated *non numero sed pondere*. Now though the greater *number* is not corrupt, the greater *weight* is corrupt, so that corruption predominates in the borough, taken *collectively*, though, perhaps, taken *numerically* the greater part may be uncorrupt. That borough, which is so constituted as to act corruptly, is in the eye of reason corrupt, whether it be by the uncontrollable power of a few, or by an accidental pravity of the multitude. The objection, in which is urged the injustice of making the innocent suffer with the guilty, is an objection not only against society but against the possibility of society. All societies, great and small, subsist upon this condition — that as the individuals derive advantages from union, they may likewise suffer inconveniences; that as those who do nothing, and sometimes those who do ill, will have the honors and emoluments of general virtue and general prosperity, so those likewise who do nothing, or perhaps do well, must be involved in the consequences of predominant corruption." (2.373-374.)

The Lords upheld the Court of Session, though Boswell thought it "a very nice case." Nowadays, I suppose no one would deny the legality of punishing the innocent with the guilty as far as setting aside an election, though not to any further extent, such as fine or imprisonment. Johnson's position merely assumes the legality, as decided by the courts, and is concerned with the equitable basis of the decision.

Early in 1776 Boswell was much exercised by his father's wish to entail the family estate to heirs general, instead of to heirs male, however remote, which was Boswell's romantic and rather unpaternal desire. The nucleus of the property had come from Boswell's great-great-great-uncle, who had passed over four daughters and a brother to leave it to a nephew. Boswell felt that this should be followed as a precedent, and he had other scruples as to whether daughters transmitted the blood of the fanily at all, since "some distinguished naturalists" were of the opinion that "our species is transmitted through males only [2.414]." Having muddled himself further with references to the Bible and to Blackstone, Boswell at length appealed to Johnson for advice, hoping, I think, that Johnson would support him, since Johnson had previously ridiculed Langton for devising his estate to three sisters rather than to a remote male. But Johnson recognized the seriousness of the problem, perhaps because he knew that the relations between Boswell and his father were strained, and did not rush headlong into a decision. He did not know whether he was "quite equal to it." It was a case "compounded of law and justice, and requires a mind versed in juridical disquisitions." Could not Boswell ask the opinion of Lord Hailes, who was "both a Christian and a Lawyer"? But Johnson implied that he would think it over: "Write to me, as anything occurs to you; and if I find myself stopped by want of facts necessary to be known, I will make inquiries of you as my doubts arise." (2.415.)

Some three weeks later Johnson had made up his mind, against Boswell:

I am going to write upon a question which requires more knowledge of local law, and more acquaintance with the

general rules of inheritance, than I can claim; but I write,
because you request it.

Land is, like any other possession, by natural right wholly
in the power of its present owner; and may be sold, given,
or bequeathed, absolutely or conditionally, as judgment
shall direct or passion incite.

But natural right would avail little without the protection
of law; and the primary notion of law is restraint in the
exercise of natural right. A man is therefore, in society, not
fully master of what he calls his own, but he still retains
all the power which law does not take from him.

In the exercise of the right which law either leaves or
gives, regard is to be paid to moral obligations.

Of the estate which we are now considering, your father
still retains such possession, with such power over it that
he can sell it and do with the money what he will, without
any legal impediment. But when he extends his power
beyond his own life, by settling the order of succession,
the law makes your consent necessary.

Let us suppose that he sells the land to risk the money in
some specious adventure, and in that adventure loses the
whole; his posterity would be disappointed, but they could
not think themselves injured or robbed. If he spent it upon
vice or pleasure, his successors could only call him vicious
and voluptuous; they could not say that he was injurious or
unjust.

He that may do more, may do less. He that, by selling or
squandering, may disinherit a whole family, may certainly
disinherit part, by a partial settlement.

Laws are formed by the manners and exigencies of particular times, and it is but accidental that they last longer
than their causes: the limitation of feudal succession to the
male arose from the obligation of the tenant to attend his
chief in war.

As times and opinions are always changing, I know not
whether it be not usurpation to prescribe rules to posterity,
by presuming to judge of what we cannot know; and I know
not whether I fully approve either your design or your
father's, to limit that succession which descended to you
unlimited. If we are to leave *sartum tectum* to posterity,
what we have without any merit of our own received from
our ancestors, should not choice and free-will be kept
unviolated? Is land to be treated with more reverence than
liberty? If this consideration should restrain your father
from disinheriting some of the males, does it leave you the
power of disinheriting all the females?

Can the possessor of a feudal estate make any will? Can he
appoint, out of the inheritance, any portions to his daugh-

ters? There seems to be a very shadowy difference between the power of leaving land, and of leaving money to be raised from land; between leaving an estate to females, and leaving the male heir, in effect, only their steward.

Suppose at one time a law that allowed only males to inherit, and during the continuance of this law many estates to have descended, passing by the females, to remoter heirs. Suppose afterwards the law repealed in correspondence with a change of manners, and women made capable of inheritance; would not then the tenure of estates be changed? Could the women have no benefit from a law made in their favor? Must they be passed by upon moral principles forever, because they were once excluded by a legal prohibition? Or may that which passed only to males by one law, pass likewise to females by another?

You mention your resolution to maintain the right of your brothers [i.e., all heirs male] : I do not see how any of their rights are invaded.

As your whole difficulty arises from the act of your ancestor, who diverted the succession from the females, you inquire, very properly, what were his motives and what was his intention; for you certainly are not bound by his act more than he intended to bind you, nor hold your land on harder or stricter terms than those on which it was granted.

Intentions must be gathered from acts. When he left the estate to his nephew, by excluding his daughters, was it, or was it not, in his power to have perpetuated the succession to the males? If he could have done it, he seems to have shown, by omitting it, that he did not desire it to be done; and, upon your own principles, you will not easily prove your right to destroy that capacity of succession which your ancestors have left.

If your ancestor had not the power of making a perpetual settlement and if, therefore, we cannot judge distinctly of his intentions, yet his act can only be considered as an example, it makes not an obligation. And, as you observe, he set no example of rigorous adherence to the line of succession. He that overlooked a brother, would not wonder that little regard is shown to remote relations.

As the rules of succession are, in a great part, purely legal, no man can be supposed to bequeath any thing, but upon legal terms; he can grant no power which the law denies; and if he makes no special and definite limitation, he confers all the powers which the law allows.

Your ancestor, for some reason, disinherited his daughters; but it no more follows that he intended his act as a rule for posterity than the disinheriting of his brother.

If, therefore, you ask by what right your father admits daughters to inheritance, ask yourself, first, by what right you require them to be excluded?

It appears, upon reflection, that your father excludes nobody; he only admits nearer females to inherit before males
more remote; and the exclusion is purely consequential.

These, dear Sir, are my thoughts, immethodical and deliber-
ative; but, perhaps, you may find in them some glimmering
of evidence. (2.416-418.)

And he ended with repeating his recommendation that
Boswell consult Lord Hailes. But Boswell had done this, and
the opinion was flatly against him: "the succession of heirs
general was the succession, by the law of Scotland, from
the throne to the cottage, as far as we can learn it by record."
Hailes added that the preference of an heir male to nearer
females had been "an arbitrary act, which had seemed to
be best in the embarrassed state of affairs at that time
[2.418-419]." Boswell sent these remarks to Johnson, who
replied with some further considerations:

Having not any acquaintance with the laws or customs of
Scotland, I endeavored to consider your question upon
general principles, and found nothing of much validity
that I could oppose to this position: "He who inherits a
fief unlimited by his ancestor, inherits the power of limiting
it according to his own judgment or opinion." If this be
true, you may join with your father.

Further consideration produced another conclusion: "He
who receives a fief unlimited by his ancestors, gives his
heirs some reason to complain if he does not transmit it
unlimited to posterity. For why should he make the state of
others worse than his own, without a reason?" If this be
true, though neither you nor your father are about to do
what is quite right, but as your father violates (I think) the
legal succession least, he seems to be nearer the right
than yourself.

It cannot but occur that "Women have natural and equitable
claims as well as men, and these claims are not to be
capriciously or lightly superseded or infringed." When
fiefs implied military service, it is easily discerned why
females could not inherit them; but that reason is now at an
end. As manners make laws, manners likewise repeal them.

These are the general conclusions which I have attained.
None of them are very favorable to your scheme of entail,
nor perhaps to any scheme. My observation [to Langton],
that only he who acquires an estate may bequeath it capriciously, if it contains any conviction, includes this position
likewise, that only he who acquires an estate may entail it
capriciously. But I think it may be safely presumed, that
"he who inherits an estate, inherits all the power legally
concomitant;" and that "he who gives or leaves unlimited

an estate legally limitable, must be presumed to give that power of limitation which he omitted to take away, and to commit future contingencies to future prudence." In these two positions I believe Lord Hailes will advise you to rest; every other notion of possession seems to me full of difficulties, and embarrassed with scruples. (2.419-420.)

A few days later Johnson wrote again, saying that he hoped the question was decided, and adding some remarks about Hailes's aversion to entails:

Hereditary tenures are established in all civilized countries, and are accompanied in most with hereditary authority. Sir William Temple considers our constitution as defective, that there is not an unalienable estate in land connected with a peerage: and Lord Bacon mentions as a proof that the Turks are Barbarians, their want of *Stirpes*, as he calls them, or hereditary rank. Do not let your mind, when it is freed from the supposed necessity of a rigorous entail, be entangled with contrary objections, and think all entails unlawful, till you have cogent arguments, which I believe you will never find. (2.421.)

The question was finally settled by a compromise which Boswell's father had originally proposed: the estate was settled on the heirs male of Boswell's great grandfather, so that all of Johnson's arguments went for exactly nothing. And the daughters were left to indigence.

We may note at the outset Johnson's interest, along with many of his contemporaries, in natural right and its modification by law. The case may, in one sense, be said to rest on this point; legally, Boswell and his father could have made almost any sort of settlement, and the legal questions are therefore peripheral. Johnson is generations in advance of Boswell in his attitude toward women: it will be observed that he did not even notice the old arguments that women do not carry on the blood. He is also insistent on the changing character of law — and this is sufficiently surprising in this crusty old Tory: "Laws are formed by the manners and exigencies of particular times, and it is but accidental that they last longer than their causes." It is but a step from this to suggest that they should be abolished when they are obsolete. This Johnson did not do, perhaps because he was well aware of the fictions common to eighteenth century courts by which obsolete old laws were by-passed. In the same paragraph from which I have just quoted, Johnson asked a rhetorical question which would have astonished those Americans who were in revolt, and against whom Johnson had written with such violence: "Is land to be treated with more reverence than liberty?" It was, generally speaking. Throughout his consideration of the case Johnson is tender of the rights of women: "Women have natural and equitable claims as well as men, and these claims are not to be capriciously or lightly superseded or infringed." And he repeats, as a stroke which should have been fatal to Boswell's romantic feudalism, "As manners make laws, manners likewise repeal them." We may observe in passing Johnson's general acquaintance with feudal tenures, and also the quotation of a phrase from civil law, *sartum tectum*, which, both appropriate and unexpected, shows his easy familiarity with at least part of that subject.

Before leaving this case it might be pointed out that Johnson by no means had a closed mind on the subject of entails. I am inclined to think that he may have been jesting in his remarks about Langton's leaving his estate to the "three dowdies." (Afterwards he "laughed immoderately" and said, "I'd have his will turned into verse, like a ballad [2.262]!") And Johnson seemed disconcerted when later Boswell turned this incident back at him: Johnson's parenthesis, "if it contains any conviction," looks like an attempt to make the best of a bad thing. Some months before Boswell's case, Johnson had told Mrs. Thrale that he was in favor of entailing the Thrale estate on young Harry Thrale, but added, "we will consult men of experience."[4] When he was in Scotland Johnson made a comment on entails which perhaps gives his settled view: "His opinion was that so much land should be entailed as that families should never fall into contempt, and as much left free as to give them all the advantages of property in case of any emergency."[5] He made a somewhat similar remark later: "Entails are good, because it is good to preserve in a country, serieses of men, to whom the people are accustomed to look up as to their leaders. But I am for

4. *Letters*, 420.
5. *Life*, 5. 101.

leaving a quantity of land in commerce, to excite industry, and keep money in the country." (2.428.)

On Boswell's next visit to London he consulted Johnson on behalf of the Rev. James Thomson, for whom Boswell was one of the counsel in a lively case. In a contested election at Dumferline, a political agent

> who was charged with having been unfaithful to his employer, and having deserted to the opposite party for a pecuniary reward — attacked very rudely in a newspaper the Reverend Mr. James Thomson, one of the ministers of that place, on account of a supposed allusion to him in one of his sermons. Upon this the minister, on a subsequent Sunday, arraigned him by name from the pulpit with some severity; and the agent, after the sermon was over, rose up and asked the minister aloud, "What bribe he had received for telling so many lies from the chair of verity." (3. 58.)

An action for defamation and damages was brought against Thomson, and in spite of counsel's defense of "liberty of the pulpit," "provocation of the previous attack," and the "instant retaliation," the Court of Session decided against the minister. Johnson, says Boswell, was satisfied that the judgment was wrong, and dictated this argument in confutation:

> Of the censure pronounced from the pulpit, our determination must be formed, as in other cases, by a consideration of the action itself, and the particular circumstances with which it is invested.

> The right of censure and rebuke seems necessarily appendant to the pastoral office. He, to whom the care of a congregation is entrusted, is considered as the shepherd of a flock, as the teacher of a school, as the father of a family. As a shepherd tending not his own sheep but those of his master, he is answerable for those that stray and those that lose themselves by straying. But no man can be answerable for losses which he has not power to prevent, or for vagrancy which he has not authority to restrain.

> As a teacher giving instruction for wages, and liable to reproach, if those whom he undertakes to inform make no proficiency, he must have the power of enforcing attendance, of awakening negligence, and repressing contradiction.

> As a father, he possesses the paternal authority of admonition, rebuke, and punishment. He cannot, without reducing his office to an empty name, be hindered from the exercise of any practice necessary to stimulate the idle, to reform the vicious, to check the petulant, and correct the stubborn.

If we enquire into the practice of the primitive church, we shall, I believe, find the ministers of the word exercising the whole authority of this complicated character. We shall find them not only encouraging the good by exhortation, but terrifying the wicked by reproof and denunciation. In the earliest ages of the Church, while religion was yet pure from secular advantages, the punishment of sinners was public censure and open penance — penalties inflicted merely by ecclesiastical authority, at a time while the church had yet no help from the civil power, while the hand of the magistrate lifted only the rod of persecution, and when governors were ready to afford a refuge to all those who fled from clerical authority.

That the Church, therefore, had once a power of public censure is evident, because that power was frequently exercised. That it borrowed not its power from the civil authority is likewise certain, because civil authority was at that time its enemy.

The hour came at length, when after three hundred years of struggle and distress Truth took possession of imperial power, and the civil laws lent their aid to the ecclesiastical constitutions. The magistrate from that time cooperated with the priest, and clerical sentences were made efficacious by secular force. But the State, when it came to the assistance of the Church, had no intention to diminish its authority. Those rebukes and those censures which were lawful before, were lawful still. But they had hitherto operated only upon voluntary submission. The refractory and contemptuous were at first in no danger of temporal severities, except what they might suffer from the reproaches of conscience, or the detestation of their fellow Christians. When religion obtained the support of law, if admonitions and censures had no effect, they were seconded by the magistrates with coercion and punishment.

It therefore appears from ecclesiastical history that the right of inflicting shame by public censure has been always considered as inherent in the Church; and that this right was not conferred by the civil power, for it was exercised when the civil power operated against it. By the civil power it was never taken away, for the Christian magistrate interposed his office, not to rescue sinners from censure but to supply more powerful means of reformation; to add pain where shame was insufficient; and when men were proclaimed unworthy of the society of the faithful, to restrain them by imprisonment from spreading abroad the contagion of wickedness.

It is not improbable that from this acknowledged power of public censure grew in time the practice of auricular confession. Those who dreaded the blast of public reprehension were willing to submit themselves to the priest, by a private accusation of themselves, and to obtain a reconciliation with the Church by a kind of clandestine absolution and invisible penance — conditions with which the priest would in times of ignorance and corruption easily comply, as they increased his influence by adding the knowledge of secret sins to that of notorious offences and enlarged his authority by making him the sole arbiter of the terms of reconcilement.

From this bondage the Reformation set us free. The minister has no longer power to press into the retirements of cons-cience, to torture us by interrogatories, or to put himself in possession of our secrets and our lives. But though we have thus controlled his usurpations, his just and original power remains unimpaired. He may still see, though he may not pry; he may yet hear, though he may not question. And that knowledge which his eyes and ears force upon him it is still his duty to use for the benefit of his flock. A father who lives near a wicked neighbor may forbid a son to fre-quent his company. A minister who has in his congregation a man of open and scandalous wickedness may warn his parishioners to shun his conversation. To warn them is not only lawful, but not to warn them would be criminal. He may warn them one by one in friendly converse, or by a paro-chial visitation. But if he may warn each man singly, what shall forbid him to warn them all together? Of that which is to be made known to all, how is there any difference whether it be communicated to each singly, or to all to-gether? What is known to all, must necessarily be public. Whether it shall be public at once, or public by degrees, is the only question. And of a sudden and solemn publication the impression is deeper, and the warning more effectual.

It may easily be urged, if a minister be thus left at liberty to delate sinners from the pulpit, and to publish at will the crimes of a parishioner, he may often blast the innocent and distress the timorous. He may be suspicious, and condemn without evidence; he may be rash, and judge without exam-ination; he may be severe, and treat slight offences with too much harshness; he may be malignant and partial, and gratify his private interest or resentment under the shelter of his pastoral character.

Of all this there is possibility, and of all this there is danger. But if possibility of evil be to exclude good, no good ever can be done. If nothing is to be attempted in which there is danger, we must all sink into hopeless in-activity. The evils that may be feared from this practice arise not from any defect in the institution but from the infirmities of human nature. Power, in whatever hands it is placed, will be sometimes improperly exerted; yet courts of law must judge, though they will sometimes judge amiss. A father must instruct his children, though he himself may often want instruction. A minister must censure sinners, though his censure may be sometimes erroneous by want of judgment, and sometimes unjust by want of honesty.

If we examine the circumstances of the present case, we shall find the sentence neither erroneous nor unjust; we shall find no breach of private confidence, no intrusion into secret transactions. The fact was notorious and indubitable — so easy to be proved that no proof was desired. The act was base and treacherous, the perpetration insolent and open, and the example naturally mischievous. The minister, however, being retired and recluse, had not yet heard what was publicly known throughout the parish; and on occasion of a public election, warned his people, according to his duty, against the crimes which public elections frequently produce. His warning was felt by one of his parishioners as pointed particularly at himself. But instead of producing, as might be wished, private compunction and immediate reformation, it kindled only rage and resentment. He charged his minister, in a public paper, with scandal, defamation and falsehood. The minister, thus reproached, had his own character to vindicate, upon which his pastoral authority must necessarily depend. To be charged with a defamatory lie is an injury which no man patiently endures in common life. To be charged with polluting the pastoral office with scandal and falsehood was a violation of character still more atrocious, as it affected not only his personal but his clerical veracity. His indignation naturally rose in proportion to his honesty, and with all the fortitude of injured honesty, he dared this calumniator in the church, and at once exonerated himself from censure, and rescued his flock from deception and from danger. The man whom he accuses pretends not to be innocent, or at least only pretends, for he declines a trial. The crime of which he is accused has frequent opportunities and strong temptations. It has already spread far, with much depravation of private morals and much injury to public happiness. To warn the people, therefore, against it was not wanton and officious, but necessary and pastoral.

What then is the fault with which this worthy minister is charged? He has usurped no dominion over conscience. He has exerted no authority in support of doubtful and controverted opinions. He has not dragged into light a bashful and corrigible sinner. His censure was directed against a breach of morality, against an act which no man justifies. The man who appropriated this censure to himself is evidently and notoriously guilty. His consciousness of his own wickedness incited him to attack his faithful reprover with open insolence and printed accusations. Such an attack made defence necessary; and we hope it will be at last decided that the means of defence were just and lawful. (3.59-62.)

Thomson wished to appeal, but Boswell sensibly first asked the opinion of Thurlow, then Attorney General, on the probability of success. On the basis of the papers presented, not including Johnson's, Thurlow advised against an appeal, partly because of the expense, and partly because "there are many chances that ... the impression will be taken to the

disadvantage of the appellant." Thurlow see-saws: the style
of the sermon was "impossible to approve," but on the other
hand the minister had originally been libeled; the minister's
behavior was to be condemned, and might be actionable *if a
wrong and damage could be proved*. But the minister committed no crime:

> The common law of England does not give way to actions
> for every reproachful word. An action cannot be brought for
> general damages upon any words which import less than an
> offence cognisable by law; consequently no action could
> have been brought here for the words in question. Both
> laws [i.e., Scots and English] admit the truth to be a justi-
> fication in actions *for words;* and the law of England does
> the same in actions for libels. The judgment, therefore,
> seems to me to have been wrong, in that the Court repelled
> that defence. (3.63-64.)

Boswell followed Thurlow's advice, and did not appeal the
case, though it would appear that the law was fully on his
side. Perhaps he realized that the question had not been
decided, and would not be decided by the Lords, wholly on
the basis of law: the Court of Session appears to have been
shocked that a minister used personalities in the pulpit, regardless of the legality of such an act, and the same sense of
shock is evident in Thurlow's remarks. It is obvious that
Thurlow was not called upon to "approve the style of that
sermon," though the style might be a relevant topic for the
presbytery. It was not properly a concern of the Court of
Session or of the Lords, but the first made it so, and the
second might have done so. It is therefore entirely clear why
Johnson spent so much of his argument on the propriety of
pastoral admonition and so little on its legality. He is thinking as he would before a jury, not so much of points of strict
law, as of points which might influence the jury in favor of
his client, and conversely is trying to obviate prejudices
against his client. In this he showed his typical shrewdness
and common sense: he did not have to be told that a solicitor's duty is to win a case, and that the members of the House
of Lords, no less than those of the Court of Session, might
need to have their minds cleared of cant. It is not surprising
that Lord Hailes felt that the Scots court was wrong (3.91),

or that Burke should have said that Johnson's argument was
done "in a workmanlike manner [3.62]."

Next year Boswell asked Johnson's help in the prosecution
of a schoolmaster for indecent behavior to his female scholars:
"There is no statute against such abominable conduct; but it
is punishable at common law [3.212]." I do not for a moment
believe that Boswell needed any assistance in such a case,
which would have depended on little more than the establishment of the facts; but he was doubtless merely "drawing"
Johnson. At any rate Johnson replied a month later, and
refused to be drawn:

> The crime of the schoolmaster whom you are engaged to
> prosecute is very great, and may be suspected to be too
> common. In our law it would be a breach of the peace and a
> misdemeanor: that is, a kind of indefinite crime, not capital,
> but punishable at the discretion of the Court. You cannot
> want matter: all that needs to be said will easily occur.
> (3.214.)

Throughout 1777 Johnson was much interested in the case
of a negro slave, Joseph Knight, who was suing for his
liberty in the Court of Session. Boswell was not on the case,
but since it involved a question in which he and Johnson
were in direct disagreement, he followed it closely. Knight,
who had been kidnapped as a child in Africa, was sold to a
Mr. Wedderburne as a personal servant. He was brought to
Scotland, learned to read, and in 1772 read a report of the
Somerset case, the celebrated decision of Lord Mansfield
which abolished slavery in England. He married, found that a
couple could not live on his allowance of sixpence a week,
and asked for regular wages. Being refused he "signified his
intention of seeking service elsewhere [3.214n.]." In this he
was restrained by the local magistrates, but was upheld by
the sheriff. Thereupon he left his master, and the case was
taken to the Court of Session. His counsel included Boswell's
friend Dundas, and Maclaurin, whose printed *Information* on
behalf of Knight Boswell sent to Johnson. Johnson replied,
citing Mansfield's decision, and a few days later wrote
again: "I have looked over Mr. Maclaurin's plea, and think it
excellent. How is the suit carried on? If by subscription, I

commission you to contribute, in my name, what is proper. Let
nothing be wanting in such a case." (3.88) A few months
later he wrote again asking for news of the case; Boswell
replied that it was still pending, but that Maclaurin was
"made happy by your approbation of his memorial [3.101] ."
Still later Boswell sent the plea of the opposing side, and
asked for Johnson's opinion "as a *Politician*, as well as a
Poet" on the subject (3.127). Finally when Boswell was next
in London, Johnson dictated to him a short argument on the case:

It must be agreed that in most ages many countries have
had part of their inhabitants in a state of slavery; yet it may
be doubted whether slavery can ever be supposed the natural condition of man. It is impossible not to conceive that
men in their original state were equal, and very difficult to
imagine how one would be subjected to another but by
violent compulsion. An individual may, indeed, forfeit his
liberty by a crime, but he cannot by that crime forfeit the
liberty of his children. What is true of a criminal   seems
true likewise of a captive. A man may accept life from a
conquering enemy on condition of perpetual servitude; but it
is very doubtful whether he can entail that servitude on his
descendants, for no man can stipulate without commission
for another. The condition which he himself accepts, his
son or grandson perhaps would have rejected. If we should
admit, what perhaps may with more reason be denied, that
there are certain relations between man and man which may
make slavery necessary and just, yet it can never be
proved that he who is now suing for his freedom ever stood
in any of those relations. He is certainly subject by no law,
but that of violence, to his present master; who pretends no
claim to his obedience, but that he bought him from a merchant of slaves whose right to sell him never was examined.
It is said that, according to the constitutions of Jamaica, he
was legally enslaved; these constitutions are merely positive, and apparently injurious to the rights of mankind,
because whoever is exposed to sale is condemned to slavery without appeal, by whatever fraud or violence he might
have been originally brought into the merchant's power. In
our own time Princes have been sold by wretches to whose
care they were entrusted, that they might have an European
education; but when once they were brought to a market in
the plantations, little would avail either their dignity or
their wrongs. The laws of Jamaica afford a Negro no redress. His color is considered as a sufficient testimony
against him. It is to be lamented that moral right should
ever give way to political convenience. But if temptations
of interest are sometimes too strong for human virtue, let us
at least retain a virtue where there is no temptation to quit
it. In the present case there is apparent right on one side,
and no convenience on the other. Inhabitants of this island
can neither gain riches nor power by taking away the liberty

of any part of the human species. The sum of the argument
is this — No man is by nature the property of another: The
defendant is, therefore, by nature free: The rights of nature
must be some way forfeited before they can be justly taken
away: That the defendant has by any act forfeited the rights
of nature we require to be proved; and if no proof of such
forfeiture can be given, we doubt not but the justice of the
court will declare him free. (3.202-203.)

The court decided in Knight's favor by a large majority.
Boswell grudgingly conceded that perhaps Johnson was in the
right in this particular case, though not at all in his general
opposition to slavery, in which, Boswell impudently says,
Johnson showed "a zeal without knowledge [3.200]." Johnson's argument is much condensed, and a little glossing may
be in order. His statement at the outset that "men in their
original state were equal" means, I think, merely that they
were equal before the law. There is ample evidence in Johnson's writings that he did not believe men equal intellectu-
ally, economically, or in many other respects, in however
primitive a society. When he speaks of the laws of Jamaica
being merely positive, he uses the word in the sense noted in
his *Dictionary:* "settled by arbitrary appointment," exempli-
fied by a quotation from Hooker: "In laws, that which is
natural, bindeth universally, that which is *positive,* not so."
Johnson shows a nice balance in this argument between the
legal and the moral; there is no casuistry here. And we may
well admire the dignity and vigor of his summing-up.

In the spring of 1778 Boswell was engaged as counsel at
the bar of the House of Commons to oppose a road bill in the
county of Stirling, and asked Johnson "what mode he would
advise me to follow in addressing such an audience." That
Johnson was aware of a lawyer's problems of this sort I have
remarked in connection with the Thomson case. His admonition
here is merely common sense:

Why, Sir, you must provide yourself with a good deal of
extraneous matter, which you are to produce occasionally,
so as to fill up the time; for you must consider that they do
not listen much. If you begin with the strength of your
cause, it may be lost before they begin to listen. When you
catch a moment of attention, press the merits of the question upon them.

As to the merits of the case: "it would be a wrong thing to deprive the small landholders of the privilege of assessing themselves for making and repairing the high roads; *it was destroying a certain portion of liberty, without a good reason, which was always a bad thing.*" (3.224.)

In 1781 Boswell was counsel for the M.P. from Ayrshire, whose election was contested before a committee of the House. In connection with the case Johnson dictated some notes on the registration of deeds:

> All laws are made for the convenience of the community; what is legally done, should be legally recorded, that the state of things may be known, and that wherever evidence is requisite, evidence may be had. For this reason the obligation to frame and establish a legal register is enforced by a legal penalty, which penalty is the want of that perfection and plenitude of right which a register would give. Thence it follows, that this is not an objection merely legal; for the reason on which the law stands being equitable, makes it an equitable objection. (4.74.)

It should be noted again how often Johnson is interested not merely in the fact that a law exists, but that it is equitable and just: his approach is broad and humane. But at the same time, he was always ready to realize the necessity of a good technique in presenting an argument, as he shows in his succeeding remarks:

> This you must enlarge on, when speaking to the committee. You must not argue there, as if you were arguing in the schools; close reasoning will not fix their attention; you must say the same thing over and over again, in different words. If you say it but once, they miss it in a moment of inattention. It is unjust, Sir, to censure lawyers for multiplying words when they argue; it is often *necessary* for them to multiply words.

A few months later Boswell brought to Johnson the last case for consideration, the third involving libel. The Society of Procurators, or attornies, practicing before the lower courts of Edinburgh, had obtained a royal charter in which they had changed their designation to Solicitors, from a notion, says Boswell, that it was more genteel. This change was ridiculed by a squib in *The Edinburgh Gazette:*

> A correspondent informs us that the Worshipful Society of *Chaldeans, Cadies,* or *Running Stationers* of this city are

resolved, in imitation, and encouraged by the singular success of their brethren, of an *equally respectable* Society, to apply for a Charter of their Privileges, particularly of the sole privilege of PROCURING, in the most extensive sense of the word, exclusive of chairmen, porters, penny-post men, and other *inferior* ranks; their brethren the R—Y—L S—LL—RS, *alias* P—C—RS, *before the* INFERIOR Courts of this City, always excepted.

Should the Worshipful Society be successful, they are farther resolved not to be *puffed up* thereby, but to demean themselves with more equanimity and decency than their *R—y—l, learned,* and *very modest* brethren above mentioned have done, upon their late dignification and exaltation. (4.128-129.)

Members of the society prosecuted Robertson, the publisher, for damages, but the Court of Session dismissed the case. A review was granted, and Boswell was to answer in Robertson's defense. Johnson furnished Boswell with the following argument, which he used entire:

All injury is either of the person, the fortune, or the fame. Now it is a certain thing, it is proverbially known, that *a jest breaks no bones.* They never have gained half-a-crown less in the whole profession since this mischievous paragraph has appeared; and, as to their reputation, what is their reputation but an instrument of getting money? If, therefore, they have lost no money, the question upon reputation may be answered by a very old position — *De minimis non curat Praetor.*

Whether it was, or was not, an *animus injuriandi,* is not worth inquiring, if no *injuria* can be proved. But the truth is, there was no *animus injuriandi.* It was only an *animus irritandi,* which, happening to be exercised upon a *genus irritabile,* produced unexpected violence of resentment. Their irritability arose only from an opinion of their own importance, and their delight in their new exaltation. What might have been borne by a *Procurator,* could not be borne by a *Solicitor.* Your Lordships well know that *honores mutant mores.* Titles and dignities play strongly upon the fancy. As a madman is apt to think himself grown suddenly great, so he that has grown suddenly great is apt to borrow a little from the madman. To co-operate with their resentment would be to promote their frenzy; nor is it possible to guess to what they might proceed, if to the new title of Solicitor should be added the elation of victory and triumph.

We consider your Lordships as the protectors of our rights, and the guardians of our virtues, but believe it not included in your high office that you should flatter our vices, or solace our vanity: and, as vanity only dictates this prosecution, it is humbly hoped your Lordships will dismiss it.

If every attempt, however light or ludicrous, to lessen
another's reputation is to be punished by a judicial sentence, what punishment can be sufficiently severe for him
who attempts to diminish the reputation of the Supreme
Court of Justice, by reclaiming upon a cause already determined, without any change in the state of the question?
Does it not imply hopes that the Judges will change their
opinion? Is not uncertainty and inconstancy in the highest
degree disreputable to a Court? Does it not suppose that the
former judgment was temerarious or negligent? Does it not
lessen the confidence of the public? Will it not be said,
that *jus est aut incognitum, aut vagum?* and will not the
consequence be drawn, *misera est servitus?* Will not the
rules of action be obscure? Will not he who knows himself
wrong today, hope that the Courts of Justice will think him
right tomorrow? Surely, my Lords, these are attempts of
dangerous tendency, which the Solicitors, as men versed in
the law, should have foreseen and avoided. It was natural
for an ignorant printer to appeal from the Lord Ordinary; but
from lawyers, the descendants of lawyers, who have practiced for three hundred years, and have now raised themselves to a higher denomination, it might be expected that
they should know the reverence due to a judicial determination; and, having been once dismissed, should sit down in
silence.(4.129-131.)

The Court of Session reversed their previous judgment, and
the society received five pounds' damages. Before presenting
Johnson's argument, Boswell had submitted it to his client,
who had altered *irritandi,* in the second paragraph to *jocandi,*
having found in Blackstone, says Boswell, that to irritate is
actionable. I do not find such a statement in Blackstone, who
says, indeed, that in both actions for words and libels damage
must be proved.[6] Thurlow's comments on the Thomson case
might also be thought applicable. Blackstone, however, does
say that in criminal libel, which is a breach of the peace, the
situation is different: here ridicule, though it does not necessarily damage a person, may incite a quarrel, and hence is a
danger to the peace.[7] I suspect that the court may have been
influenced by some such reasoning in giving damages in this
civil suit, even though the law at that time appears not to
have justified this. It is worth noting in passing that it was
the "ignorant printer," not Boswell, the learned counsel, who
looked into Blackstone for help in the case.

6. *Commentaries,* 3. 123-26.
7. *Ib.,* 4. 150.

For many years Boswell had not been satisfied to remain a Scots lawyer: he longed to practice in London. It may be suspected, in truth, that he merely wished to live in London, and used the practice as an excuse. In any event, in 1775 he entered himself in the Inner Temple, and Johnson joined in his bond. It has been stated that Johnson always threw cold water on this ambition of Boswell's, but the evidence seems otherwise. To be sure, Johnson's advice was conservative:

> You must not indulge too sanguine hopes, should you be called to our bar. I was told by a very sensible lawyer that there are a great many chances against any man's success in the profession of the law; the candidates are so numerous, and those who get large practice so few. He said, it was by no means true that a man of good parts and application is sure of having business, though he, indeed, allowed that if such a man could but appear in a few causes, his merit would be known and he would get forward; but that the great risk was, that a man might pass half a lifetime in the Courts, and never have an opportunity of showing his abilities. [8]

On a later occasion, Johnson added a corollary, telling Boswell that he might be sure that "practice is got from an opinion that the person employed deserves it best; so that if a man of merit at the bar does not get practice, it is from error, not from injustice [4.172]." Still later, in the year of Johnson's death, Boswell asked him whether an extensive acquaintance in London might not hinder a lawyer from giving enough attention to business. Johnson's advice was as sound as ever:

> Sir, you will attend to business, as business lays hold of you. When not actually employed, you may see your friends as much as you do now.... But you must take care to attend constantly in Westminster Hall, both to mind your business, as it is almost all learnt there (for nobody reads now), and to show that you want to have business. And you must not be too often seen at public places, that competitors may not have it to say, "He is always at the Playhouse or at Ranelagh, and never to be found at his chambers." And, Sir, there must be a kind of solemnity in the manner of a professional man. (4.309-310.)

Boswell was not admitted to the English bar till after Johnson's death, and his practice was a failure. He admitted

8. *Life*, 3. 179.

that during one term he attended Westminster Hall only once; he was laboring to finish the *Life of Johnson;* he was drinking too much; he was perhaps more interested in politics than in law. From these diverse causes, he never put Johnson's advice to the test.

Boswell, like Chambers, was an outlet for Johnson's interest in the law. Both men stimulated Johnson to think on legal subjects and the aspects of a legal career. The accident that Boswell was a much greater biographer than he was a lawyer has made some of Johnson's opinions on the law famous. Many of these opinions occur as scattered remarks throughout the *Life of Johnson,* and may be introduced here as a supplement to Johnson's formal arguments. I shall add a few from other sources. It will be convenient to arrange them under heads: law in general; the law of nations, foreign and military law; the king and parliament; the rights and duties of the subject.

"All our religion, almost all our law, almost all our arts, almost all that sets us above savages, has come to us from the shores of the Mediterranean." (3.36.) From this splendid tribute to the ancient world, Johnson was able to pass easily to Boswell's assertion that no man could write well on law without practice: "Why, Sir, in England, where so much money is to be got by the practice of the law, most of our writers upon it have been in practice; though Blackstone had not been much in practice when he published his *Commentaries.* But upon the Continent, the great writers on law have not all been in practice; Grotius, indeed, was; but Pufendorf was not, Burlamaqui was not." (2.430.) But with all his respect for the law, Johnson generally spoke ill of attorneys: "he did not care to speak ill of any man behind his back, but he believed the gentleman was an attorney [2.126]." As compared with other professions: "I would rather have Chancery suits upon my hands, than the cure of souls [3.304]." And: "Lawyers know life practically. A bookish man should always have them to converse with. They have what he wants." (3.306.) And some rough notes by Johnson give further insight into his attitude: "If write well, not less innocent or laudable than

prescribing — pleading — judging. . . . If ill, fails with less
hazard to the public than others. The prescriber — pleader —
judge hurt others. [9]

Johnson's interest in feudal law, evident in many places,
appears in his urging Boswell to study the subject: "The
whole system of ancient tenures is gradually passing away;
and I wish to have the knowledge of it preserved adequate and
complete."[1] As to whether barristers had more law or less in
the past: "Nay, Sir, they had more law long ago than they
have now. As to precedents, to be sure they will increase in
course of time; but the more precedents there are, the less
occasion is there for law; that is to say, the less occasion is
there for investigating principles." (2.158.) And on the tenure
of judges: "There is no reason why a Judge should hold his
office for life, more than any other person in public trust. A
judge may be partial otherwise than to the Crown: we have
seen judges partial to the populace. A judge may become
corrupt, and yet there may not be legal evidence against him.
A judge may become froward from age. A judge may grow unfit
for his office in many ways." (2.353.)

There is a single reference to ancient law: "In Sparta,
theft was allowed by general consent: theft, therefore, was
there not a crime, but then there was no security, and what a
life must they have had, when there was no security." (3.293.)

When Johnson visited Paris, he noted with interest that
"The French have no laws for the maintenance of their poor."
And again: "We heard the lawyers plead." (2.390,393.)
He was also interested in French military law: "The magistrate cannot seize a soldier but by the Colonel's permission [p.391] ." A few years later when he visited Langton in
camp with the militia, he sat, "with a patient degree of attention, to observe the proceedings of a regimental court-martial,"
and later wrote to Langton to enquire the outcome. (3.361,365.)
He also interested himself in a court-martial of Lord Charles
Hay, and wrote something for him which is lost (3.9). He
thought Hay "had nothing to fear from a court-martial," but

9. *Works*, 1. 268n.
1. *Life*, 2. 202.

in later years his judgment of such tribunals was not high: "he expresses much doubt of an enlightened decision; and said, that perhaps there was not a member of it, who in the whole course of his life, had ever spent an hour by himself in balancing probabilities [4.12]."

Goldsmith's view that the dogma that the king can do no wrong is morally false was thus rebutted by Johnson:

> Sir, you are to consider that in our constitution, according to its true principles, the King is the head; he is supreme; he is above everything, and there is no power by which he can be tried. Therefore it is, Sir, that we hold the King can do no wrong; that whatever may happen to be wrong in government may not be above our reach, by being ascribed to Majesty. Redress is always to be had against oppression, by punishing the immediate agents. The King, though he should command, cannot force a Judge to condemn a man unjustly; therefore it is the Judge whom we prosecute and punish. (1.423-424.)

Once during an argument, Johnson heatedly said, "The crown has not power enough," but yet he was unwilling to approve the Royal Marriage Bill, "Because (said he) I would not have the people think that the validity of marriage depends on the will of man, or that the right of a King depends on the will of man," (2.170, 152.) One aspect of the King's power particularly interested Johnson: "He detested the idea of governing by parliamentary corruption, and asserted most strenuously, that a prince steadily and conspicuously pursuing the interests of his people could not fail of parliamentary concurrence. A prince of ability, he contended, might and should be the directing soul and spirit of his own administration; in short, his own minister, and not the mere head of a party: and then, and not till then, would the royal dignity be sincerely respected [2.117].

On the succession: "A right to a throne is like a right to anything else. Possession is sufficient, where no better right can be shown." (3.157.) But that was not the case in 1688: "What we did at the Revolution was necessary: but it broke our constitution." (4.170.)

Johnson's interest in the constitution was so extensive

that he once projected a history of it, as he once also planned
a history of parliament for Cave.[2] Hawkins gives a revealing
account of this interest:

> For the English constitution, as originally framed, he ever
> expressed a profound reverence. He understood it well, and
> had noted in his mind the changes it had at various periods
> undergone, that is to say, first, in the reign of Hen. VII
> when the yeomanry were put into a state of competition
> with the nobility; afterwards, when by the abolition of ten-
> ures, and the putting down the court of wards and liveries,
> occasion was given to Sir Harbottle Grimston to say that, in
> that transaction, neither did the crown know what it lost,
> nor the people what they had gained; and lastly, by the
> erecting of a monied, in opposition to the landed, interest,
> and the introduction of the science and practice of funding.

> He, therefore, looked not on Magna Charta as the palladium
> of our liberties, . . . but to the subsequent concessions of
> the crown in favor of the people, such as are the petition
> of right, the habeas corpus act, the bill of rights, and num-
> erous other statutes of a like beneficial tendency.[3]

On the ancient function of the Commons:

> The House of Commons was originally not a privilege of
> the people, but a check for the Crown on the House of
> Lords. I remember Henry the Eighth wanted them to do
> something; they hesitated in the morning, but did it in the
> afternoon. He told them, "It is well you did; or half your
> heads should have been upon Temple Bar.[4]

As to the expulsion of Wilkes by a resolution of the Commons,
he said: "Parliament may be considered as bound by law, as
a man is bound where there is nobody to tie the knot. As it is
clear that the House of Commons may expel, and expel again
and again, why not allow of the power to incapacitate for that
parliament, rather than have a perpetual contest kept up between parliament and the people." (3.408.) Later, Wilkes was
careless enough to suggest that the Commons might evade the
law against exporting specie by ordering it sent to the Colonies; Johnson caught him very wittily: "Sure, Sir, *you* don't
think a *resolution of the House of Commons* equal to *the law
of the land.*" (4.104.)

2. *Ib.*, 4. 382n., 1. 155
3. *Works*, 1. 505-506
4. *Life*, 3. 408

Boswell once asked Johnson whether the influence exercised by the Scots peers in electing members of the Commons by means of fictitious qualifications ought not to be resisted, and Johnson naturally agreed (4.248, 250). But on another occasion he observed that "the statutes against bribery were intended to prevent upstarts with money from getting into Parliament;" adding that "if he were a gentleman of landed property, he would turn out all his tenants who did not vote for the candidate whom he supported[2.339-340]." So much for force as compared with fraud. But the legal rights of the Lords Johnson acknowledged readily enough: when the peers were criticised for opposing the opinion of the judges in a case before the Lords, he said: "Sir, there is no ground for censure. The Peers are judges themselves: and supposing them really to be of a different opinion, they might from duty be in opposition to the judges, who were there only to be consulted[3.345]."

On the rights and duties of the subject, Johnson has many comments. In his capacity of Thrale's executor, he advised the widow, "You are in your civil character a man. You may sue and be sued."[5] But as to the rights of women whose husbands were living,—and adulterous,—Johnson is not in advance of his era: "Confusion of progeny constitutes the essence of the crime; and therefore a woman who breaks her marriage vows is much more criminal than a man who does it. A man, to be sure, is criminal in the sight of God: but he does not do his wife a very material injury, if he does not insult her . . . ."[6] He repeated this opinion when Boswell brought up the subject of legitimation by subsequent marriage: "I think it a bad thing; because the chastity of women being of the utmost importance, as all property depends upon it, they who forfeit it should not have any possibility of being restored to good character; nor should the children, by an illicit connection, attain the full rights of lawful children, by the posterior consent of the offending parties [2.457]." Johnson's views on fornication are characteristic: "I would punish

5. *Letters*, 725
6. *Life*, 2. 55-6

it much more than is done, and so restrain it. In all countries
there has been fornication, as in all countries there has been
theft; but there may be more or less of the one, as well as of
the other, in proportion to the force of law . . . . Depend upon
it, Sir, severe laws, steadily enforced, would be sufficient
against those evils, and would promote marriage." (3.17-18.)
To the notion that a husband's infidelities released a wife
from her obligations, Johnson replied:

> This is miserable stuff, Sir. To the contract of marriage, be-
> sides the man and wife, there is a third party — society;
> and, if it be considered as a vow — God: and, therefore, it
> cannot be dissolved by their consent alone. Laws are not
> made for particular cases, but for men in general. A woman
> may be unhappy with her husband; but she cannot be freed
> from him without the approbation of the civil and ecclesias-
> tical power. A man may be unhappy because he is not so
> rich as another; but he is not to seize upon another's prop-
> erty with his own hand. (3.25.)

Where morals were not involved, Johnson's views on law
were sometimes ahead of those of his contemporaries. When a
friend attacked the law which gave a bounty for the export of
Irish corn, as prejudicial to the English trade, Johnson said:
'you talk the language of a savage: what, Sir? would you prevent any people from feeding themselves, if by any honest
means they can do it?" (2.130-131.)

The question of copyright was brought to a head during this
period by a Scots bookseller, Donaldson, who published books
in defiance of the supposed common law right of literary property. Johnson denied this right, but opposed Donaldson on
another ground:

> He is a fellow who takes advantage of the law to injure his
> brethren; for, notwithstanding that the statute secures only
> fourteen years of exclusive right, it has always been under-
> stood by *the trade*, that he who buys the copyright of a book
> from the author obtains a perpetual property; and upon that
> belief numberless bargains are made to transfer that prop-
> erty upon the expiration of the statutory term. Now Donald-
> son, I say, takes advantage here of people who have really
> an equitable title from usage; and if we consider how few of
> the books of which they buy the property succeed so well
> as to bring profit, we should be of opinion that the term of
> fourteen years is too short; it should be sixty years. (1.438.)

The courts decided against Donaldson, whose appeal to the Lords was, however, upheld. Before the final decision, Johnson expressed himself many times on the matter, once thus

> There seems ... to be in authors a stronger right of property than that by occupancy; a metaphysical right, a right, as it were, of creation, which should from its nature be perpetual but the consent of nations is against it, and indeed reason and the interests of learning are against it; for if it were to be perpetual, no book, however useful, could be universally diffused among mankind, should the proprietor take it into his head to restrain its circulation. (2.259.)

His final opinion was expressed in a letter written apparently to be used in the argument before the Lords:

> The author has a natural and peculiar right to the profits of his own work.
>
> But as every man who claims the protection of society must purchase it by resigning some part of his natural right, the author must recede from so much of his claim as shall be deemed injurious or inconvenient to society.
>
> It is inconvenient to society that an useful book should become perpetual and exclusive property.
>
> The judgment of the Lords was therefore legally and politically right.
>
> But the author's enjoyment of his natural right might without any inconvenience be protracted beyond the term settled by the statute. And it is, I think, to be desired
>
> 1. That an author should retain during his life the sole right of printing and selling his work.
>
> This is agreeable to moral right, and not inconvenient to the public, for who will be so diligent as the author to improve the book, and who can know so well how to improve it?
>
> 2. That the author be allowed, as by the present act, to alienate his right only for fourteen years.
>
> A shorter time would not procure a sufficient price, and a longer would cut off all hope of future profit, and consequently all solicitude for correction or addition.
>
> 3. That when after fourteen years the copy shall revert to the author, he be allowed to alienate it again only for seven years at a time.
>
> After fourteen years the value of the work will be known and it will no longer be bought at hazard. Seven years o

possession will therefore have an assignable price. It is proper that the author be always incited to polish and improve his work, by that prospect of accruing interest which those shorter periods of alienation will afford.

4. That after the author's death his work should continue an exclusive property capable of bequest and inheritance, and of conveyance by gift or sale for thirty years.

By these regulations a book may continue the property of the author, or of those who claim from him, about fifty years, a term sufficient to reward the writer without any loss to the public. In fifty years far the greater number of books are forgotten and annihilated, and it is for the advantage of learning that those which fifty years have not destroyed should become *bona communia*, to be used by every scholar as he shall think best.

In fifty years every book begins to require notes either to explain forgotten allusions and obsolete words, or to subjoin those discoveries which have been made by the gradual advancement of knowledge, or to correct those mistakes which time may have discovered.

Such notes cannot be written to any useful purpose without the text, and the text will frequently be refused while it is any man's property.'

On the rights of the individual, Johnson made many comments. Indifferent to such matters as the duration of parliaments, he was sure that "the *habeas corpus* is the single advantage which our government has over that of other countries."[8] It followed that "unless civil institutions insure protection to the innocent, all the confidence which mankind should have in them would be lost [4.252]." Yet he did not fear general warrants: "Such a power (he observed) must be vested in every government, to answer particular cases of necessity; and there can be no just complaint but when it is abused, for which those who administer government must be answerable [2.72]." The accusations against Hastings brought from Johnson a sensible remark on evidence: "What foundation there is for accusation I know not, but they will not get at him. Where bad actions are committed at so great a distance, a delinquent can obscure the evidence till the scent becomes cold; there is a cloud between, which cannot be penetrated: therefore all distant power is bad." (4.213.) And when a member of parliament said that he disregarded the arguments of counsel because they were paid for speaking, Johnson's common sense showed again: "You cannot help paying regard to their arguments, if they are good. If it were testimony, you might disregard it, if you knew that it were purchased." (4.281.)

Motive in crime is handled rather summarily by Johnson. He agreed with Blackstone that a murderer's being furnished with two pistols was a proof that he meant to shoot two persons (3.384). Likewise, when Boswell defended Rousseau's intentions, Johnson replied: "We cannot prove any man's intentions to be bad. You may shoot a man through the head, and say you intended to miss him; but the judge will order you to be hanged. An alleged want of intention, when evil is committed, will not be allowed in a court of justice." (2.12.) Although Johnson thought at one time that the greatest lack of the Highlanders in 1745 was the lack of law (2.126), he was later inclined in one instance to believe that Scotland had too much. When a Scots judge allowed the lapse of twenty years since the commission of a crime to be pled in bar, he at first disapproved. Then, says Boswell, "he thought there was something in it, if there had been for twenty years a neglect to prosecute a crime which was *known*. He would not allow that a murder, by not being *discovered* for twenty years, should escape punishment." (5.24.) A few days later he analyzed the notion further:

A jury in England would make allowance for deficiencies of evidence on account of lapse of time; but a general rule that a crime should not be punished, or tried for the purpose of punishment, after twenty years, is bad. It is cant to talk of the King's advocate delaying a prosecution from malice. How unlikely is it the King's advocate should have malice against persons who commit murder, or should even know them at all. If the son of the murdered man should kill the murderer who got off merely by prescription, I would help him to make his escape; though, were I upon his jury, I would not acquit him. (5.87.)

The same respect for a juryman's duty, coupled with a rough wish for more summary treatment, is found in his remark about a man who, apparently in self-defence, shot another on whose land he was trespassing: "Whoever would do as Campbell did, deserves to be hanged; not that I could, as a juryman, have found him legally guilty of murder; but I am glad they found means to convict him [3.189]."

From Johnson's many comments on liberty, I have selected three which are typical: "They make a rout about *universal* liberty, without considering that all that is to be valued, or indeed can be enjoyed by individuals, is *private* liberty. Political liberty is good only so far as it produces private liberty." (2.60.) Again: "Every society has a right to preserve peace and order, and therefore has a good right to prohibit the propagation of opinions which have a dangerous tendency. To say the *magistrate* has this right, is using an inadequate word: it is the *society* for which the magistrate is agent. He may be morally or theologically wrong in restraining the propagation of opinions which he thinks dangerous, but he is politically right." (2.249.) Finally: "This is the gradation of thinking, preaching, and acting: if a man thinks erroneously, he may keep his thoughts to himself, and nobody will trouble him; if he preaches erroneous doctrine, society may expel him; if he acts in consequence of it, the law takes place and he is hanged." (2.252.)

The final liberty of man, the residual right of revolution, is acknowledged by Johnson: "if the abuse be enormous, Nature will rise up, and claiming her original rights, overturn a corrupt political system [1.424]." He paraphrased this on another occasion: "If a sovereign oppresses his people to a great degree, they will rise and cut off his head. There is a remedy in human nature against tyranny, that will keep us safe under every form of government." (2.170.) But concerning one revolutionary, Johnson was very sane: he was glad that Lord George Gordon had escaped, "rather than that a precedent should be established for hanging a man for *constructive treason* [4.87]."

A number of miscellaneous matters may be brought together in concluding this chapter. "The law against usury is for the protection of creditors as well as of debtors," since it tends to keep them from lending to desperate persons (3.26). On

libel: "Damages will be given to a man who is calumniated in
his lifetime, because he may be hurt in his worldly interest,
or at least hurt in his mind: but the law does not regard that
uneasiness which a man feels on having his ancestor calumniated. That is too nice." (3.15.) Speaking of unlimited
estates, "The right of an heir at law is only this, that he is
to have the succession to an estate, in case no other person
is appointed to it by the owner. His right is merely preferable
to that of the King [2.432]." His knowledge of 9 Geo. 2. c. 36
prevented his leaving his Lichfield house to his native city:
"I cannot live a twelve-month, and the last statute of mort-
main stands in the way."[9] His knowledge of the law of
settlement, on the other hand, made possible another act of
charity, when he solicited admission for a woman into the
workhouse of St. Martin's in the Fields, "to which she has a
claim by her husband's settlement."[1] Hawkins makes the
puzzling remark that Johnson, at a loss in the steps to be
taken by an executor, did not understand what was meant by
proving the will.[2] I think this can be explained in part. *Prove*
in this sense does not appear in the *Dictionary*, but *probate*
does, correctly defined, and the word *proof* occurs in the
definition. Johnson was therefore surely familiar with the
general process of probate, and some of the terms used. I
suggest that he merely wanted to know the exact steps, and
Hawkins misunderstood. Finally a note on the possibility
that perjured oaths may avoid worse crimes: "I once said ...
that perhaps a Nonjuror would have been less criminal in taking the oaths imposed by the ruling power, than refusing
them; because refusing them, necessarily laid him under an
almost irresistible temptation to be more criminal; for a man
must live, and if he precludes himself from the support furnished by the establishment, will probably be reduced to very
wicked shifts to maintain himself."[3]

9. *Works*, 1. 582
1. *Letters*, 844
2. *Works*, 1. 549
3. *Life*, 2. 321

On such a note of humanity, we may close the chapter of Johnson as counsel to the lawyer Boswell, marked by the dozen formal cases in which Boswell sought advice, ranging from the injured dignity of Dr. Memis and the Society of Solicitors, through Boswell's self-torment over male succession and lay patrons, to the slavery case which stirred Johnson so deeply.

Johnson, the Law, and Lawyers, 1760-1784

This chapter will overlap chronologically the two preceding, and will complete the survey of Johnson's experience with law and lawyers. Chambers and Boswell were more important than any others in Johnson's legal career, if I may use the term, because they called forth such extensive observations on the law from him. But many of his acquaintances were more famous as lawyers, and had some influence on his continuing education in the law. Ballow, who had first taught him about the law, drops out of the picture during this time, but his friendships with Hawkins, Murphy, Chambers, and Burke lasted till his death. Welch predeceased him by a few months, but was till the end "one of my best and dearest friends," as Johnson wrote to him.[1]

Among his newer friends was the young William Jones, elected to the Club in 1773, and called to the bar in 1774. Although Jones owes his fame to his Sanskrit studies, he wrote a well received book on Bailments. Another lawyer was Edmond Malone, who was called to the Irish bar in 1767 and came to London in 1774. Perhaps the most expert Shakespeare scholar of the period, he was also the man whose energy and encouragement pushed Boswell over every obstacle to the triumphant completion of the *Life of Johnson*. A man more successful in the practice of the law than either of these was John Dunning, first Lord Ashburton, elected to the Club in 1777. Johnson called him "the great lawyer," because of his immense popularity, and Lord Eldon recalled an anecdote about that success: "Mr. Dunning, ... being in very great business, was asked how he contrived to get through it all. He said, 'I do one third of it — another third does itself —

1. *Life*, 3. 217

and the remaining third continues undone.'" (3.128.) The two
men respected each other; Dunning remarked to Boswell,
apropos of the fact that most persons listened to Johnson
instead of conversing with him: "One is always willing to
listen to Dr. Johnson [3.240]."

About Johnson's personal acquaintance with Blackstone,
very little is known, but something substantial may be conjectured. Only one meeting between them is recorded: on
30 April 1778 they were both present at a dinner at the Old
Bailey to the "judges, counsel, and a few guests."[2] —
Johnson's presence at such a dinner is worthy of note as a
proof of his high standing with the legal profession. — And
"Mr. Justice Blackstone conversed with Johnson on the subject of Sir Robert Chambers," who had gone to India as a
judge. Now Chambers had not only been a protégé of Johnson
since 1754 but had also been Blackstone's protégé during
that same period — as Vinerian scholar, fellow, and professor
succeeding Blackstone at Oxford. It is inconceivable to me
that on one of Johnson's many visits to Oxford Chambers did
not introduce the two men, though I should not pretend that
Johnson and Blackstone were close friends. Johnson's library contained several of Blackstone's books, and it is possible that some of them were presented by the author. One last
tenuous connection is that Goldsmith for several years before
his death in 1774 occupied chambers in the Temple directly
above Blackstone's, and is said to have annoyed Blackstone
with his noisy parties. Did Johnson occasionally meet Blackstone on the stairs as he visited his old friend?

One of Johnson's firm friendships was with William Scott of
Doctors' Commons, afterwards Lord Stowell. Scott, like
Chambers, was a native of Newcastle, and Croker says that
Johnson met him through Chambers at Oxford, probably in the
'sixties when Scott was a tutor at University College. At any
rate, by 1772 they were sufficiently intimate that Scott, still
in his twenties, could remark to Johnson: "What a pity it is,
Sir, that you did not follow the profession of the law. You

2. Croker, *Life*, 4. 202

might have been Lord Chancellor of Great Britain." Johnson, much agitated, replied, "Why will you vex me by suggesting this when it is too late."[3] Two years later, Chambers having conducted Johnson as far as Newcastle on his Scottish tour, Scott took over and accompanied him to Edinburgh. Scott later told Croker that when Chambers went to India Scott "seemed to succeed to his place in Johnson's friendship [2.25n.]." In 1778 Boswell records a long conversation, not on legal matters, between himself, Johnson, and Scott in Scott's chambers in the Temple. Scott became a member of the Club, and at Johnson's death was an executor and a legatee.

His younger brother John, afterwards Lord Eldon, was like William and Chambers, a member of University College. He was lecturing on law there in 1775 when Johnson visited the college,[4] and knew Johnson at least as early as 1773, in which year Scott placed an anecdote concerning his walking in a garden with Johnson and Chambers.[5] Little is known of the relationship of John Scott and Johnson, partly because Boswell does not mention him, perhaps from pique at a practical joke played on him by Scott. From other sources, however, we hear of Mrs. Scott pouring Johnson fifteen cups of tea of an evening, and when Johnson was on his deathbed he sent a message to Scott urging him to attend church regularly on Sundays. So well at least did Johnson know the rising young barrister who was later to be Lord Chancellor.

Many other lawyers among Johnson's acquaintance, several of whom were members of his various clubs, we must pass by. It may be remarked that from 1759 to 1765 he lived successively in Staple Inn, Gray's Inn, and Inner Temple Lane, in close proximity with lawyers. From 1765 to 1782 Johnson lived much of the time with the Thrales, and there he became acquainted with still other lawyers, both socially, as with W. W. Pepys, a Master in Chancery, and in professional matters with the Thrales' solicitor, Scrase. Of Scrase he had a

3. *Life*, 3.309-10
4. *Letters*, 383n.
5. *Life*, 2. 268n.

high opinion, and with him he was associated for several
years in problems connected with the brewery and with
Thrale's estate, of which Johnson was later an executor.

One case with which Johnson was particularly concerned
was that involving Bach-y-Graig, the Welsh estate of John
Salusbury, Mrs. Thrale's father. This was entailed, barring
direct heirs male, on John's brother Thomas and his sons; in
default of heirs male of Thomas, on Hester, later Mrs. Thrale.
The estate had been mortgaged — Mrs. Thrale says "in
effect" to pay Thomas's expenses when a student at Cambridge — and when Thomas by marrying an heiress was able
to pay off the mortgage in 1755 John gave him a written
acknowledgment of the whole sum.[6] John died in 1762, before
Hester's marriage; Thomas died in 1773, without issue, and
the estate passed to Mrs. Thrale. Then the trouble began.
Thomas's widow, not the heiress whose money had been used,
but a second wife, brought suit in chancery for the loan. Mrs.
Thrale had wanted the estate entailed on her son, with remainder to the sons of her daughters or other heirs of her
husband, and at first Johnson, who had been consulted, was
not averse to such a plan.[7] But he had urged getting legal
advice, and Scrase, the solicitor, had objected to an entail.
Finally Mrs. Thrale kept discretionary power over the estate,
and Johnson was appointed a trustee. After Thrale's death in
1781 Lady Salusbury pressed the suit. The question at issue
was whether Thomas's loan had been a bona fide loan or
whether he was merely protecting the estate from foreclosure
for the benefit of himself and his heirs. It may be noted that
he did not press for payment during his lifetime. His rather
offhand promise of a dowry for Hester was never performed,
and it may be that he felt that this estate would serve as an
equivalent. But a loan had been made, documents existed —
which Johnson examined with great care and endorsed afterwards. In October, 1782, Johnson's diary shows that he was
writing something which he calls merely "Answer;" he says

6. *Misc.*, 1. 339n.
7. J.L. Clifford, *Piozzi*, Passim.

that he completed twenty-eight pages of it in a few days. It is
my supposition that this was an answer for Mrs. Thrale's
solicitors to use in chancery for this case; the document is
otherwise unknown and unidentified. Whether such a document
was ever used is uncertain, but within a few months a compromise payment of about £7500 had been decided on and paid.

Another case in which Johnson was briefly involved for
Mrs. Thrale is enigmatically mentioned by him in a letter
(No. 745) of 31 October, 1781. As executor, he is busy with
claims on Thrale's estate:

> It almost enrages me to be suspected of forgetting the dis-
> covery of the papers relating to Cummins's claim. These
> papers we must grant the liberty of using, because the law
> will not suffer us to deny them. We may be summoned to de-
> clare what we know, and what we know is in those papers.
> When the evidence appears, Lady Lade will be directed by
> her lawyers to submit in quiet.

A Mrs. Cumyns was mistress of a school at Kensington where
Susan Thrale had been placed between 1774-1776, and she is
mentioned in connection with Susan later in this same letter.
It is possible that this represents a claim for board. Johnson's spelling of proper names is wholly unreliable, but his
advice in this case seems as sound as ever. Lady Lade,
Thrale's sister, had lent Thrale money in 1772, and perhaps
she had, therefore, or thought she had, some claim on the estate. I suspect that there is no connection between her claim
and "Cummins's."

During these same years Johnson was consulted from time
to time by his old friend Taylor, who, it will be remembered,
had been an attorney before taking orders. Three cases in
particular occupied much of Johnson's attention, the first
being Taylor's separation. In 1763 he wrote Johnson that his
wife had left him. He had apparently been accused of incon-
tinence with a servant, Hannah. Johnson, as yet knowing no
details, gave him some general advice:

> The tale of Hannah I suppose to be false, not that if it be
> true it will justify her [Mrs. Taylor's] violence and precipi-
> tation, but it will give her consequent superiority in the
> public opinion and in the courts of justice, and it will be
> better for you to endure hard conditions than bring your
> character in to a judicial disquisition....

> You know that I have never advised you to anything tyranni-
> cal or violent, and in the present case it is of great import-
> ance to keep yourself in the right, and not injure your own
> right by any intemperance of resentment or eagerness of
> reprisal. For the present I think it prudent to forbear all
> pursuit, and all open inquiry, to wear an appearance of
> complete indifference, and calmly wait the effects of time,
> of necessity, and of shame. I suppose she cannot live long
> without your money, and the confession of her want will
> probably humble her. Whether you will inform her brother, I
> must leave to your discretion, who know his character and
> the terms on which you have lived. If you write to him, write
> like a man ill treated but neither dejected nor enraged.
> (Letter 156.)

His next letter urged Taylor to act "as a man injured, and
instead of making defense, to expect submission." Further,

> You inquire what the fugitive lady has in her power. She
> has, I think, nothing in her power but to return home and
> mend her behavior. To obtain a separate maintenance she
> must prove either cruelty to her person or infidelity to her
> bed, and I suppose neither charge can be supported. Nature
> has given women so much power that the law has very
> wisely given them little.

He advised against writing Taylor's brother-in-law, since it
was his part to write first. Moreover,

> If a separate alimony should come to be stipulated I do not
> see why you should by an absurd generosity pay your wife
> for disobedience and elopement. What allowance will be
> proper I cannot tell, but would have you consult our old
> friend Mr. Howard. His profession has acquainted him with
> matrimonial law, and he is in himself a cool and wise man.

(Howard was a proctor practicing in the Ecclesiastical Court
of Lichfield, and an early friend of Johnson's.) Nevertheless
he would not rule out the possibility of a reconciliation: "If
there is any hope of living happily or decently, cohabitation
is the most reputable for both." (No. 157.)

A fortnight later Johnson wrote that he was glad Taylor had
given up the mediation of a man who had tried to intimidate
him: "What have you to dread from the law? The law will give
Mrs. Taylor no more than her due and you do not desire to
give her less." Taylor had apparently not consulted Howard,
their proctor friend, and therefore Johnson recommended another friend and a higher authority on this branch of the law,
Dr. Smalbroke, advocate, of Doctors' Commons, whose name
will be recalled from an earlier chapter:

I do not see that you have anything more [to do]than to sit
still, and expect the motions of the lady and her friends. If
you think it necessary to retain counsel, I suppose you will
have recourse to Dr. Smalbroke, and some able man of the
common law or chancery, but though you may retain them
provisionally, you need do nothing more; for I am not of
opinion that the lady's friends will suffer her cause to be
brought into the courts.

And he again recommended Howard:

In affairs of this kind it is necessary to converse with some
intelligent man, and by considering the question in all
states to provide means of obviating every charge. It will
surely be right to spend a day with Howard. (No. 159.)

Within the next three weeks Mrs. Taylor and her friends had
apparently offered terms, and Johnson seems to have drafted a
letter for Taylor to send them in reply. After commenting on
it he adds:

I no more desire than you to bring the cause before the
courts, and if they who are on the lady's side can prove
nothing, they have in reality no such design. It is not likely
that even if they had proof of incontinency they would
desire to produce it, or make any other use of it, than to
terrify you into their own conditions.

He then remarks that the breach between the couple was
greater than he had previously realized, and concludes:

Your determination against cohabitation with the lady I
shall therefore pass over, with only this hint, that you must
keep it to yourself, for as by elopement she makes herself
liable to the charge of violating the marriage contract, it
will be prudent to keep her in the criminal state, by leaving
her in appearance a possibility of return, which preserves
your superiority in the contest, without taking from you the
power of limiting her future authority, and prescribing your
own conditions. (No. 161.)

Eight months later a settlement had been reached, evidently on terms favorable to Taylor, and Johnson was able to con-
gratulate him on the happy ending, "the happiest that could
be next to reformation and reconcilement[No. 165]." Throughout the case Johnson had combined the good offices of a
friend with the cool and astute advice of a good legal mind.

In 1776 Taylor brought suit "to establish his rights to the
reversion of certain lands acquired from his relative Ralph
Wood."[7a] He asked Johnson for help, and received this advice:

7a. H. Liebert, "New Letters," *Harvard Lib. Bul.*, 3 (1949), 146.

> The case which you sent me contains such vicissitudes of settlement and rescission that I will not pretend yet to give any opinion about it. My advice is, that it be laid before some of the best lawyers, and branched out into queries, that the answer may be more deliberate, and the necessity of considering made greater. (No. 455.)

Taylor wished to bequeath a reversion to the son of Richard Green, the Lichfield apothecary and owner of the Lichfield Museum, well known to Johnson. His second wife and Taylor's first wife were sisters, and Green's son was third in remainder to Taylor's estates. Johnson advised Taylor to come to London and talk to counsel, but he was not optimistic:

> Unless skilful men give you hopes of success, it will be better not to try it; you may still triumph in your ill-success. But supposing that by the former compact between you and Wood, she had it for her life, she had as much as she ought to have. I never well understood the settlement he and you concerted between you. Do you know what is become of her, and how she and the [word obliterated] live together? What a wretch it is! (No. 461.)

Later that same month Johnson visited Taylor at Ashbourne and no doubt discussed the case. It appears that briefs were then drawn up (by Johnson?), which Johnson took back to London to present to the Attorney General, Thurlow, and the Solicitor General, Wedderburn, for an opinion. A fortnight later he had not yet presented the briefs, because Thurlow was busy with a trial. But there was no hurry: "The opinion is as good and as useful a month hence, unless you found [name effaced] alienating the land." (No. 473.) Then Johnson was off to Bath. (If he had been the solicitor, he could not have acted more in the traditional character of a lawyer.) From Bath he wrote Boswell in London asking him to look in Johnson's house for "two cases; one for the Attorney General, and one for the Solicitor General," and shortly thereafter Taylor came up to London. Boswell wrote to a friend that Taylor had begged Johnson to come back to town "to assist him in some interesting business, and Johnson loves much to be so consulted, so comes up."[8] A fortnight later Wedderburn

8. *Life*, 3.44

gave an opinion directly against Taylor. Said Johnson, "He thinks of the claim much as I think."[9] A solicitor bluntly confirmed this opinion. Two days later the case was no forwarder: Johnson commented, "His solicitor says he is sick, but I suspect he is sullen [No. 479]." And again, to Mrs. Thrale:

> All this while the Doctor is hurt only in his vanity. He thought he had supplanted Mrs. Wood, and Mrs. Wood has found the means of defeating him. He really wanted nothing more than to have the power of bequeathing a reversion to Mr. Green's son.... This purity of intention, however, he cannot prove, and the transaction itself seems pactum iniquum. I do not think that he can, or indeed that he ought to prevail. (No. 483.)

Taylor, in disgust, went home to Ashbourne, and after a month Johnson wrote him:

> Some time ago I had a letter from the solicitor, in which he mentioned our cause with respect enough, but persists in his opinion, as I suppose your attorney has told you. He is, however, convinced that nothing fraudulent was intended: I would be glad to hear what the attorney says. (No. 492.)

Taylor lost the case. In 1779, Johnson wrote that he had seen Green, who "said nothing of the affair of Wood, nor was it mentioned." (Liebert, p. 146.)

In 1782 Johnson and Taylor were interested in a case involving a dispute between two young women named Collier and their step-father, Thomas Flint, Taylor's clerk. Mrs. Collier, apparently related to Johnson, had brought Flint about £200 a year. After her death her daughters, thinking that Flint was trying to keep part of their mother's property from them, appealed to Johnson for help. Langley, the headmaster of the Ashbourne Grammar School, was also interested in the dispute. Langley was inclined to doubt Flint's veracity, but Johnson thought that the girls had better accept an offer which Flint had made them.[1] The dispute dragged on for nearly a year, complicated by the fact that Johnson was unable to come at the facts in the case. At one point the girls appeared to wish to sue Flint and at the same time to want him to pay

9. *Letters*, 478

1. *Misc.*, 2. 452

them something on account — which would have been equivalent to his underwriting a suit against himself — a proposal which Johnson accurately described as "wild."[2] Johnson was helpful, however: if they would send him their grandfather's will, he would get an opinion on it, and would assume any charges up to £10 to procure it from the registry. He was sent a copy of the will — but it had no attestation of authenticity — and an abstract of Flint's marriage settlement, but that was in Flint's hand and lacked, therefore, "any legal credibility [No. 807]." For a former attorney, Taylor was unbelievably slipshod. Into this muddle Johnson then injected some sense:

> What seems to me proper to be done, but you know much better than I, is to take an exemplification of the will from the registry. We are then so far sure. This will I entreat you to send. If it be clear and decisive against the girls, there can be no farther use of it. If you think it doubtful, send it to Mr. Madox, and I will pay the fee.

> When the will is despatched, the marriage settlement is to be examined, which if Mr. Flint refuses to show, he gives such ground of suspicion as will justify a legal compulsion to show it.

> It may perhaps be better that I should appear busy in this matter than you, and if you think it best, I will write to Lichfield that a copy of the will may be sent to you, for I would have you read it. I should be told the year of Mr. Dunn's death.

> I think the generosity of Mr. Flint somewhat suspicious. I have, however, not yet condemned him nor would irritate him too much, for perhaps the girls must at last be content with what he shall give them. (No. 807.)

Taylor became petulant, as old men sometimes will, when pressed for specific action, but Johnson continued to press him:

> That a silly, timorous, unskilful girl has behaved improperly, is a poor reason for refusing to tell me what expectations have been raised by the will, and what questions I must ask the lawyers, questions which if you do not like to answer them, I must ask elsewhere. (No. 821.)

In the last letter on the case, the questions are still unanswered:

2. *Letters*, 806

I would show the lawyers the papers, but that I know not what questions to ask nor can state the case, till I am informed with regard to some particulars.

What do Miss Colliers suppose will be discovered in the writings?

Had Mr. Flint a son by their mother? I think he has. What had he with their mother? I think about £200 a year. What do they ask from Mr. Flint?

What does he offer them? This you have told me, but my memory is not distinct about it, and I know not how to find your letter. Tell me again.

All that has a bad appearance on Flint's part is his requisition of a discharge from future claims. If they have no claims, what is the discharge? Yet this may be only unskilfulness in him.

I think there is no reason to suppose that Mrs. Flint's estate could be settled by her father exclusively upon Collier's children, or that she should be advised at her marriage with Mr. Flint to debar herself from providing for her future children, whatever they might be, in their due proportions.

Do answer this, and add what it is necessary for me to know, and I hope to trouble you no more about it. When I have your answer I will transact with Mr. Flint and Miss Collier; or with as little trouble to you as I can. (No. 823.)

Finally Johnson received the answers, and drew up for the lawyers a brief "case," which is in the Hyde collection. Whether the girls received any satisfaction is not known; they were not named in Flint's will when he died in 1787.

During the years when Johnson was aiding his friends in these cases, his writings continue to show his study of the law. In the notes to his edition of Shakespeare (1765), references to legal matters are rather infrequent, partly because he is satisfied to quote some previous commentator when he is accurate. Of some forty-seven notes original with Johnson — a small number, scattered through eight volumes — the great majority are definitions or glosses, brief and pointed. Thus in the first two volumes, "terms for common justice," "retort your manifest appeal," "quit the fine," "apparitor," "sue," "action," and "extent" are explained.[3] If these seem rather

3. 1. 265, 372, 465; 2. 147, 204, 258, 426

obvious, it might be noted that Johnson in some cases is pointing out that Shakespeare is using the word in its legal not its ordinary sense, with a consequent shift in meaning. In commenting on a well known passage from *Measure for Measure,*

> Isabel: Yet shew some pity.
> Angelo: I shew it most of all, when I shew justice;
>   For then I pity those, I do not know . . .

Johnson cites Sir Matthew Hale's similar words: "When I find myself swayed to mercy, let me remember, that there is a mercy likewise due to the Country[1.297]." This is especially interesting when we remember Johnson's own version of this idea, already cited from the *Rambler,* No. 81: "The magistrate, therefore, in pardoning a man unworthy of pardon, betrays the trust with which he is invested, gives away what is not his own, and, apparently, does to others what he would not that others should do to him." There remain in the two volumes three miscellaneous bits of legal learning: that the punishment of perjury included "wearing a paper expressing the crime," that "one of the legal tests of a *natural* is to try whether he can number," and that "one method of qualifying a dog according to the forest laws, is to cut his tail, or make him a curtail."[4]

In the third volume there are six more glosses,[5] in one of which Johnson remarks, "It is now almost forgotten in England that the heirs of great fortunes were the king's wards [p. 277]." In a later note, on *III Henry VI,* he returned to the subject:

> It must be remembered, that till the restoration the heiresses of great estates were in the wardship of the king, who in their minority gave them up to plunder, and afterwards matched them to his favorites. I know not when liberty gained more than by the abolition of the court of wards. (5.187.)

After glossing "multiplying medicine," he quotes an old law: "In the reign of Henry the Fourth a law was made to forbid

4. 2. 165, 207, 477
5. pp. 12, 277, 306, 325, 394, 462

all men thenceforth to multiply *gold, or use any craft of* multiplication." (3.390.)

The fourth volume contains eight more definitions or glosses,[6] and as before a smaller number of more interesting comments. In a note on the divine right of kings in *Richard II*, Johnson remarks that Shakespeare did not learn the doctrine in the reign of James I, "to which it is now the practice of all writers, whose opinions are regulated by fashion or interest, to impute the original of every tenet which they have been taught to think false or foolish." He reiterates this point later in another note on the same play (pp. 54, 77). A note on *I Henry IV* presents a curious application of the notion of self-defense to international law:

> The lawfulness and justice of the holy wars have been much disputed; but perhaps there is a principle on which the question may be easily determined. If it be part of the religion of the Mahometans to extirpate by the sword all other religions, it is, by the law of self-defense, lawful for men of every other religion, and for Christians among others, to make war upon Mahometans, simply as Mahometans, as men obliged by their own principles to make war upon Christians, and only lying in wait till opportunity shall promise them success [p. 111].

In another note on the same play, Johnson refers to the law of Henry VII which "made it safe to serve the king regnant," however false his title should later prove to be (p. 165).

In the fifth volume, besides four definitions[7] and the comment on the court of wards already quoted, Johnson has some pertinent remarks on oaths, a subject which he took very seriously. Richard, in *III Henry VI*, says:

> An oath is of no moment, being not took
> Before a true and lawful magistrate;
> That hath authority o'er him that swears.

> Johnson: The obligation of an oath is here eluded by very despicable sophistry. A lawful magistrate alone has the power to exact an oath, but the oath derives no part of its force from the magistrate. The plea against the obligation of an oath obliging to maintain an usurper, taken from the unlawfulness of the oath itself in the foregoing play, was rational and just. (p. 130.)

6.   pp. 30, 33, 40, 118, 310, 336, 585, 587

7.   pp. 91, 262, 331, 424

In the next volume, in addition to four glosses,[8] Johnson cites at length and by title the law of James I against witch-craft — the "infection" which turned the minds of so many otherwise sober citizens. He is able to conclude with satis-faction, "This law was repealed in our time [p. 371]."

In the seventh volume, along with four more glosses,[9] Johnson illustrates a word by using its legal sense, a rather unusual proceeding. Shakespeare wrote, "our jealousy does yet depend," i.e., is not yet determined. Johnson: "We now say, the cause is depending [p. 365]." The last volume shows a single definition (p. 290).

Five years after publishing his edition of Shakespeare, Johnson wrote the first of his political pamphlets, *The False Alarm,* on the Wilkes case and the Middlesex election. The pamphlet, like those that followed, is a mixture of legal and political arguments, and it is not easy to separate them. The constitutional question, says Johnson, is clarified by history:

> by a train of precedents sufficient to establish a custom of parliament, the House of Commons has jurisdiction over its own members; . . . the whole has power over individuals; and . . . this power has been exercised sometimes in im-prisonment, and often in expulsion.

> That such power should reside in the House of Commons in some cases, is inevitably necessary, since it is required by every polity, that where there is a possibility of offence, there should be a possibility of punishment. A member of the House cannot be cited for his conduct in parliament before any other court; and, therefore, if the House cannot punish him, he may attack with impunity the rights of the people, and the title of the king.

> This exemption from the authority of other courts was, I think, first established in favor of the five members in the long parliament. It is not to be considered as an usurpa-tion, for it is implied in the principles of government. If legislative powers are not co-ordinate, they cease in part to be legislative; and if they be co-ordinate, they are un-accountable; for to whom must that power account, which has no superior?

> The House of Commons is indeed dissoluble by the king, as the nation has of late been very clamorously told; but while

8. pp. 20, 61, 95, 437
9. pp. 120, 316, 351, 453

it subsists it is co-ordinate with the other powers, and this co-ordination ceases only when the House by dissolution ceases to subsist.

As the particular representatives of the people are in their public character above the control of the courts of law, they must be subject to the jurisdiction of the House; and as the House, in the exercise of its authority, can be neither directed nor restrained, its own resolutions must be its laws, at least if there is no antecedent decision of the whole legislature.

This privilege, not confirmed by any written law or positive compact, but by the resistless power of political necessity, they have exercised, probably from their first institution, but certainly, as their records inform us, from the 23d of Elizabeth, when they expelled a member for derogating from their privileges....

The first laws had no law to enforce them, the first authority was constituted by itself. The power exercised by the House of Commons is of this kind, a power rooted in the principles of government, and branched out by occasional practice; a power which necessity made just, and precedents have made legal.[1]

As to the claim that the Commons might expel but not exclude, Johnson has this answer:

Laws which cannot be enforced, can neither prevent nor rectify disorders. A sentence which cannot be executed can have no power to warn or to reform. If the Commons have only the power of dismissing for a few days the man whom his constituents can immediately send back, if they can expel but cannot exclude, they have nothing more than nominal authority, to which perhaps obedience never may be paid.

The representatives of our ancestors had an opinion very different: they fined and imprisoned their members; on great provocation they disabled them forever; and this power of pronouncing perpetual disability is maintained by Selden himself....

The Commons cannot make laws, they can only pass resolutions, which, like all resolutions, are of force only to those that make them, and to those only while they are willing to observe them.

The vote of the House of Commons has therefore only so far the force of a law, as that force is necessary to preserve the vote from losing its efficacy; it must begin by operating upon themselves, and extends its influence to others, only by consequences arising from the first inten-

1. *Works*, 10. 6-8

tion. He that starts game on his own manor, may pursue it
into another. (pp. 12-13.)

The next year, Johnson published *Thoughts on the Late
Transactions respecting Falkland's Islands*. On the complicated question of the ownership of those islands, even now
disputed, Johnson has some pertinent remarks. He concedes
the probability of prior English discovery, doubts the priority
of English settlement, but really rests his argument on a sort
of de facto sovereignty:

> If sovereignty implies undisputed right, scarce any prince
> is a sovereign through his whole dominions; if sovereignty
> consists in this, that no superior is acknowledged, our king
> reigns at Port Egmont with sovereign authority. Almost
> every new acquired territory is in some degree controvert-
> ible, and till the controversy is decided, a term very diffi-
> cult to be fixed, all that can be had is real possession and
> actual dominion. (10. 56.)

He was impatient with the faction which wished more and
would go to war to obtain it: "They have hitherto shown no
virtue, and very little wit, beyond that mischievous cunning
for which it is held by Hale that children may be hanged
[p. 59]."

The last two pamphlets, *The Patriot* and *Taxation No
Tyranny*, both on the American question, may be considered
together. Johnson derives England's authority over the colonies from three facts: they "were settled under English
protection; were constituted by an English charter; and have
been defended by English arms [10. 88]." From this he
deduces the next position: "the supreme power of every
community has the right of requiring from all its subjects,
such contributions as are necessary to the public safety or
public prosperity[p. 94]." As to the nature of authority:

> In sovereignty there are no gradations. There may be limited
> royalty, there may be limited consulship; but there can be
> no limited government. There must in every society be some
> power or other from which there is no appeal, which admits
> no restrictions, which pervades the whole mass of the
> community, regulates and adjusts all subordination, enacts
> laws or repeals them, erects or annuls judicatures, extends
> or contracts privileges, exempt itself from question or
> control, and bounded only by physical necessity.

By this power, wherever it subsists, all legislation and
jurisdiction is animated and maintained. From this all legal
rights are emanations which, whether equitably or not, may
be legally recalled. It is not infallible, for it may do wrong;
but it is irresistible, for it can be resisted only by rebellion, by an act which makes it questionable what shall be
thenceforward the supreme power. (10. 106-107.)

He summarizes his position in another paragraph:

To him that considers the nature, the original, the progress,
and the constitution of the Colonies, who remembers that
the first discoverers had commissions from the crown, that
the first settlers owe to a charter their civil forms and regular magistracy, and that all personal immunities and legal
securities, by which the condition of the subject has been
from time to time improved, have been extended to the col-
onists, it will not be doubted but the parliament of England
has a right to bind them by statutes, and *to bind them in all
cases whatsoever,* and has therefore a natural and constitutional power of laying upon them any tax or impost, whether
external or internal, upon the product of land, or the manufactures of industry, in the exigencies of war, or in the
time of profound peace, for the defense of America, *for the
purpose of raising a revenue,* or for any other end beneficial to the empire. (10. 109-110.)

Approaching the problem from a somewhat different angle,
Johnson argues:

The less is included in the greater. That power which can
take away life, may seize upon property. The parliament
may enact for America a law of capital punishment; it may
therefore establish a mode and proportion of taxation.
(10. 89.)

After defining taxation, Johnson proceeds to discuss the
nature of charters and corporations, as applied to the colonies:

An English colony is a number of persons, to whom the
king grants a charter permitting them to settle in some
distant country, and enabling them to constitute a corporation, enjoying such powers as the charter grants, to be
administered in such forms as the charter prescribes. As a
corporation they make laws for themselves, but as a corporation subsisting by a grant from higher authority, to the
control of that authority they continue subject....

"To their charters the Colonies owe, like other corporations,
their political existence. The solemnities of legislation,
the administration of justice, the security of property, are
all bestowed upon them by the royal grant. Without their
charter there would be no power among them, by which any
law could be made, or duties enjoined, any debt recovered,
or criminal punished.

A charter is a grant of certain powers or privileges given to
a part of the community for the advantage of the whole, and
is therefore liable by its nature to change or to revocation.
Every act of government aims at public good. A charter,
which experience has shown to be detrimental to the nation,
is to be repealed; because general prosperity must always
be preferred to particular interest. If a charter be used to
evil purposes, it is forfeited, as the weapon is taken away
which is injuriously employed. (10. 107-108.)

And concerning the limitations of corporations:

A corporation is considered in law as an individual, and
can no more extend its own immunities than a man can by
his own choice assume dignities or titles.

The legislature of a colony, let not the comparison be too
much disdained, is only the vestry of a larger parish, which
may lay a cess on the inhabitants, and enforce the payment;
but can extend no influence beyond its own district, must
modify its particular regulations by the general law and,
whatever may be its internal expenses, is still liable to
taxes laid by superior authority. (10. 117.)

In reply to the American argument of no taxation without
representation, drawn, says Johnson, from "the fanciful
Montesquieu, that *in a free state every man being a free agent
ought to be concerned in his own government,*" Johnson
brusquely counters, "Whatever is true of taxation is true of
every other law, that he who is bound by it, without his consent, is not free, for he is not concerned in his own government [p. 111]." He then states his well known doctrine of
virtual representation, that those of us without franchise are
"helpless spectators," and that even the electors who happen
to be in the minority are governed "not only without, but
against their choice [p. 112];" nevertheless we all have a
sort of representation, and the legislature generally acts in
the interest of the whole public. Then he cites a parallel
case:

In the controversy agitated about the beginning of this
century, whether the English laws could bind Ireland,
Davenant, who defended against Molyneux the claims of
England, considered it as necessary to prove nothing more
than that the present Irish must be deemed a colony.
(10. 118.)

And he further notes that "by the 6 Geo. I. chap. 5. the acts
of the British parliament bind Ireland [p. 120]."

For those who fear that the innocent will be punished with the guilty in forcing compliance with the laws, Johnson has some comments on national crimes:

> But there are some who lament the state of the poor Boston-
> ians, because they cannot all be supposed to have com-
> mitted acts of rebellion, yet all are involved in the penalty
> imposed. This, they say, is to violate the first rule of
> justice, by condemning the innocent to suffer with the
> guilty.
>
> This deserves some notice, as it seems dictated by equity
> and humanity, however it may raise contempt, by the ignor-
> ance which it betrays of the state of man and the system of
> things. That the innocent should be confounded with the
> guilty is undoubtedly an evil; but it is an evil which no
> care or caution can prevent. National crimes require nation-
> al punishments, of which many must necessarily have
> their part, who have not incurred them by personal guilt. If
> rebels should fortify a town, the cannon of lawful authority
> will endanger equally the harmless burghers and the crim-
> inal garrison. (10. 89.)

We may now turn to a scarcely less controversial book, *A Journey to the Western Islands*, published in 1775. Johnson interested himself in the changes in the law in the Highlands, particularly since the '45. These are his observations:

> In the Highlands it was a law, that if a robber was sheltered
> from justice, any man of the same clan might be taken in
> his place. This was a kind of irregular justice, which,
> though necessary in savage times, could hardly fail to end
> in a feud....
>
> Mountaineers are thievish, because they are poor, and
> having neither manufactures nor commerce, can grow richer
> only by robbery....
>
> By a strict administration of the laws, since the laws have
> been introduced into the Highlands, this disposition to
> thievery is very much repressed....
>
> Mountainous regions are sometimes so remote from the seat
> of government, and so difficult of access, that they are
> very little under the influence of the sovereign, or within
> the reach of national justice. Law is nothing without power;
> and the sentence of a distant court could not be easily
> executed, nor perhaps very safely promulgated, among men
> ignorantly proud and habitually violent, unconnected with
> the general system, and accustomed to reverence only their
> own lords. It has therefore been necessary to erect many
> particular jurisdictions, and commit the punishment of
> crimes, and the decision of right, to the proprietors of the
> country who could enforce their own decrees. It immediately
> appears that such judges will be often ignorant, and often

partial; but in the immaturity of political establishments no
better expedient could be found. As government advances
towards perfection, provincial judicature is perhaps in
every empire gradually abolished.

Those who had thus the dispensation of law were by consequence themselves lawless....

In the Highlands, some great lords had an hereditary jurisdiction over counties, and some chieftains over their own
lands, till the final conquest of the Highlands afforded an
opportunity of crushing all the local courts and of extending
the general benefits of equal law to the low and the high,
in the deepest recesses and obscurest corners.

While the chiefs had this resemblance of royalty, they had
little inclination to appeal, on any question, to superior
judicatures. A claim of lands between two powerful lairds
was decided like a contest for dominion between sovereign
powers....

The Highland lords made treaties, and formed alliances, of
which some traces may still be found, and some consequences still remain as lasting evidence of petty regality.
The terms of one of these confederacies were that each
should support the other in the right, or in the wrong,
except against the king. (10. 366-370.)

Johnson's assessment of the changes wrought by the British government is singularly dispassionate:

Whether by disarming a people thus broken into several
tribes, and thus remote from the seat of power, more good
than evil has been produced, may deserve inquiry. The
supreme power in every community has the right of debar-
ring every individual, and every subordinate society, from
self-defence, only because the supreme power is able to
defend them; and therefore where the governor cannot act,
he must trust the subject to act for himself. These islands
might be wasted with fire and sword before their sovereign
would know their distress.... Laws that place the subjects
in such a state contravene the first principles of the compact of authority: they exact obedience, and yield no
protection....

The abolition of the local jurisdictions, which had for so
many ages been exercised by the chiefs, has likewise its
evil and its good. The feudal constitution naturally diffused
itself into long ramifications of subordinate authority. To
this general temper of the government was added the peculiar form of the country, broken by mountains into many sub-
divisions scarcely accessible but to the natives, and
guarded by passes, or perplexed with intricacies, through
which national justice could not find its way....

When the chiefs were men of knowledge and virtue, the
convenience of a domestic judicature was great. No long

journeys were necessary, nor artificial delays could be practiced; the character, the alliances, and interests of the litigants were known to the court, and all false pretences were easily detected. The sentence, when it was passed, could not be evaded; the power of the laird superseded formalities, and justice could not be defeated by interest or stratagem.

I doubt not but that since the regular judges have made their circuits through the whole country, right has been everywhere more wisely and more equally distributed; the complaint is, that litigation is grown troublesome, and that the magistrates are too few and therefore often too remote for general convenience.

Many of the smaller islands have no legal officer within them. I once asked, if a crime should be committed, by what authority the offender could be seized, and was told that the laird would exert his right — a right which he must now usurp, but which surely necessity must vindicate, and which is therefore yet exercised in lower degrees by some of the proprietors, when legal processes cannot be obtained.

In all greater questions, however, there is now happily an end to all fear or hope from malice or from favor.... All trials of right by the sword are forgotten, and the mean are in as little danger from the powerful as in other places. No scheme of policy has, in any country, yet brought the rich and poor on equal terms into courts of judicature. Perhaps experience, improving on experience, may in time effect it. (10. 427-431.)

Various aspects of land tenure engaged Johnson's attention in Scotland. In one place he found an old widow occupying the remains of a building which her husband's ancestors had possessed for four generations. The right, he says, was considered as established by legal prescription   (p. 321). Another and more common tenure was that of the tacksman, an intermediary between the laird and the smaller tenants, paying rent and reverence to the laird, and receiving them from the tenants (p. 421). On occasion the undertenants cultivated the tacksman's ground on shares (p. 476). On the isle of Ulva, Johnson found the survival of the custom of *mercheta mulierum*, "a fine in old times due to the laird at the marriage of a virgin," and remarked that the origin of the claim, "as of our tenure of *borough English*, is variously delivered [pp. 493-494]."

Among the papers Johnson wrote for the forger-clergyman Dodd in a vain attempt to secure a pardon, there is little

reference to the law. In Dodd's *Last Solemn Declaration* he is
made to say: "I repent that I have violated the laws by which
peace and confidence are established among men," and in a
communication to the newspapers Johnson observed that "in
all communities penal laws have been relaxed as particular
reasons have emerged."[2]

Johnson's last great work, the *Lives of the Poets*, contains
a scattering of comments on law, as well as noting that some
nine of his subjects (or their near relatives) studied the law.
Occasionally Johnson goes rather afield in this respect, once
saying that Rowe's father, a sergeant-at-law who published
Benlow's and Dallison's *Reports*, "ventured to remark how
low his authors rated the prerogative."[3] Johnson also sought
information about his subjects from his legal acquaintance,
Herbert Croft and Clark of Lincoln's Inn, and Walmsley, his
old patron of Lichfield.

One of the famous passages in the *Lives* is the comment on
Milton's *Areopagitica*:

> The danger of such unbounded liberty, and the danger of
> bounding it, have produced a problem in the science of
> government, which human understanding seems hitherto un-
> able to solve. If nothing may be published but what civil
> authority shall have previously approved, power must
> always be the standard of truth; if every dreamer of innova-
> tions may propagate his projects, there can be no settle-
> ment; if every murmurer at government may diffuse discon-
> tent, there can be no peace; and if every sceptic in theology
> may teach his follies, there can be no religion. The remedy
> against these evils is to punish the authors; for it is yet
> allowed that every society may punish, though not prevent,
> the publication of opinions which that society shall think
> pernicious; but this punishment, though it may crush the
> author, promotes the book, and it seems not more reasonable
> to leave the right of printing unrestrained, because writers
> may be afterwards censured, than it would be to sleep with
> doors unbolted, because by our laws we can hang a thief.
> (2.102.)

The troubled days of the Civil War called forth other observations. Of Waller's contention that grievances ought to be
redressed before the Commons grants supplies, Johnson says
that it "is agreeable enough to law and reason[2.230]," and
he adds that Hampden's sentence "seems generally to be

2. *Papers written by Dr. Johnson and Dr. Dodd*, 1926, pp.23,26.
3. *Works*, 3. 28

thought unconstitutional [p. 231]." Equal justice, difficult to
guarantee in any age, was not attained when the Earl of
Northumberland proved "too great for prosecution [p.242]."
The constitutional dilemma in which Cromwell found himself
is neatly described: "It was certainly to be desired that the
detestable band should be dissolved, which had destroyed the
church, murdered the King, and filled the nation with tumult
and oppression; yet Cromwell had not the right of dissolving
them, for all that he had before done could be justified only
by supposing them invested with lawful authority." He adds
that Cromwell was restrained from taking the title of king
"partly by fear of the laws, which, when he should govern by
the name of King, would have restrained his authority [pp.245-
246]."

Johnson's dislike of Cromwell did not make him an uncrit-
ical friend of the Stuarts, as he shows when he points out that
Settle wrote a panegyric on the infamous Judge Jeffries, and
asks, "what more could have been done by the meanest
zealot for prerogative [p.348]?" The troubles of the times
are again reflected in his remark that Halifax argued warmly
in the House in favor of a law granting the assistance of
counsel in trials for high treason (3.14). A quiet interlude
appears in the life of Rowe, who "was entered a student of
the Middle Temple, where, for some time he read statutes and
reports with proficiency proportionate to the force of his mind,
which was already such that he endeavored to comprehend
law, not as a series of precedents, or collection of positive
precepts, but as a system of rational government, and impartial justice [3.29]."

The parliamentary maneuvers of the Whigs brought forth
these remarks, in the *Life of Addison:*

> The Earl of Sunderland proposed an act called "The Peer-
> age Bill," by which the number of peers should be fixed,
> and the King restrained from any new creation of nobility,
> unless when an old family should be extinct. To this the
> lords would naturally agree; and the King, who was yet
> little acquainted with his own prerogative, and, as is now
> well known, almost indifferent to the possessions of the
> Crown, had been persuaded to consent. The only difficulty
> was found among the Commons, who were not likely to

approve the perpetual exclusion of themselves and their posterity....

The Lords might think their dignity diminished by improper advancements, and particularly by the introduction of twelve new peers at once, to produce a majority of Tories in the last reign; an act of authority violent enough, yet certainly legal, and by no means to be compared with that contempt of national right with which some time afterwards, by the instigation of Whiggism, the Commons, chosen by the people for three years, chose themselves for seven. But, whatever might be the disposition of the Lords, the people had no wish to increase their power. The tendency of the bill, as Steele observed in a letter to the Earl of Oxford, was to introduce an aristocracy; for a majority in the House of Lords, so limited, would have been despotic and irresistible. (3.74-75.)

The powers of investigating committees, which Johnson had discussed in the *Parliamentary Debates* many years earlier, are again touched on in the *Life of Prior* in reference to a committee of the Privy Council:

They are represented as asking questions sometimes vague, sometimes insidious, and writing answers different from those which they received. Prior, however, seems to have been overpowered by their turbulence, for he confesses that he signed what, if he had ever come before a legal judicature, he should have contradicted or explained away. The oath was administered by Boscawen, a Middlesex justice, who at last was going to write his attestation on the wrong side of the paper. (3.138.)

Prior remained in custody over two years, without trial.

In the *Life of Pope* Johnson shows his human fallibility. Speaking of the translation of the *Iliad*, he says:

Of the quartos it was, I believe, stipulated that none should be printed but for the author, that the subscription might not be depreciated; but Lintot impressed the same pages upon a small folio, and paper perhaps a little thinner, and sold exactly at half the price, for half a guinea each volume, books so little inferior to the quartos that, by a fraud of trade, these folios, being afterwards shortened by cutting away the top and bottom, were sold as copies printed for the subscribers. (4.22.)

Johnson fails to castigate Lintot for this sharp dealing, but rather, so great was his prejudice in favor of the trade, commiserates with Lintot, who, by a piracy, "after all his hopes and all his liberality, was, by a very unjust and illegal action, defrauded of his profit " when an edition was printed in

Holland and clandestinely imported into England to undersell
the authorized edition (p.23). At the end of the same life,
Johnson finds a more proper object for his sympathy in John
Bernardi, who, suspected of complicity in a plot to kill
William III, was imprisoned without trial for almost forty
years (p.145).

And so through the last chapter of Johnson's life, his
interest in the law continued, watching William and John
Scott enter the career chosen by Chambers and Boswell, helping Taylor and Mrs. Thrale in their legal difficulties, and
commenting on divers legal topics in the edition of Shakespeare, the political pamphlets, the *Journey to the Western
Islands*, and the *Lives of the Poets*.

Conclusion

> When an acquaintance was one day exclaiming against the
> tediousness of the law and its partiality, "Let us hear, sir
> (said Johnson), no general abuse; the law is the last result
> of human wisdom acting upon human experience for the
> benefit of the public."[1]

Such a warm tribute to the law from Johnson should be no
surprise to the reader of this book. Now we may look back
briefly and inquire how Johnson's study of the law influenced
his thinking. Before 1739 the materials for judgment are scant.
In 1738 he was still a violent anti-Hanoverian, and in *London*
spoke of "rigid law" and the "fell attorney." In April of the
next year, in the same mood and of the same politics, "a true-
bred lawyer never contents himself with one sense when there
is another to be found," and explains wills "into a sense
wholly contrary to the intention of the testator." But in the
summer of the same year, when he prepared the "Considerations" on the legality of abridgment for the use of Cave, he
was obliged to approach a legal problem soberly and carefully. This appears to be an important turning point. From this
time on, his anti-Hanoverianism diminishes sharply, and no
one but an incurable romantic could believe the legend of his
going off to fight with Bonnie Prince Charlie six years later.
His attitude toward the law and the constitution is respectful,
and remains so for the rest of his life. Even the *Parliamentary
Debates* were not used to show off his wit at the expense of
the Whigs, but rather show him tackling the legal and constitutional problems with fairness and impartiality. I think it is
not too much to suggest that his respect for tradition and
authority, so evident in his later life, has its foundation in
this period, as it was buttressed with his later study.

1. *Misc.*, 1. 223

This same respect for tradition is clear in Johnson's religion, but I am inclined to consider its origin in the law, particularly when one remembers the insistence which Johnson placed on the credibility of the evidence for historical Christianity, where he thinks and talks very much like a lawyer.

Johnson's interest in tradition brings us to his many inquiries about the history of law, the progress and decline of feudal law, and the relations between law and commerce. This was not mere antiquarianism. Commercial law was in its infancy in the eighteenth century, but Johnson saw its great importance to the island which was becoming an empire, and knew that a study of its origins would illuminate problems of his day. And though many of the vestiges of feudal law had been removed under Charles II, many still remained, particularly concerning real property. In a sense, Johnson's concern with Boswell's entail is an example of his interest in feudal law, as well as evidence that he would not have the *dead* hand of tradition (when it was really dead) operate against common sense or progress.

Progress was a word not often in Johnson's mouth, but it seems to me that in the field of law Johnson did believe in it. After remarking, anent Frederick's plan to reform the Prussian courts, "Laws often continue when their reasons have ceased," he shows his approval of filling their defects and lopping off their superfluities.

His liberalism is further shown in his attitude toward the rights of women, again in the dispute about Boswell's entail, at least once in his implied support of relaxing the laws against papists (*Idler*, No. 10), and most outstandingly in his consistent opposition to negro slavery, which he described in 1756 as "unlawful in itself," a position much amplified twenty years later in his argument for Boswell on behalf of the negro Knight. In all of these he was ahead of his times, and in all of these his study of the law had its share.

We have seen Johnson's interest in the law developing from young manhood — silent at first, though he later told Boswell that he would have taken a law degree at Oxford except for his poverty — writing a brief for Cave on the copyright question when he was not yet thirty, inquiring of Adams whether he might be admitted to practice at Doctors' Commons, and rebuffed for lack of a degree, turning to hackwork which yet allowed him to study out the constitutional questions of the day as he composed the Parliamentary Debates for the *Gentleman's Magazine*, serving another sort of apprenticeship as he toiled through seven long years on the *Dictionary*, reading through law books for that purpose and comparing his results with the law dictionaries then available, when in his middle fifties settling down to study law as a background for helping Hamilton — perhaps hoping that he might be given some sort of legal office as a reward — turning his great talents to the actual composition of lectures on the English law for the young Chambers, satisfied that he was helping a young man on the path which he himself would have chosen, then helping Boswell with his numerous briefs whenever that erratic genius called on him, still pained when one of his young lawyer friends thoughtlessly wished that he might have been Lord Chancellor.

It is useless to resist imagining what sort of lawyer Johnson might have been. His quick wit, his powerful physique, his thundering voice would have been great assets to a trial lawyer, and he possessed the true lawyer's belief that there is something to be said on both sides of a question, and that it is his duty to present the best case for his client because his client has a right to such aid. I do not believe that his physical defects, his poor sight and the markings of scrofula, or his nervous twitchings, which he could apparently control and which besides have been much exaggerated, would seriously have hampered his career. His essential fairness and his basic humaneness would have made him valuable on the bench, and in his steadfast opposition to slavery he was at least in step with such men as Lord Mansfield, and far in advance of such sentimentalists as Boswell. His attitude toward entails is also modern, and there is no trace of his so-called Jacobitism in his position on the prerogative.

But who would lose the Rambler in the advocate or judge? In a busy legal career Johnson might have left us some splen-

did decisions, but his impact on his contemporaries — and
upon us — could scarcely have been greater, and might have
been much less. And we still have his thoughts on the law,
some random and casual, some carefully considered, some
ringing affirmations, like the one at the head of this chapter.
In their total, they are much more than we could have expected
from one whose career was at first glance so far from the law.
Indeed, they are enough — enough perhaps to make Johnson
the great lawyer-layman of his century.

Index

Abingdon, Earl of, 26
Adam, R.B., Catalogue of his
   library, 66 ff.
Adams, Dr. William, 8-10
Alfred, Code of, 88, 101
ambassadors, rights of, 83
American colonies, taxation of,
   9, 105, 128, 149, 189-191
American Indians, councils of,
   100; visit to France, 107
Arbuthnot, Dr. John, 141
Argyle, Duke of, 16, 20, 26
Aristotle, 60
attorney general, 48
Attorney General Ryder, 23,24
attorneys, 3, 4, 8, 9, 37, 40,
   44, 48, 53, 199
Auchinleck, living of, 140
Ayliffe, John, *Parergon juris*,
   6, 47, 62

Bach-y-Graig, 177
Bacon, Francis, 47, 64, 148
Bacon, Nathaniel, *Historical
   Discourse on the Laws*, 36
Bailey, Nathaniel, *Dictionary*,
   48
Ballow, Henry, 30, 67, 174;
   Treatise of Equity, 31, 63
Barnard, Sir Frederick, King's
   Librarian, 61, 120
Barnard, Sir John, 19, 20, 24,
   26, 28
barraters, 53
Barrington, Daines, 63, 97, 98
barristers, 2, 3, 163
Bathurst, Lord, 25, 26
Benlow's *Reports*, 195
Bentham, Jeremy, 63
Bernardi, John, 198
Bill of Rights, 165

Blackstone, William, 2-5, 56,
   57, 67, 80, 81, 121, 122,
   144, 162, 170, 175
   *Analysis of the Laws of
      England*, 4, 65, 73-80
   Commentaries, 2-5, 14, 57,
      63, 65, 73, 74, 121, 136,
      160
   The Great Charter, 62
Blount, Thomas, 48
Boerhaave, Herman, 141
Boerius, Nicholas, *Decisiones
   Burgedalenses*, 61
"borough English," 194
Boscawen, Justice, 197
Boswell, James, 8, 71, 123-173,
   181
   his cases:
   Ayrshire election, 158
   Hastie of Campbelltown,
      128-131
   lay-patron's presentation of
      minister to parish, 137-140
   Memis vs. Royal Infirmary
      of Aberdeen, 141-143
   Paterson *et al.* vs. Alexand-
      er *et al.*, 143-144
   schoolmaster's indecent be-
      havior, 155
   Society of Solicitors vs. Ro-
      binson, 143, 158-160
   Stirling road bill, 157
   Rev. James Thomson, 150-155
   Wilson vs. Smith and Armour,
      131-136
   B. and the English bar, 161
   his entail, 144-150
   his scruples rebutted by
      Johnson, 124
   Johnson on addressing the
      House of Commons, 157,
      158

203